W9-CLI-173

Praise for *Distilled Spirits*

"This remarkable book deserves the widest readership it can get, for more clearly than any other book I know, it shows the depth to which the human spirit can descend and still rebound. Aldous Huxley and Gerald Heard were close friends and my most important mentors, and I spent one memorable afternoon with Bill Wilson. Don Lattin's astonishing book brings their life stories alive. It is carefully researched and disarmingly honest."

—Huston Smith, author of *The World's Religions*

"The painful journey from addiction to relapse to recovery has become the *Pilgrim's Progress* of our era. In this riveting fusion of memoir and tripartite biography, the noted religion reporter Don Lattin aligns his own pilgrimage to sobriety with the inspiration offered by three transformative twentieth-century figures who also found spiritual value as the basis for corrective action."

—Kevin Starr, University of Southern California

"It is difficult for me to hide my enthusiasm for this book. It is a fascinating biography/memoir with an abundance of heart—courageously honest, philosophically nuanced, and peppered with the most delightful sense of humor. It's easy to be romantic about drugs and mysticism—tougher to be both morally rigorous *and* honestly ecstatic about the real openings they offer. I'm grateful that Lattin can hold this tension while also weaving a mesmerizing story."

—Jeffrey Kripal, author of *Esalen: America and the Religion of No Religion*

"An eye-opening and mind-expanding read. I highly recommend this book to anyone and everyone who is interested in consciousness, spiritual exploration, recovery, and awakenings. Don is a masterful storyteller and writer. He weaves together the lives of these men in a way that is intriguing and wise. Read it, then start a revolution!"

—Noah Levine, author of *Dharma Punx*

"This extraordinary book blends careful historical research with rich personal reflections. Lattin describes the intersecting lives and lasting influence of three men who helped transform American spirituality. *Distilled Spirits* offers readers a rare opportunity to gain both knowledge and wisdom."

—Marion Goldman, author of *The American Soul Rush: Esalen and the Rise of Spiritual Privilege*

"Don Lattin writes knowledgeably and elegantly about these three brilliant yet troubled men, while candidly chronicling his own demons. A hard-nosed reporter, here he reveals a softer side, and thank God for that. A quiet wisdom infuses every page of this lovely book."

—Eric Weiner, author of *Man Seeks God: My Flirtations with the Divine*

"Don Lattin knows how to tell a ripping good story, and there are many in this book. The scene of Lattin interviewing the Pope as their plane lands in Miami is alone worth the price of admission. Add to that some fascinating stories about Aldous Huxley and Bill Wilson, the founder of Alcoholics Anonymous, and you've got yourself a great read. There is some irony in the fact that Don Lattin was doing drugs and drinking heavily while reporting on religion for the *San Francisco Chronicle*. But it all comes together in this book, which explores the connections between the spiritual search and the substances that produce altered states of consciousness. It's a trip, as they used to say, and a great read."

—Wes "Scoop" Nisker, Buddhist teacher, performer, and author of *The Essential Crazy Wisdom*

Distilled Spirits

Distilled Spirits

Getting High, Then Sober, with a Famous Writer,
a Forgotten Philosopher, and a Hopeless Drunk

DON LATTIN

UNIVERSITY OF CALIFORNIA PRESS
Berkeley   Los Angeles   London

University of California Press, one of the most distinguished
university presses in the United States, enriches lives around the
world by advancing scholarship in the humanities, social sciences,
and natural sciences. Its activities are supported by the UC Press
Foundation and by philanthropic contributions from individuals
and institutions. For more information, visit www.ucpress.edu.

University of California Press
Berkeley and Los Angeles, California

University of California Press, Ltd.
London, England

Library of Congress Cataloging-in-Publication Data

Lattin, Don, 1953–
    Distilled spirits : getting high, then sober, with a famous writer, a
forgotten philosopher, and a hopeless drunk / Don Lattin.
        p.   cm.
    Includes bibliographical references (p.   ) and index.
    ISBN 978-0-520-27232-3 (cloth : alk. paper)
    1. Spiritual biography.   2. Religious biography.   3. Lattin, Don,
1953–   4. Huxley, Aldous, 1894–1963.   5. Heard, Gerald, 1889–1971.
6. W., Bill.   I. Title.
    BL72.L34   2012
    200.92'2—dc23
NO [B] (Lattin\   2012013931

Manufactured in the United States of America

21   20   19   18   17   16   15   14   13   12
10   9   8   7   6   5   4   3   2   1

In keeping with a commitment to support environmentally responsible
and sustainable printing practices, UC Press has printed this book
on Rolland Enviro100, a 100% post-consumer fiber paper that is FSC
certified, deinked, processed chlorine-free, and manufactured with
renewable biogas energy. It is acid-free and EcoLogo certified.

To my parents,
who tried their best to love
and be loved in return

Contents

Photographs follow page 170

Introduction

The Life Force is like a juggler; it is always contriving that
we shall watch the hand with which the trick is not being
done. When we look back, we often discover that it was the
symptom we were studying, not the cause.

Gerald Heard, *Narcissus*, 1924

You've probably never heard of Gerald Heard. The first person to tell me
about him was Michael Murphy, the cofounder of Esalen Institute at Big
Sur. That retreat center on the California coast was the birthplace of the
human potential movement—a heady blend of psychology and spirituality that captivated so many people in my generation of seekers. Murphy
and I were at his home in Marin County, across the Golden Gate Bridge
from San Francisco, sitting in the sun on a vine-covered deck just off his
kitchen. Mount Tamalpais rose up behind us.

We were talking about the roots of Esalen Institute, which opened its
doors at the dawn of that wonderfully weird decade, the 1960s. Murphy
told me a story about how he and Dick Price, his founding partner at
Esalen, had traveled down to Southern California in the summer of 1961
to visit Gerald Heard at his cottage in Santa Monica. Price and Murphy

spent four hours with Heard, a British philosopher who enraptured the two young men with tales of esoteric Old Testament rituals, inspiring stories about obscure Christian mystics, and amazing accounts of new scientific research into paranormal activity and psychic phenomena. New ideas seemed to pop into Heard's head as he recounted his still-developing theories about the evolution of human consciousnesses.

Heard was seventy-two years old, nearing the end of a long career during which he had published more than three dozen books, from deep philosophical tomes to weird mystery tales. Murphy had already been to India on his spiritual search, and Price was looking for a more humanistic approach to helping people struggling with mental disorder. Heard told them about a short-lived interfaith retreat center, Trabuco College, that he'd started in the 1940s in the Santa Ana Mountains south of Los Angeles. At the time of his encounter with Heard, Murphy was wondering what to do with an old hot springs resort his family owned up the coast at Big Sur. Heard went into a reverie about the spiritual power of such a place, overlooking the vast Pacific, the perfect setting to bring together East and West.

"Gerald knew Big Sur very well and had this whole theory about this westward movement toward the cutting edge of social change," Murphy said. "That was it. We left that meeting with Gerald and decided to push the 'go' button for Esalen. Gerald was a big part of the inspiration. That meeting was the tipping point."

The next time I heard the name Heard was from Huston Smith, a renowned scholar of world religions. We were sitting in two armchairs in the bay window of Huston's home in Berkeley, talking about Smith's early influences, about what had inspired him to write *The World's Religions*, which has sold more than two million copies since it was first published in 1958, and which is still widely used as a religious studies text. Smith explained how he discovered Gerald Heard. It was back in the 1940s. Smith was writing his PhD thesis at the University of California, Berkeley, and was fascinated by Heard's idea that humanity had the potential for a breakthrough in human consciousness. He read every book Heard had written and then tracked him down in Trabuco Canyon.

When Huston Smith talks about his first encounter with Gerald Heard, he sounds as impassioned as Michael Murphy. That meeting led to another event that would change Smith's life. Heard introduced Huston to his friend Aldous Huxley, the famous English writer who had recently published *The Perennial Philosophy*, his extended 1945 essay that explores the common mystical truth running through all religions. Sitting there that day in Berkeley, I realized that I might want to learn more about this Gerald Heard character, who, it turned out, was one of Huxley's closest friends and a major influence on him.

Huxley was my favorite writer in the late 1960s and early 1970s, when I was coming of age and starting to think about the meaning of life. I began with Huxley's last book, *Island*, his 1962 novel about a cynical reporter who gets shipwrecked on an island where the natives live in cosmic harmony. After *Island*, I started working my way back through Huxley's body of work, first with *Brave New World*, his best-known novel, then *The Doors of Perception*, his long essay recounting his mescaline trip in the spring of 1953. I was in my mother's womb in New Jersey when Huxley had his psychedelic baptism in his home in the Hollywood Hills, but something was born in me, years later, when I read *The Doors of Perception*. I was still a teenager. It was 1970, but for me "the sixties" were only beginning.

My life over the next few decades was marked by a number of inspiring highs and a few soul-shattering lows. By the time the new millennium rolled around, my choice of drugs had progressed from mushrooms and marijuana to alcohol and cocaine. I'd had a satisfying career as a religion reporter for the *San Francisco Examiner* and the *San Francisco Chronicle*. I'd met and interviewed all manner of enlightening people, including the Dalai Lama, Pope John Paul II, Thich Nhat Hanh, Mother Teresa, J. Krishnamurti, and Billy Graham. I'd won awards and had three books published. But there was a little problem. I was an alcoholic, and I was addicted to cocaine, and it was all starting to come crashing down. Today that seems like another life. In the fall of 2004, I checked myself into a hospital in Oakland, California, to try to detox my body and heal my soul.

My recovery involved going to meetings of Alcoholics Anonymous— something I did *not* want to do. I had lots of preconceived ideas about

AA, something its members call "contempt prior to investigation." I was different. I'd written newspaper stories about the recovery movement and twelve-step spirituality. I knew enough to know AA wasn't for me. It was fine for evangelical Christian drunks, but not for an enlightened drunk like me. I'd written countless stories about cults, and I didn't feel like joining one. But at the same time, I didn't see many effective alternatives. So I decided to set aside a lifetime of finely honed skepticism—at least for a few months. I checked myself into that substance abuse center in Oakland for a twenty-eight-day treatment program. I started going to meetings. I started "working the program." But, being a newspaper reporter, I couldn't resist the temptation to investigate the story behind the founding of AA.

What I learned amazed me. It turns out that Bill Wilson, the cofounder of Alcoholics Anonymous, had been deeply involved with Gerald Heard. They met at Trabuco College in the 1940s and began a lifelong correspondence. They even took LSD together. In fact, Gerald Heard was Bill Wilson's guide on Wilson's first LSD trip in the summer of 1956. Wilson didn't simply try LSD. He started a salon in New York City where he and a group of friends continued to investigate the spiritual potential of psychedelics.

At the time the drug was legal and thought to be a potential treatment for a variety of maladies, including alcoholism. Huxley, Wilson, and Heard thought LSD, used cautiously, could help some people deepen their spiritual lives. They saw direct spiritual experience—whatever inspired it—as the foundation for an ethical, compassionate life. Psychedelics could help some alcoholics and other selfish individuals see beyond the limited, egocentric worldview that limits our spiritual potential. Drugs could give us a glimpse of another way of seeing the world. Then the hard work would begin.

That hard work is the rest of our lives.

Huxley, Wilson, and Heard have been dead for decades, but their body of work continues to shape the way we envision the sacred and live our lives. My current spiritual practice includes a Saturday morning gathering with a small group, some in recovery and some not. It's a blend of Christian mysticism and Zen Buddhism. We meet for about two hours to socialize, meditate, and read scripture. One week we may reflect on a passage from the Bible. At the next meeting we may study a Buddhist sutra or hear a dharma talk from our teacher. I may be the only one of us who realizes it, but our little group would never have come together without the work of Huxley, Wilson, and Heard. In our approach to God, we, like these three men, draw wisdom from several faiths, seek spiritual experience over religious doctrine, and focus on personal growth. We—like so many other seekers in our generation—see ourselves as "spiritual but not religious."

.   .   .   .   .

Aldous Huxley, Gerald Heard, and Bill Wilson are a bridge between two worlds.

Queen Victoria was still on her throne when Huxley (1894–1963) was born into a famous family of British writers and intellectuals. He died the same day President John F. Kennedy was gunned down in Dallas. Huxley's early novels and collections of poetry quickly established him as the leading prophet and spokesman for a generation of young Europeans searching for a new way of living following the horrors of World War I. Aldous's long, happy, and unorthodox marriage to Maria Nys, a bisexual born in Belgium, prefigured the later breakdown of the traditional American family and the rise of the sexual revolution of the 1960s and 1970s. Huxley spent the final twenty-five years of his life in Southern California, where his early experimentation with psychedelic drugs and his writings on their spiritual potential inspired another generation of alienated young people to question the consumerism, materialism, and conservative values of the 1950s.

Heard (1889–1971) was Huxley's best friend and one of his most important mentors. They met in London in 1929 and came to the United States together in 1937. These two men may have been the last great polymaths of Western culture. In an era of increasing specialization, they were interested in everything. Heard was a leading writer, philosopher, and cultural critic in the years between the First and Second World Wars. He was the first science commentator for BBC radio in the 1930s and wrote one of the first popular books about flying saucers in the 1950s. Under two different pseudonyms, Heard wrote a series of detective novels and pioneering articles on gay spirituality. But Heard, the so-called godfather of the New Age movement, was above all a mystic. His belief in the power of humanity to evolve spiritually and reach new levels of consciousness laid the foundation for the human potential movement of the 1960s and 1970s.

Wilson (1895–1971) was the main force behind the growth of Alcoholics Anonymous, one of the most successful spiritual movements of the twentieth century. AA's twelve-step program for religious renewal and psychological well-being inspired the larger recovery movement and a new approach to spiritual fellowship, one that builds on the redemptive power that can be found when small groups of like-minded believers come together for solace and support. Wilson's interest in the writings of Gerald Heard inspired him to seek out Heard during Wilson's first visit to California in the winter of 1943–44. Their friendship and spiritual collaboration continued over the next two decades.

Wilson's practical, open-minded approach to religion helped change the way Americans envision the divine. At first glance, he may seem an unlikely partner in Huxley and Heard's crusade. Wilson began his adult life as a hard-drinking Wall Street speculator with little interest in religion. After nearly drinking himself to death in the 1920s and early 1930s, "Bill W.," as he became known, was reborn with a revelation that alcoholics and other troubled souls must connect with some sort of "higher power" before they can overcome their selfishness and obsessions. Gerald Heard and Aldous Huxley came to this same realization, but it was Wilson who put the philosophy into practice, founding a no-nonsense, self-help movement that has inspired millions of people around the world to find "God *as we understand Him.*"

Huxley and Heard settled in Los Angeles in the late 1930s with a group of displaced Englishmen who came to be known as the "British mystical expatriates of Southern California." Wilson came to the West Coast from New York battling depression but eager to embark on his own pilgrimage of self-discovery.

Heard and Huxley had come to believe that humanity had the potential for a breakthrough in consciousness. In the three decades leading up to the 1960s, they emerged as the leading evangelists of a philosophy that mixed meditation, mysticism, psychology, psychedelic drugs, and a utopian vision of an enlightened society. At the same time, their spiritual program was a utilitarian approach to living a more fulfilling life. Wilson called it "a faith that works."

Wilson founded AA before he met Heard and Huxley, but Wilson's later life and writings were deeply influenced by both men. And it was a mutual admiration society. Aldous Huxley called Bill Wilson "the greatest social architect of the twentieth century." Each of these men independently led an inspiring life, but it's only when we consider the three collectively, pausing at those moments where their lives intersect, that we fully appreciate their cumulative power. Huxley saw the social problem. Heard charted the spiritual course. Wilson recruited passengers for the journey.

For me, and for many others in my generation, that journey was the proverbial long, strange trip. Huxley's writings on the spiritual dimension of the psychedelic drug experience inspired us to seek mystical enlightenment through the wonders of modern chemistry. We didn't want to worship God. We wanted to *experience* God. Some of us wanted to *be* God. We were not interested in doctrine, dogma, or religious denominations. We wanted instant insight. We wanted to leave ordinary reality behind—to break on through to the other side—and there was no time to waste.

Gerald Heard was at least as enthusiastic as Huxley about the transcendent power of an LSD experience, but he also knew that an altered state of consciousness does not automatically lead to an altered way of life. It took me too many years to learn that lesson. True spiritual change involves hard work and an understanding that we are all in this together. Religious insight means little if it's not shared and experienced with others. Drugs, including alcohol, can give us a taste of bliss, but many of us do not know when to stop. We find ourselves falling into isolation and addiction—not communion or enlightenment. Bill Wilson fell so far that he barely made it back.

Carl Jung, the famous Swiss psychiatrist, corresponded with Bill Wilson in the early 1960s. In a letter to the cofounder of Alcoholics Anonymous, Jung pointed out that the Latin word for alcohol is *spiritus*. "You use the same word for the highest religious experience," Jung wrote, "as for the most depraving poison."

Distilled spirits, like psychedelic drugs, are double-edged swords. They can illuminate the ecstasy, but they can also unleash the agony. They certainly did both in my life. *Distilled Spirits*, the book, blends my story with those of Huxley, Wilson, and Heard.

All biography is in a sense autobiography, and that is especially the case in this book.* Biographers are always, at some level, trying to understand themselves, and that's the main reason I wrote this book. I never met Huxley, Wilson, or Heard. They were members of my grandparents' generation. But they were at least two generations ahead of their time, and their lives still provide a template for us to better understand our own.

Huxley shows me a way to break through the wall of cynicism, which is the first step toward cultivating compassion and connection. Wilson provides a step-by-step program to break the cycle of addiction by taming the ego and surrendering to a power greater than oneself. Heard offers a program of prayer and meditation, a way to live with and sometimes rise above the sadness and melancholy that shadowed their lives—and mine.

At their best, religion and spirituality are about interconnectedness—about looking for the similarities, not the differences, and being open to inspiration. I must confess up front that these qualities do not describe my natural state of mind. Most of my religious exploration occurred

---

*My inspiration for this approach comes, in part, from Lytton Strachey, the iconoclastic biographer and critic who came to know Huxley and Heard in the incestuous artistic and literary scene that enlivened London and its environs in the first decades of the twentieth century. Strachey's work was a reaction against the ponderous biographical work of his era. His technique was to "row out over the great ocean of material, and lower down into it, here and there, a little bucket, which will bring up to the light of day some characteristic specimen, from those far depths, to be examined with a careful curiosity." Strachey was a firm believer in "brevity—a brevity which excludes everything that is redundant and nothing that is significant—that, surely, is the first duty of the biographer." Strachey (1918) 2000, pp. 1, 2.

when I was a reporter for the secular press. I was not getting paid to get inspired. As a newspaper reporter, I was supposed to keep my distance and remain objective. As a religion reporter, I had the tough assignment of writing about faith while sticking to the facts.

Inspired religion is about transcendence and reconciliation, but the territory religion writers explore tends to involve the endless conflict of the American culture wars. We are on a constant search for scandal, especially sex scandal. Newspaper reporters revel in writing about religious hypocrisy, and God knows that's never hard to find. But after nearly three decades, I had to turn in my press pass. Skepticism is an honorable trait, especially for journalists, but I'd spent enough time hanging out in that dim alley where cynicism meets skepticism, looking for a little light.

What I learned writing this book is what I found in my own recovery from alcoholism and drug addiction—the redemptive power of storytelling and the strength of fellowship. It's something we see at every meeting of Alcoholics Anonymous. We can argue about whether twelve-step programs really work, or whether people in Alcoholics Anonymous are merely trading one addiction for another, replacing their cocktails with some amorphous higher power.

It's actually much simpler than that. AA and other recovery programs work because they inspire some people to change their social networks, to start hanging out with another crowd, and most important, to shut up and start listening. We find someone willing to listen to our story. We tell it as honestly as we can and try to live a more compassionate life one day at a time.

ONE **Wounded**

Is there a "God gene," a strand of DNA that brings us into this world pre-disposed toward metaphysical longing? Such a theory was postulated in 2004 by a geneticist at the U.S. National Cancer Institute. He claimed to have discovered a gene that predicts a person's underlying tendency toward spirituality. Our faith, he said, is hardwired. He speculated that religious belief arises in a population because neurobiology and natural selection favor individuals with a strong sense of spirituality.

Other geneticists questioned the science behind the claim, but let's say for a moment that there is a God gene. For if there is, we might also assume that Aldous Huxley was born without one.

Most of us begin our lives with some kind of religious heritage. My mother is Jewish. My father was Presbyterian. Neither of them did much to cultivate that spiritual legacy in their children, but that religious heritage is there, whether or not my genetic makeup has anything to do with it.

Aldous Huxley was born into a family with a legacy of doubt and disbelief. If there is a gene for skepticism, we might want to obtain some DNA samples from his progeny and run some tests.

Huxley was born on a small country estate southeast of London on July 26, 1894. He was the third son of two private-school teachers, Leonard Huxley and Julia Arnold. His genetic skepticism dates back to his grandfather Thomas Henry Huxley, a famous zoologist who coined the term *agnosticism*. Huxley seems to have exhibited his grandfather's scientific curiosity at an early age.

One morning, at age four, Aldous was staring out the window into the garden.

"What are you thinking about, Aldous dear?" his mother asked.

"Skin," he replied.

Aldous Huxley's maternal lineage includes Matthew Arnold, one of the great Victorian poets, and Thomas Arnold, Julia's father, another Englishman infamous for switching religions long before "shopping for faith" was in vogue. Thomas Arnold was a prominent educational reformer who twice left the Anglican Church and converted to Catholicism. It so upset Julia's Protestant mother that she smashed the windows of the chapel at one of her husband's Roman Catholic confirmations. Being raised in a family torn by such religious strife left Huxley's mother with what his biographer termed "a very deep faith, but perhaps no conventional religion."

Thomas Henry Huxley, the grandfather, was widely known in England as "Darwin's bulldog." He was an early and fierce supporter of the theory of evolution who engaged the religious leaders of his time in spirited public debate, but he was never an ideologue. Open-mindedness was his creed, especially in matters of religion. "I neither affirm nor deny the immortality of man," he told a friend. "I see no reason for believing it, but, on the other hand, I have no means of disproving it."

When I reached intellectual maturity and began to ask myself whether I was an atheist, a theist or a pantheist; a materialist or an idealist; Christian or freethinker; I found that the more I learned and reflected, the less ready was the answer; until, at last, I came to the conclusion that I had neither art nor part with any of these denominations, except the last. The one thing in which most of these good people were agreed was the one thing in which I differed from them. They were quite sure they had attained a certain "gnosis," had more or less successfully solved the problem of existence; while I was quite sure I had not, and had a pretty strong conviction that the problem was insoluble.

Leonard Huxley followed his agnostic father's example in raising Aldous and his two older brothers, Julian and Trev. They were baptized in the Church of England and given just enough religious education so they might learn "the mythology of their time and country."

· · · · ·

My religious upbringing was, in a way, similar. As far as I know, my father was not following the example of Thomas Henry Huxley, but he thought his children should be exposed to organized religion, much like kids should be exposed to certain childhood diseases in order to build up their immune systems.

I was baptized into the Christian fold at the First Presbyterian Church in Ramsey, New Jersey, and later sent to Sunday school, but I always knew I wasn't supposed to really *believe* what I heard from the pulpit. It was America and it was the 1950s, and *not* going to church was a stepping-stone to Communism. My religious education abruptly ended when I was twelve. It was 1965. The times they were a-changin'. We were living in Southern California, and my parents were about to get a divorce.

My father asked me if I wanted to keep going to church. "Not really," I replied. "Good," he said. "Then we don't have to take you." Devotion to Jesus was never a big thing in our house. We had daily communion, but the sacrament was a mystically dry gin martini.

One of the first things they ask you to do in drug rehab is to write out your substance abuse history. They ask you to try to remember when that first sip of alcohol crossed your lips and how you felt about it. My early memories of alcohol are my earliest memories, period. And they are fond memories.

Before I even started kindergarten, when I was four or five years old, I used to wait around all day for my dad to come home from work. It seemed like an eternity. I'd hide in his closet, behind the rows of dark woolen suits, forty-eight extralong, and wait to hear the sound of his car pulling up the gravel driveway outside our house in Chesterland, Ohio. We were out in what seemed like the country. It was the last place we lived that wasn't a soulless new subdivision. There were still dirt roads on the last stretch of the way home and lots of woods to explore.

Dad would walk into the bedroom, and I'd jump out of the closet and yell, "Boo!" He always acted like he was surprised. I'd watch him pull his keys and spare change out of his pockets and carefully place them in an old ashtray on his dresser. The faded yellow porcelain tray was molded in the form of a grinning skeleton leaning back on his elbows, encouraging you to snub out your cigarette butts where his stomach used to be. I'd watch Dad take off his long pants and hang them up in his closet. Then I'd follow him back out to the family room as he faithfully approached the bar, his altar of alcohol.

That's where Dad displayed all the shiny paraphernalia of the sophisticated drinking man—the silver cocktail shaker, cut-glass pitcher, long elegant spoons, and his solid-glass swizzle sticks of many colors. I especially liked the array of tiny golden swords he used to skewer the three olives that went with each martini. The centerpiece of the altar was a bottle of Beefeater gin glistening in the glow of the early evening.

Dad would dip a larger glass tumbler into a silver ice bucket, fill it to the brim, and then slowly pour in the gin, like a priest consecrating the wine. He'd wave a bottle of vermouth over the gin, like incense, allowing no more than a drop to fall into the frosty glass. Then he'd skewer his three olives and begin the procession over to his favorite chair. I'd climb into his lap, and I always got to pull the first gin-soaked olive off the tiny sword. It was there, in the safety of my father's lap, that I acquired an early appreciation for this wondrous elixir.

Then Dad would unfold the evening newspaper, wrapping it around my little body like a curtain protecting us from the rest of the world. He would read me the funnies and perhaps a bit of the day's news.

No wonder I became a newspaper reporter and an alcoholic.

.   .   .   .   .

Gerald Heard had a very different childhood experience. He had a strict religious upbringing. Actually, it was more than strict; it was abusive.

He was born in London on October 6, 1889, and given the name Henry Fitzgerald Heard. Like Aldous Huxley, he was the youngest of three boys, but he was not raised to question the faith of his forefathers. Gerald's father, the Reverend Henry James Heard, was a priest in the Church of England, as was his paternal grandfather, the Reverend John Bickford Heard. Gerald's father adhered to a harsh form of Anglican evangelicalism.

It was not a happy home. Gerald was beaten by his father, his brothers, and a drunken nursemaid whose abusive behavior would later spark Heard's interest in the teachings of Alcoholics Anonymous. Heard's mother died when he was four years old. He was put in the care of his maternal grandmother, a Christian fundamentalist from County Clare, Ireland, who believed that "a child's will must be broken." Heard recalled later in life that his grandmother's "belief in eternal damnation had a strong and painful presence on my early life."

There was a respite in 1899, when Gerald was ten years old. His evangelical father remarried, and his stepmother shielded him from further abuse. "Although his stepmother was fond of him, his excessive need for love made him emotionally vulnerable and overly responsive to the slightest show of kindness," observed Jay Michael Barrie, a man who spent many years as Heard's private secretary and knew him better than most. "This heightened sensitivity coupled with his uncommonly precocious mind made him an irresistible target of the sadistic teasing for which the English public-school boy is notorious."

Gerald was a frail child with little interest in athletics, a central element of life at his boarding school. The school has been described as a "bullying haven of athleticism," and Gerald often received the brunt of that bullying. It was a rough chapter in his young life, but Heard survived by finding power in his ability to spin a tale. It was at school that he learned how telling a good story could "keep the bullies at bay."

As a young student, Gerald was fascinated by science and technology and the writings of H.G. Wells. Heard's father expected his son to follow him into the Christian ministry; later, when Gerald began his college education at Cambridge, he began with serious theological studies and the intention of following that path. He learned Hebrew and the Greek New Testament. But Heard was soon drawn to a less orthodox spirituality.

Cambridge was also the home of the Society for Psychical Research, which was formed in 1882 to study psychic phenomena and other paranormal activity. Heard would later serve on the society's governing council, from 1934 to 1937, after which he left England and emigrated to the United States.

．   ．   ．   ．   ．

Bill Wilson was born on the other side of the Atlantic, in the Vermont village of East Dorset, on November 26, 1895, which makes him sixteen months younger than Huxley and six years Heard's junior. His parents ran a small inn, and the cofounder of Alcoholics Anonymous was born, fittingly enough, in a room behind the bar.

Bill's parents, Gilman "Gilly" Wilson and Emily Griffith, were of solid New England stock, but they were not solid parents. Recalling his own childhood beatings, Bill Wilson sounds a lot like Gerald Heard.

"My mother was a disciplinarian, and I can remember the agony of hostility and fear that I went through when she administered her first good tanning with the back of a hairbrush," Wilson said. "Somehow I never could forget that beating. It made an indelible impression upon me, for I really think that she was angry."

Bill's father worked in the marble quarries of the Green Mountains, drank, and chased women. Gilly and Emily divorced when Bill was ten years old, and then they both abandoned him. Gilly headed north to Canada, and Emily took off to Boston to go to college. She took Bill's sister with her but left him with his grandparents. Young Bill was devastated. "It was an agonizing experience for one who apparently had the emotional sensitivity that I did," he recalled decades later. "I hid the wound and never talked about it with anybody."

Bill was sent off to Burr and Burton Academy, a private boarding school founded in 1829 in Manchester, Vermont, about five miles from East Dorset. He stayed there five days a week, returning to his grandparents' home on weekends. It was at school that he found his first love, sixteen-year-old Bertha Banford, the daughter of a local minister. Bill's mood changed. His grades went up. Someone loved him, and everything was right in the world.

Then suddenly she was gone. Bertha had gone off one weekend to New York with her parents. On a Tuesday morning in November, only weeks before Bill's seventeenth birthday, the students gathered in the academy chapel. The headmaster pulled out a telegram and told the students the awful news. Bertha had undergone surgery over the weekend at a Manhattan hospital and died of internal bleeding. Her death sparked a personal and spiritual crisis in young Bill's life.

It is a matter of debate as to whether Bill Wilson had much of a religious upbringing. He says nothing about it in his autobiography. His maternal grandfather, probably the chief influence on Bill in his early years, was well versed in the writings of the New England transcendentalists and was an admirer of Roger Ingersoll, the nineteenth-century orator, freethinker, and defender of agnosticism. Ingersoll was as notorious in America as Thomas Henry Huxley was in Britain. In response to these transcendentalist ideas, it is said in one account, Bill "left the church at about age twelve on a matter of principle."

Wilson learned about the Judeo-Christian tradition by taking the required four-year Bible study course at Burr and Burton Academy. And, as the boyfriend of a preacher's kid, he started getting more involved in Christian activities. But that ended with Bertha's death. Wilson became depressed. He didn't graduate. And according to one of his biographers, Bertha's death "erased any vestiges he might have had of belief in God."

For years to come, Wilson would use the words *atheist* or *agnostic* to describe his personal philosophy. But there was one religious experience that would have a profound impact on young Bill. His paternal grandfather, William "Willy" Wilson, was one of the founding members of the East Dorset Congregational Church. Grandpa Willy was also a ferocious drunk. He was struggling with his alcoholism just as the Christian temperance movement was beginning to flourish in New England, a crusade that would culminate in the Eighteenth Amendment and the enactment of Prohibition in 1920. Willy attended revival meetings and signed temperance pledges, but he kept falling off the wagon until one Sunday morning, when he climbed to the top of a mountain and begged for God's help. He saw a blinding light and felt an enlivening breeze. Bill Wilson's grandfather rushed down to East Dorset Congregational Church, ordered the minister to leave the pulpit, and told the dramatic story of his sudden conversion. He lived another eight years, and it is said that he never had another drink.

Bill grew up hearing this story about his grandfather, and he would never forget it. It would, decades later, provide the template for his own revelatory tale, a story that would become the founding myth of Alcoholics Anonymous.

· · · · ·

Huxley, Wilson, and Heard all hail from some combination of British or Irish ancestry.

Heard was born in London, but his family was Irish gentry going back more than four centuries. The family name is "Heard of Kinsale, County Cork." According to family lore, John Heard of Wiltshire came to Ireland with Sir Walter Raleigh in 1579.

The Wilson name can be traced back to Scotland, then to the north of Ireland. Wilson's great-grandfather brought the family to America, originally settling in Manchester, Vermont.

My family passed through England on its way to the New World. Thanks to the genealogical obsession of my great aunt Jennie, the Lattin family can trace its ancestry back to sixteenth-century Flanders.

Pierre Lettin, my earliest known ancestor, lived in Malines, Flanders, now Belgium. His son, grandson, and great-grandson all worked as secretaries and registrars for the Supreme Tribunal of Malines. The Lettins became Protestants and were driven from their native land in 1567 by the northern arm of the Spanish Inquisition and the persecutions of the Duke of Alva.

They escaped to Norwich, England, where they remained for a few generations. Then Richard Lettin (sometimes spelled "Lattin" or "Latting") left England in 1638 and settled in Concord, Massachusetts. One of his sons brought the family down to Long Island, New York, where he finagled a deed for a large tract of land from the Matinecock Indians and founded a hamlet known as Lattingtown. My ancestors stayed in New York for the next three hundred years.

Yes, I'm the original white Anglo-Saxon Protestant, at least on my father's side.

My mother never liked to talk about her family of origin. I pieced together what I could over the years from her siblings, most of whom were just as reluctant to talk about their childhood. Here's what I know: Muriel Lilian Kubey was born in Passaic County, New Jersey, on March 27, 1920, the second of four children born to Joseph Henry Kubey and Fanny Blumenthal. Joe and Fanny were Jewish, but no one's sure where their parents were from. Perhaps Russia, maybe Poland, possibly Latvia. My mom grew up in an apartment house on Linden Avenue in East Orange, New Jersey. Her dad owned a candy store called the Sugar Bowl on Main Street in Paterson, New Jersey.

An experienced genealogist once told me that the American name *Kubey* is derived from the Czech or Slavic name Kubycheck. It means "God protect." That may be, but God did not protect Joseph Kubey. He died after a sudden illness in 1930, leaving Fanny to raise four children in the midst of the Great Depression. From what I can deduce, Fanny also struggled with emotional depression, and the family barely made it. That may explain why the adult children of Joe and Fanny Kubey were so reluctant to talk about the past.

My mother's thirteen-year-old brother had to find work to support the family, and my ten-year-old mother became a surrogate parent for her little brother and sister. She prepared the meals and learned to sew to bring in a little money. There was no time or money for, or interest in, religious education, and besides, they were reluctant Jews and did not observe Jewish holidays. In fact, Fanny was obsessed with concealing her Jewish heritage. That was not uncommon back in those fiercely anti-Semitic times, but my grandmother went so far as to join a club that did not allow Jewish members. My mother once told me that the only reason she knew she was Jewish was that my grandmother wouldn't let the kids bring in a Christmas tree for the holidays. As a compromise, she was allowed to set up a dollhouse.

Spiritually speaking, the Kubey kids were scattered to the four winds. My mother became the wife of a lapsed Presbyterian, while her younger sister married into an Irish Catholic family. My mom's older brother chose an atheist. They brought up the children as secular humanists. My mother's little brother married a Jew and raised a daughter in that faith.

·　　·　　·　　·　　·

We may or may not be born with a "God gene," but it seems like some of us *are* born with a genetic predisposition to alcoholism.

The love of drink in Bill Wilson's family goes back at least two generations, as it does in my family. Walk into any meeting of Alcoholics Anonymous or Narcotics Anonymous or Cocaine Anonymous and you will soon hear a story of intergenerational addiction.

My grandfather Albert C. Lattin wasn't much of a drinker, but his wife, Bessie "Lulu" Pritchard, is another story. Lulu was born in 1896, a few months after Bill Wilson. She and my grandfather met in New York City in 1915. He was a thirty-two-year-old reporter working at the New York Stock Exchange, where Bill Wilson also began his own business career around the same time. Grandpa, who would later become a sports promoter and earn the moniker "Big Al Lattin from Manhattan," loved to drive up and down Broadway in his open-topped Buick and his bowler hat.

Lulu was a nineteen-year-old dancer in a Broadway revue, a brunette with tight curls, a small mouth, and a slender waist. They moved into an apartment not far from the spot where the George Washington Bridge lands on the western shore of Manhattan Island. My father, Warren C. Lattin, was born in that building, at 112 Nagle Avenue, on November 8, 1917. Photographic evidence yellowed and curled around the edges indicates that they had a few good years.

There were play days in the snow with my proud grandparents pulling a sled upon which my toddler father sat with a wool cap pulled over his ears and a perplexed look on his face. There were trips to the beach at Atlantic City. Lulu—attired in one of those tight, full-body bathing suits worn in the 1920s—sits perched atop the broad shoulders of my grandfather, their arms extended like gymnasts' in a coordinated routine. My six-year-old dad, his hair falling down onto his face, looks up with a smile. There were sailing trips on the Hudson River in the *Wanderer*, my grandfather's boat. Another photo shows Lulu and two of her flapper girlfriends in the cabin of the boat with that dazed, glazed look of young ladies who have had too much to drink and have no intention to stop.

Lulu started hiding bottles. Grandpa did not approve. America was a few years into that thirteen-year "Noble Experiment" known as Prohibition, but the marriage didn't last that long. There would be no more children. My grandmother moved to Miami and in with a man who ran a bar. She stayed in Florida until her alcoholism finally killed her. According to her Dade County death certificate, she died in 1957 of gastrointestinal hemorrhage and cirrhosis of the liver. If there is a gene for alcoholism, Lulu passed it down to my father, and through him, to me.

I have no memory of Grandma Lulu, but I know I met her at least once, and I see her every day. There's a small black-and-white photo on my bedroom dresser that shows her with my mother and my sister pushing a baby stroller down a street in New York City. Judging by the clothes they're wearing and the age of the baby, I suspect the photo was taken in the summer of 1954. I assume my father took the photograph and I am the baby. I'm looking up out of the stroller with a perplexed expression on my face, not unlike the one my father has in the picture of that play day in the snow. Some decades later, I was poking around what is now Spanish Harlem, searching for the apartment building where my father was born. I found it and realized that the photo of me in the stroller was taken in front of 112 Nagle Avenue. My dad had taken Grandma Lulu back for one last look.

My father once told me that there was a Jewish tailor in the ground-floor storefront of that six-story, redbrick apartment building. Dad got his first job there, as a *shabbos goy*. His duties included visiting the tailor's apartment to turn on the lights and fire up the stove, tasks the tailor's family was forbidden to perform on the Jewish Sabbath. The Jewish tailor shop is long gone.

Today, the storefront is occupied by *Las Tunas Botanica,* a Latino spiritual supply shop full of votive candles, good luck charms, and dusty shelves cluttered with colorful statues of Catholic saints, little bottles of magic potions, and a fine assortment of pagan paraphernalia. There's a giant statue of Jesus in the window where the Jewish tailor once plied his trade. My father was not a religious man, nor am I, but I couldn't resist the temptation to tap into the spiritual power of that place. So I purchased a small statue of Saint Francis, climbed into my rental car, and headed across the Hudson River to the Lattin family grave in Ramsey, New Jersey.

.   .   .   .   .

All families are wounded, some worse than others. Our childhood wounds, someone once told me, fall like a shadow across the face of God.

Aldous Huxley's wounds began to fester in 1908, shortly after he was sent off to Eton College for his secondary school studies. His beloved mother, Julia, learned that she had cancer and was dead within months. Aldous was fourteen years old. Three years later, the teenager was struck with an eye disease that blinded him for several years and seriously impaired his vision for the rest of his life. Then, in 1914, just after he recovered some of his eyesight and was about to begin his studies at Oxford, Aldous was crushed by the final act in a cruel trilogy.

Aldous's twenty-three-year-old brother, Trev, had fallen into a deep depression and had to interrupt his postgraduate work at Oxford. All three of the Huxley boys struggled to live up to the legacy of their famous grandfather, but that family pressure hit Trev the hardest. He'd fallen in love with one of the family's housemaids, a young girl below his station. The affair was doomed, and she was given notice. Trev was sent to a rest home in Surrey, but it was too late. One day in the summer of 1914, Noel Trevenen Huxley walked out of that home, into the woods, and hanged himself.

His younger brother's reaction is telling. "There is—apart from the sheer grief of the loss—an added pain in the cynicism of the situation," Aldous wrote in a letter. "It is just the highest and best in Trev—his ideals—which have driven him to his death—while there are thousands who shelter their weakness from the same fate by a cynical, unidealistic outlook on life. Trev was not strong, but he had the courage to face life with ideals, and his ideals were too much for him."

Aldous's surviving brother, Julian Huxley, who would later become Sir Julian, the famed biologist, also suffered from depression. While that disease did not seriously impair Aldous, he found other ways to wall off his emotions. "This meaningless catastrophe was the cause of the protective cynical skin in which [Aldous] clothed himself and his novels in the twenties," Julian explained. Another friend much later in life said Aldous Huxley was "to the last suspicious of the scars left by the emotional ties of the family."

.   .   .   .   .

Gerald Heard's childhood wounds would not—like Huxley's—turn him into a cynic, but they would spark a crisis of faith. World War I was on the horizon when Heard left Cambridge, without a theological degree, and began working in London as the private secretary of a retired liberal politician. But just as Europe was erupting in flames, Heard had a nervous breakdown. He was twenty-seven years old. Decades later, Heard's private secretary would blame this breakdown on the fact that Gerald was "on a collision course with doubt as to many of the doctrines of Christianity."

After a long illness, Heard finally recovered and found new direction in his life. The young man who had felt called to the priesthood had become a scientific materialist with a strong sense of social responsibility and "an equally strong conviction that the world could be tidied up, that justice could and must prevail, and that it was his duty to dedicate his life and efforts to a frontal attack on the obstacles to these ends."

Another church doctrine that Heard may have struggled with was the church's condemnation of homosexuality, for Heard was also coming to terms with his own sexuality. His breakdown began in 1916, around the time he was introduced to the pleasures of bohemian London, especially as practiced by the Bloomsbury group of writers and artists who'd gathered in one of that city's leafier neighborhoods.

It must have been a strange time for Gerald. He was surrounded by freethinkers and free love while he struggled with feelings of repression and depression. Looking back on this time later in life, Heard said it felt like he was suffocating under "the heavy pressure of inhibition." It would take him a number of years to reconcile his sexual feelings and his strict Christian upbringing.

.   .   .   .   .   .

Physical and emotional maladies kept Huxley and Heard off the battlefields of World War I, and they would later become two of the leading pacifists in England in the years leading up to World War II.

Bill Wilson was sent to Europe and briefly saw action just as the First World War was ending. He shipped out of New York on the British troop carrier the *Lancashire,* arriving in England in the summer of 1918. Wilson was quartered outside of Winchester and got a chance to visit that city's famous cathedral before heading across the English Channel to face the Germans in France. He was, of course, extremely anxious about what lay ahead. He'd been on an emotional roller coaster, riding waves of patriotism, duty, dread, and fear. So it's not surprising that Wilson would have a powerful religious experience inside that silent sanctuary of stone and stained glass.

"I was lifted into a sort of ecstasy," he writes in his autobiography. "And though I was not a conscious believer in God at the time—I had no defined belief—yet I somehow had a mighty assurance that things were and would be all right. . . . I didn't define it, but it was a valid spiritual experience and had the classic mechanism: collapsed human powerlessness, then God coming to man to lift him up to set him on the high road to his destiny."

.   .   .   .   .

Spending most of my career working for daily newspapers rarely allowed me to write about myself or my own spiritual search, and I still tell my own story with some hesitation. *I* is a dirty word among newspaper reporters, or at least it used to be. We were taught to keep ourselves out of our stories.

But my reluctance to write a memoir began to change when my mother moved into a nursing home that provides assisted living and memory care to about a hundred seniors in the suburbs north of Sacramento. My mother lives there. Her memories have died there, and visiting her shows me that I may have no choice but to write mine down before they're gone.

Having a parent with Alzheimer's disease or another form of dementia or memory loss can be a painfully long and sad way to say good-bye. It also reaffirms the adage about laughing to keep from crying. There is great sorrow in having a parent with no memory, but it can also be a great adventure. My older sister and I never know how much of Mom will be there when we visit. It changes from moment to moment, which is exactly how my mother lives now, from moment to moment. Buddhists spend their whole lives trying to live in the moment. By that standard, Mom is enlightened.

Her existence in the moment also provides my sister and me with a running comedy routine, and like all great humor, it's funny and tragic. One minute my mother will be introducing me to the other ladies in the memory unit as "my son, Don." Two minutes later, she'll turn to me and say, "Where did we meet?"

Where *did* we meet? Actually, it's a good question.

This chapter is titled "Wounded." My family's fatal wound was inflicted on January 23, 1953, about ten months before I was born. I was a bereavement baby, and I've come to believe that the single most important event of my childhood occurred on that day. It's most certainly *why* I was born.

Since I wound up spending most of my life as a newspaper reporter, let me begin the story with a newspaper clipping that my sister and I found when we were going through my mother's things after we sent her off to memory care. It was clipped from the January 24, 1953, edition of a New Jersey newspaper, headlined "Ramsey Boy, 4, Falls from Car, Dies of Injuries." Here's the story:

Little Alan Lattin met death yesterday because he was unwilling to accompany his mother, Mrs. Muriel Lattin of 147 Myrtle Avenue, in her car to pick up his sister at elementary school, the boy's father, Warren, said today.

Alan, 4, took the back seat of his mother's 2-door sedan protesting that he wanted to stay with the neighbor they were visiting.

Mrs. Lattin prepared to get into the driver's seat when, with the car standing still, the boy thrust the hinged front seat forward.

The impact somehow opened the right hand door and he was catapulted, head first, onto the driveway. He picked himself up, resumed his position in the car, and lost consciousness.

Mrs. Lattin drove her boy to the Good Samaritan Hospital in Suffern, where he died a few minutes later. Cause of the death is still not determined.

On November 15, 1953, I was born in that same hospital in Suffern, New York. My parents named me "Donnie" after Alan's imaginary friend—a little boy he would blame for his minor misdeeds. "I didn't do it," Alan would insist. "Donnie did it."

When I was about four years old, I started talking about my own imaginary friend. His name was Russell. "I didn't do it," I'd insist. "Russell did it." Like most kids who go through this stage of childhood projection, I grew up, stopped talking about "Russell," and found more mature ways to project my feelings onto other people.

Our family appeared to resume the normal routines of suburban life in the 1950s. My parents had cocktail parties. My father began a long career as a salesman and sales manager for Thomas J. Lipton, the people with the "flow-through teabag." My mother stayed at home, cooking, cleaning, and raising my sister and me.

My family rarely talked about Alan, and never mentioned the details of his death. My sister and I didn't know the whole story until my mother lost her memory of it and we found that newspaper clipping in a box of keepsakes. When we were growing up, Alan's name was spoken only when we'd look at old family photos and my parents would try to figure out if the little boy with the pointy ears in that picture was Alan or Donnie. We could have been twins.

We were, if you believe in reincarnation.

My family picked up and moved every three to four years, bouncing across the country like we were running away from the past, first to Ohio, then Colorado, and on to California, where we ran out of places to run and my parents got divorced. They'd managed to keep up the appearance of an intact family until we got to California and my sister got married in the fall of 1965. Many years later, my father and I got very drunk and he told me that he never really forgave my mother for Alan's death.

Like his father, Big Al Lattin from Manhattan, my father was a large man, six foot, six inches tall. He told me about how he had picked up little Alan in his arms that cold January day and wept like a baby, something he had never done before and hadn't done since. We had another drink, and I told Dad about the time I overheard an argument he and my mother had shortly before they got divorced. My mother had cried out in anger, "I'm not the one who wanted to have another kid after Alan died!"

Mom and Dad had been arguing about whether they should keep the marriage intact until I'd left home. I was thirteen years old, and neither of them could put up with another five years of the charade. A few years later, when my dad told me he and my mother were getting a divorce, I replied, "It's about time," and walked away. It may have been the first really cruel and cynical thing I said. It wouldn't be the last.

My family never dealt with the psychological trauma of my brother's passing. They just got another puppy, and I grew up in the long shadow of the tragic events of January 23, 1953. My mother tried to forget what happened by turning her attention to me. She was a good mother, loving and—not surprisingly—overprotective. Mom was a nervous driver for the rest of her life. I can still see her hands tightly clutching the steering wheel and her thumbs twitching back and forth. We were the first people in the neighborhood to have seat belts installed in our car.

As a boy, I was not allowed to roam far from home—a restriction I would more than make up for in my teenage years.

When I left home for good to go to college in the early 1970s, Mom needed another surrogate son, someone else she could care for, someone else to keep her from thinking about what happened to Alan on that driveway back in Ramsey, New Jersey. She found him in the form of her second husband. My sister and I could never really figure out what Mom saw in the guy until I connected the dots back to Russell, my imaginary friend from the 1950s. For the man my mother married was named Gideon "Russ" Russell. I'm convinced that my mother didn't really marry Russ Russell. She married "Russell," my imaginary friend. It was the only way to keep her connection to "Donnie" and, through that imaginary figure, to the son she lost.

Now my mother doesn't remember why she is named Russell. She doesn't remember either of her husbands. But she does remember Donnie. There are some days on the memory care unit when she calls everyone "Donnie." My sister is "Donnie." The nurses are "Donnie." Her stuffed animals are "Donnie." Everyone is "Donnie," except for me. She's not sure who I am, and come to think of it, neither am I.

·   ·   ·   ·   ·

Most of us leave our family of origin licking our wounds. Some of us spend the rest of our lives picking at the scabs.

Bill Wilson was wounded by his abandonment by both parents. Like many kids from broken homes, young Bill blamed himself for their divorce. If only he could have been better, more lovable, his parents would have loved him enough to stay together.

Gerald Heard was burned by the fire and brimstone of his father's faith and the fundamentalism of an abusive grandmother. This early spiritual abuse left him repressed and depressed.

Aldous Huxley began his adult life scarred by his mother's death and his brother's suicide.

Each of these men found a way to move on with life—and their lives would come together three decades later in the mountains southeast of Los Angeles. They were on the road to Trabuco Canyon, but there would be a few more stops along the way.

Bloomsbury

The Muses, in Greek mythology, were the daughters
of Memory, and every writer is embarked, like
Marcel Proust, on a hopeless search for time lost.
But a good writer is one who knows how "to give
the purer meaning to the words of the tribe." . . .
Time lost can never be regained; but in his search
for it he may reveal to his readers glimpses of timeless reality.

Aldous Huxley, *Knowledge and Understanding*, 1956

My quest to understand the lives and times of Gerald Heard and Aldous
Huxley began early one morning outside a four-story Georgian apartment building on Endsleigh Place in London. I wouldn't have found
the place at all if I hadn't tracked down Stawell Heard, one of Gerald's
distant cousins. We'd met the night before at the Blackbird, a pub on
Earl's Court Road in South Kensington. Stawell rarely gets phone calls
from people interested in his long-dead cousin, who's as forgotten in his
native England as he is in his adopted home of California, where he lived
out the final thirty-four years of his life. Stawell was glad to hear from
someone still interested in Gerald, for he too finds in this man a life that
deserves to be remembered.

Heard and Huxley met for the first time one evening in January 1929
at the home of Raymond Mortimer, an English literary critic and mem-

ber of the Bloomsbury circle. My immediate goal in London was to set foot in the room where Heard and Huxley had their first encounter. I knew from earlier research that Mortimer lived at 6 Gordon Place in Bloomsbury in early 1929, but I found no such street on any London map. That stumbling block was cleared when Stawell Heard consulted a directory that listed the previous names of London streets. "Mystery solved," he told me when we met in the pub. "Gordon Place is now known as Endsleigh Place."

Endsleigh Place is one of the London streets that define Gordon Square and Tavistock Square Gardens, two little parks that form the nucleus of the Bloomsbury district. Like most of the charming London squares, these quadrangles were originally designed as private gardens for people living in the surrounding homes. Today, Gordon Square is owned by the University of London and is open to all visitors, as is Tavistock, which is now a city park. I walked through the Tavistock gate just after dawn and was greeted by two drunks sitting on a park bench, passing a bottle. It wasn't clear whether they were getting an early start or finishing up a long night, but I quickly walked by them and into the grassy square. The most prominent monument in the park is a statute of Gandhi, sitting cross-legged atop a little mountain of stone.

I roamed around a bit more and found a bust of Virginia Woolf, one of the founding members of the Bloomsbury circle, which also included the economist John Maynard Keynes, the artist Clive Bell, the biographer Lytton Strachey, and Virginia's husband, the critic Leonard Woolf. Virginia is remembered for, among many other things, the observation "A woman must have money and a room of her own if she is to write fiction." The line comes from her book-length essay *A Room of One's Own*, which was published in 1929, a few months after Heard and Huxley had their first encounter. Woolf and her husband lived at 46 Gordon Square and later at 52 Tavistock Square, down the street from the building and the room I was trying to find on that damp London morning.

The building is now known as Passfield Hall, and for most of the year it houses students from the London School of Economics. I sat down on the stoop and waited for someone to walk out the locked front door. Someone did, and I slipped inside, trying to look like I had a reason to be there. The place has been remodeled a few times since Raymond Mortimer called it home, but standing in the entry hall I immediately recognized the gracefully curved stairway from which Aldous Huxley walked into the life of Gerald Heard in the first few weeks of 1929.

"Aldous Huxley sailed into my view," Heard would later recall. "His approach, his 'port,' had about it something of a galleon's. He came in, as it were, under full sail, a long coat billowing around him. The voice, however, was as neat as a seamstress's stitching. And, indeed, the long fingers made the precise movements of a needlewoman handling thread and seam. The discourse was not only ironic and entertaining, but fantastically informed."

Mortimer knew this would be an extraordinary meeting of minds, so he had invited no other guests. One of Huxley's verbal tics was to punctuate his conversation with *extraordinary* and *incredible*, and we can safely assume those words were frequently uttered that night. We may also assume that Huxley was struck by Heard's eyes, which were a dazzling light blue. The two men probably talked about Heard's book *The Ascent of Humanity*, which would be published later in the year. That ambitious work would trace the evolution of human consciousness over millennia—from a time when man had no sense of himself as a separate individual to the sometimes crippling self-obsession of modern man. Heard would spend the rest of his life laying out the course mankind must follow to achieve a futuristic "super-consciousness." But I'm sure lots of gossip also enlivened that first conversation. Huxley's latest novel, *Point Counter Point*, a cutting caricature of London's aristocratic dilettantes, was just out. Bloomsbury's leading lights were poring over its pages, trying to figure out who was whom in Huxley's semifictional satirical account of their incestuous existence.

"We stayed talking till past 1 A.M.," Heard recalled, "when all the buses had finished their routes, all taxis ceased their cruising. Consequently each of us had before him a more than three-mile walk. To my surprise, for our directions were divergent, Huxley accompanied me all the way to my block of flats and then, changing tack, sailed off for another couple of miles of solitary striding to his own rooms. But not before he had invited me to another session the following week."

Huxley met Heard just as the other great male friend of his life, D. H. Lawrence, was dying. That friendship began in 1926, when Huxley was traveling in India and received a surprise letter from Lawrence praising him for his travel writing. Huxley visited Lawrence in Florence in the fall of that year.

They were in some ways an odd couple. Lawrence was as earthy and emotional as Huxley was transcendent and cerebral. Huxley and Lawrence would harshly critique each other's work, and even their differing philosophies of life, but maintained a deep mutual respect. They had really come together during a long holiday in Switzerland the winter of 1927. The two men would each write in the mornings, then relax or go on outings with Maria, Huxley's first wife, and Lawrence's impetuous mate, Frieda. Huxley was working on *Point Counter Point* and Lawrence was finishing up his great novel *Lady Chatterley's Lover*. Aldous was the first reader of that work. Maria was given the job of typing up the handwritten manuscript of the book, which would be banned as obscene in a number of countries and not published in the United States until 1959, four years after Maria's death.

Aldous and Maria were both at Lawrence's bedside when he died in France on March 2, 1930. Aldous dealt with his grief over his friend's passing by collecting and editing *The Letters of D. H. Lawrence*, which was published the following year in England and the United States. Lawrence was the basis for the character of Rampion in *Point Counter Point*. "Being with Rampion rather depresses me; for he makes me see what a great gulf separates the knowledge of the obvious from the actual living of it," says Philip Quarles, the overly intellectual writer in *Point Counter Point*, a character Huxley seems to have based on himself. "If I could only capture something of his secret."

Huxley had met Lawrence briefly in England in 1915. They were brought together by Lady Ottoline Morrell, the woman who had baptized Aldous into the Bohemian London scene when he was a twenty-one-year-old Oxford undergraduate. Morrell and her husband, Philip, a Liberal member of Parliament, presided over Garsington Manor, an Oxfordshire estate that provided some of the most memorable settings and characters in modern English literature. Lady Ottoline was the model for Hermione, a character in the D. H. Lawrence novel *Women in Love*, and was the object of a cutting caricature in Huxley's first novel, *Crome Yellow*. Lady O did not appreciate her portrayal. She'd been a gracious hostess and opened many doors for young Aldous. It was through her that he'd met Maria. Lady Ottoline was also Huxley's connection to Virginia Woolf and the Bloomsbury set—not to mention a few of Aldous's more memorable lovers and mistresses.

Ottoline and Philip Morrell also maintained a London home on Bedford Square, where they hosted such guests as Winston Churchill, whom Virginia Woolf recalled as "very rubicund, all gold lace and medals, on his way to Buckingham Palace," and the philosopher Bertrand Russell, one of Ottoline's lovers. Woolf commented on the role Ottoline played in the larger scene: "When the history of Bloomsbury is written . . . there will have to be a chapter, even if it is only in the appendix, devoted to Ottoline," she wrote in her diary. "Lady Ottoline is a great lady who has become discontented with her own class and is trying to find what she wants among artists and writers. For this reason, as if they were inspired with something divine, she approaches them in a deferential way and they see her as a disembodied spirit escaping from her world into one where she can never take root."

Ottoline was the most flamboyant and self-consciously Bohemian star in the Bloomsbury galaxy. Katie Roiphe, in her book about literary London in the early years of the twentieth century, notes that Ottoline wore "outlandish, fairy-tale clothes, from giant feathered hats to Turkish harem pants to flowing satin tunics . . . dressing as if she were about to be painted, and she often was." Her affair with her gardener was the basis for the scandalous *Lady Chatterley's Lover*. But even Ottoline managed to be shocked when her husband confessed one day that he had not one but two pregnant mistresses—his secretary and a former maid.

Aldous Huxley first met Ottoline in late 1915. "I had an amusing day on Sunday," he said in a letter to his father, "going out to Garsington for luncheon to the Philip Morrells, who have bought the lovely Elizabethan manor there. Lady Ottoline, Philip's wife, is quite an incredible creature—arty beyond the dreams of avarice and a patroness of literature and the modern. She is intelligent, but her affectation is overwhelming."

Aldous was introduced at the luncheon as "the grandson of Thomas

Henry Huxley." Someone present at the table described Aldous as "very silent, very young," going on to note that his height of "six foot four seemed even taller because of the slenderness of his body and his slight stoop. Under the thick brown hair, his wide face was pale with full lips and blue eyes which had an inward look. . . . He did not talk much at his first visit, but as soon as he was gone, everyone agreed about the deep impression of unique quality, of gentleness and depth."

Huxley started hanging out at the manor and soon took a room there while finishing up his Oxford studies. It was a living arrangement that would have a profound effect on the young man's view of love, sex, and marriage. Garsington and Bloomsbury were more than intellectual and artistic incubators. They were hotbeds of freethinking and free love.

"Everything was going to be new; everything was going to be different. Everything was on trial," Virginia Woolf explained. "The old sentimental views of marriage in which we were brought up were revolutionized. . . . There is nothing shocking in a man's having a mistress, or in a woman's being one. Perhaps the fidelity of our parents was not the only or inevitably the highest form of married life. Perhaps indeed that fidelity was not so strict as one had supposed."

Huxley proposed to Maria Nys at Garsington in the late summer of 1916, a few months after their first meeting. Maria had been born in the Flemish town of Courtrai in the fall of 1898. To escape the German advance in World War I, she fled to England with her mother and sisters. Maria's uncle, an art professor at Glasgow University, knew Lady Ottoline and arranged for the teenage girl to take a room at Garsington.

Maria had a alluring appeal, and not only to Aldous. Lady Ottoline was drawn to her. So was Mary Hutchinson, a Bloomsbury writer and socialite, who could not resist Maria's "Persian" qualities. "Her eyes were almond-shaped and very beautiful," said Hutchinson, "her expression languid, her nature innocent, sensual, uncomplicated, her heart warm and loyal. Her hair was dark. She always seemed to be sweetly scented, oiled and voluptuous." Hutchinson would later become a lover of both Aldous and Maria, but that ménage à trois was still some years off. In December 1916, Maria left for Italy with her mother. She wouldn't set eyes on Aldous again until the spring of 1919.

Meanwhile, Huxley tried to find his own footing in London. He took a couple of dreary desk jobs as part of the British war effort. He tried his hand at poetry, publishing two collections, titled *The Burning Wheel* and *The Defeat of Youth*. The reviews were mixed. The *Times* found his work "pleasantly offensive." Huxley also began writing his own critical reviews for the *New Statesman and Nation*, beginning his more success-ful career as a literary journalist. He returned to Eton to try his hand at teaching, but decided, "God never intended for me to do any regular work." He told a friend, "I am just a mildly clever fool, educated from the earliest age to be 'blasé,' for in England one isn't supposed to be refined, unless one is blasé and cynical."

Eton could not compete with the social whirl of London, where Hux-ley sat at the feet of Bertrand Russell, who inspired Huxley's later paci-fism, and T. S. Eliot, who advised Aldous to stick to prose. There was no shortage of female companionship or galleries to visit.

Yet his heart belonged to Maria. As soon as the war ended, Aldous sailed off to the continent to see her. They were married in the sum-mer of 1919 at the little seventeenth-century Hôtel de Ville at Bellem, Belgium, beginning an extraordinary partnership that continued for the next thirty-five years, ending only with Maria's death from cancer in California in the winter of 1955. Maria's dedication to Aldous was as deep as it was unconventional. She was, in many ways, his eyes, but also his ears. She was his secretary and his chauffeur. She was his gatekeeper and protector. She kept some people away from Aldous and provided access for others—including beautiful young women to share his bed.

Why did Maria become a wife whose duties included the procure-ment of her husband's lovers? In her 1974 biography of Aldous, Sybille Bedford, Aldous and Maria Huxley's close friend and confidante, asks and answers the question:

Why did she do it? Well first of all, as she has said, for Aldous. For his work. It was also part of her generosity, and her sense of realism. . . . Maria took what I should call the aristocratic view of sex. And she knew that she was wise—it never got out of hand. She did see to *that*. Not that it was necessary. And Aldous? Men have asked me: "Allowing one's wife to help one getting a girl—isn't that terribly undermining for a man?" They were shocked. Well Aldous did not feel in the least diminished, he never seemed to feel the need to assert his manhood. . . . It was a measure of how certain they were, and how free, and of the great niceness that there was between them. There was some brother and sister element in their relation; they could share each other's escapades.

That is about as close as Bedford comes in her biography to addressing the issue of Maria Huxley's bisexuality. In later years, she was more direct. "Maria was bisexual and she did have a series of short-term, passionate relationships with other people while she was married to Aldous."

Mary Hutchinson—best known in the Bloomsbury saga for her affair with Clive Bell—was the most notorious paramour to enter Huxley's bedchamber. In his 2002 biography of Huxley, Nicholas Murray unearths letters Huxley wrote to Hutchinson showing that the affair with Hutchinson was deeper, longer, and more complicated than most of Huxley's liaisons. "How much I enjoyed last Friday," Aldous wrote. "I always used, in the past, to be so terribly shy and nervous of you. Why I hardly know—unless it was your air of impenetrable serenity that disquieted me. What are you really like?"

Hutchinson's seductions were legendary. Virginia Woolf called her "a crafty devil" who "hunts like a beast of prey." In fact, Hutchinson may have been using Aldous to get to his wife. "Maria was the one I loved," she later confessed. "Aldous was gentle, aloof, affectionate and even ardent sometimes, but it was Maria who attracted and charmed me."

. . . . .

My fascination with the Huxley marriage is not purely prurient. I'll confess that the young scoundrel in me would love a wife who cares so much about her husband's need to concentrate on his writing that she provides a needed diversion by bringing beautiful women to his door. I feel blessed when my wife, Laura, knocks on my door with a demitasse of espresso and a chocolate chip cookie.

What I find most fascinating about Bloomsbury in the 1920s and 1930s is how much it reminds me of San Francisco in the 1960s and 1970s.

Huxley's open marriage and his disdain for "traditional family values" prefigured the sexual revolution and social upheaval that rocked American society when I was coming of age. John Maynard Keynes, the highly influential economist and member of the Bloomsbury circle, described the quandary that faced both generations. "We all want both to have and not to have husbands and wives."

Keynes had love affairs with Lytton Strachey and Bloomsbury artist Duncan Grant and then married a famous Russian ballerina. What was most unusual about the Roaring Twenties and the Swinging Sixties was not so much that people were having lots of sex, but that they were so open about it. "Many of them believed that if they told the truth— often ugly cutting truths—then nothing they did could be considered wrong," Roiphe writes. "In this they were reacting against what they saw as the hypocrisy fostered by their parents' generation, but they may have placed too much faith in the redemptive power of communication for its own sake."

Aldous Huxley, a product of Victorian England, had a front-row seat for the Roaring Twenties and lived to see the dawn of the Swinging Sixties. And he was prophet for all seasons, a social commentator whose writing still inspires. Huxley would seek to reconcile sex and spirituality, science and religion, but in the end he was as mistrustful of technological progress as he was of organized religion, wary of sexual repression *and* free love. He would become the satiric muse of the "Lost Generation," but his cynicism was never crippling. He would search for a way to move beyond the nihilism and hedonism of his social circle, to cultivate a new kind of conscious awareness.

Huxley lived on the edge of Bohemian London. He tested the waters, but he kept his distance. During the early 1920s, Huxley's main source of income was his journalism. He parodied the bourgeois Bohemians of his time in his novels while providing more serious commentary in his essays in the literary and popular press.

By the late 1920s, Huxley was clearly disillusioned with the "puerilities of the jazzing libertine." Sexual freedom as practiced in his day was not the answer to the puritanical repression of the Victorian era. He offered the following observation in an article published in the May 1928 issue of *Vanity Fair:* "There has probably never been so much of casual intimacy between the sexes as at the present time; nor ever, probably, so little genuine warmth of feeling or wholehearted abandonment to passion." Huxley seems to be saying that the young ladies Maria brought into his chamber were sexually freer than they used to be, but not free enough. "Thus the modern young woman gets the best of both worlds, she succeeds in being fashionable and rational about sex, without running any risk of being swept off her conscious feet by the physical-instinctive biological forces which a genuine warm, wholehearted abandonment might so dangerously let loose."

Huxley had equal contempt for the traditional family, which, according to his reckoning, was already in decline in England and the United States. "Throughout at least the Nordic sections of the Anglo-Saxon world, the family is a declining institution," he wrote in the next issue of *Vanity Fair*, in June 1928. "It is a fact which I number among the greatest of our Anglo-Saxon blessings." By now, Huxley had a family of his own. Maria had given birth to their only child, Matthew, in the spring of 1920. Huxley saw some value in the immediate family, but he describes it in rather cold terms. "Most children become attached by force of habit to those who surround them," he wrote. "Circumstance and feeling will always ensure the existence of some sort of family." Huxley was a big believer in the British boarding school, which kept children of a certain class away from their parents for most of the year between the ages of nine and nineteen. These schools have "done much to accelerate the break-up of the family system in England," a welcome development in Huxley's view.

Huxley's opinions about the value of family cannot be separated from his own experience of it. There were the deaths of his mother and his brother, and the constant pressure to live up to the legacy of his famous grandfather. Looking into the future, Huxley foresaw a continued "decrease in the size and power of the family circle," which will mean "the growing individual will have an unprecedented freedom."

Maybe, or maybe not. Huxley ends his June 1928 essay, titled "The Decline of the Family," on a prophetic note. He foresees another scenario in which the breakdown of the family gives rise to a fierce nostalgia for its return. And he was right—witness the repressive political agenda of the Christian right today in its crusade for a return to "traditional family values." "We may be quite sure," Huxley wrote, "that the young people of the coming generation will be no more satisfied with the family system of 1950 than we were satisfied with the family system of 1910 or our fathers with that of 1880. What their complaints will be, it is hard to prophesy. Perhaps—for such is the perversity of the human heart—they will look with envy on the luxuriant and inextricably united family."

.   .   .   .   .

My philosophy about marriage and family flowed, like Huxley's, from my own experience and environment. I grew up with a cynical view of marriage. For many years I looked at monogamy as little more than a stepping-stone to hypocrisy. It was the 1970s, the era of open relationships. The marching orders were: "Love the one you're with." Promiscuity was fine; dishonesty was not. My father was not faithful to my mother, nor was he honest with her. One of his affairs was the stated reason for their divorce, which came as my adolescent hormones were in full blossom. I was old enough that—under California law—I was to be consulted about the child custody arrangements. I had a say as to whether I would live with my mom or dad. It was the first hard decision of my life. I had this fantasy of my dad and me sharing a cool bachelor pad in Hollywood or Venice Beach. We'd sit around drinking martinis and reading *Playboy* magazine. But I could not conceive of my mother living alone. My sister had already married and left home, and my mother simply did not seem like an independent unit. She needed a man to take care of her.

What should I do? Should I do what I wanted to do, or what I thought I *should* do? I fretted about it for weeks. Around that time, I'd started writing songs and playing guitar. I was fifteen years old, and I knew what I wanted to be when I grew up. I wanted to be Bob Dylan.

Forty-two years later, sitting at my computer, I am trying to remember how it felt to be fifteen years old. There's really only one way to recover the memory. It's been many years since I pulled out the battered spiral notebook in which I scribbled teenage lyrics full of anger and angst. The notebook has a red cover torn at the top. The name "Diploma Theme

Book" is printed on the front. You could pick these up for forty-nine cents back in the summer of 1969.

There are twenty-three songs inside, and I start tearing up just looking at the titles. The songs are all so sweet and stupid, cynical and sincere. The first song is titled "Practice What You Preach." Try to imagine a teenage impersonation of Bob Dylan: "They tell him that his promises just should not be broke / Yet they treat the marriage promise like a joke / If you ever want him to learn what you have to teach / You better start a-practicin' what you preach."

There's a song called "Caught in the Middle." It starts: "Either way my decision makes someone sad. / I have to choose between my mom and dad. / One will wind up glad. / The other will be so sad. / I'm caught in the middle of a family feud."

I decided that I wanted to live with my dad. It wasn't my fault that I'd been put in this situation, so I was going to do what I wanted to do. I didn't have the nerve to tell my mother, so I told my dad. We were sitting in his 1968 Chevy Impala outside our house on the Palo Verdes Peninsula in Southern California. He'd already moved out. He tried not to look surprised when I told him I wanted to move in with him. I immediately sensed that wasn't the choice I was supposed to make.

"Okay," he said, pausing. "Have you told you mother?"

"I can't," I replied. "You tell her."

School had just ended, and we'd already decided that I would spend part of the summer with a friend whose family had a farm in Illinois. Dad was supposed to give Mom the news, but only after I was safely out of town. A few days after I'd arrived at the farm, the phone rang. My mother didn't say hello. She said, "Your father tells me you refuse to live with me."

I don't remember much about the rest of the phone call, but I do remember what happened. My mother guilt-tripped me into changing my mind. I wound up staying in the house with her. But I came back from the Midwest that summer with a wall around my heart.

My memories of my feelings in the summer of 1969 were confirmed by some letters I found as my sister and I went through my mother's things when we sent her off to memory care. I'd mailed the first one to her from the farm in Illinois, a week before I returned to California. "I know this whole thing is tough on you, but put yourself in my place. Whoever I stay with after everything is settled shouldn't make any difference to the other person because the whole thing isn't my fault and I'm just caught in the middle of it," I wrote. "But however it comes out I love you and Dad as much as I ever did—which is a lot even though it probably doesn't seem that way to you sometimes. You can both do me one favor—don't fight, and still be friends—at least in front of me."

My mother got her way. I would live with her. But I wouldn't talk to her. Days went by without a word. At the time, I didn't really know the details of my brother's death and how it must have devastated my mother. If I had, I might have shown more compassion or been less cynical. But as I saw it then, my parents had lied to me: I really had no choice about where I was to live.

.   .   .   .   .

Back on the farm, I'd earned some money over the summer loading bales of hay onto flatbed trucks. Over the next few months I put those funds together with a little money I'd scraped together working at a car wash and at my brother-in-law's Shell station and bought a 1965 Mustang, red with a white vinyl roof. The following summer I decided it was time for a road trip. I tore all the seats out except the driver's seat, gathered up my guitar and my dog, and headed up Highway 1.

My road trip in the summer of 1970 lasted a couple of weeks. Somewhere south of Santa Barbara, I pulled over to pick up a hippie girl. She hopped in the car, but not before her boyfriend jumped out of the bushes to join her. This wasn't exactly the fantasy I had in mind.

They sat where the backseat used to be, leaning against my sleeping bag and playing with my dog, Alvin, a beagle I'd named after the cartoon chipmunk with the squeaky voice. Alvin had less than a year left to live. He'd been my loyal companion since I was a five-year-old boy living in Chesterland, Ohio. He moved with us to Colorado and then California and was the only friend I had until I could make new friends. I kept looking back at Alvin and the hippies in the rearview mirror, and

I didn't like what I saw. The hippie chick's boyfriend looked more like Charlie Manson than a proponent of peace and love. I didn't trust him. He had a big knife strapped to his belt and a funny look in his eye. I made up a story about having to head back down south for something and ditched them at a gas station, terrified that I'd run into them again on my northern journey of self-discovery.

My mother had agreed to let me head up the coast after I told her I would stay with the parents of Patty Smith, who'd been my best friend during the four years we lived in Colorado. Patty was the ultimate tomboy, so we got along great as kids. We loved to dress up as cowboys, strap on our pistols, and head into the dirt hills on the edge of our freshly minted Littleton subdivision. Behind us, the Rockies rose up in purple mountain majesty. It always looked like you could walk to the Rocky Mountains from the fort we fashioned from scrap lumber and cardboard boxes we found in the hills. We headed for the mountains many times, collecting pieces of petrified rock along the way with Alvin the beagle at our side, but the Rockies were always just another mile away.

Patty's family moved out to Los Altos, an upper-middle-class suburb south of San Francisco, shortly before my family moved to Palos Verdes, an upper-middle-class suburb south of Los Angeles. I did reconnect with Patty on my journey up the coast, but my first stop on that trip was not Los Altos but Big Sur.

Looking back, I'm not sure what first drew me to this spectacular stretch of the central California coast. Big Sur had had a Bohemian reputation since at least the 1940s, when Henry Miller, the great writer and unapologetic libertine, moved there and inspired an enclave of likeminded artists, writers, and freethinkers to join him. *Harper's* magazine blew the whistle in 1947 with a breathless story titled "The New Cult of Sex and Anarchy," which revealed how the Millerites were cultivating a new strain of erotic mysticism above the rugged California cliffs. If you listened carefully you could hear echoes of Bloomsbury bouncing off the canyon walls.

In the early 1960s, Michael Murphy and Richard Price opened Esalen Institute at Big Sur. Gerald Heard and Aldous Huxley, who came to lecture and visit, had been among the first guests. But I knew nothing of this in the summer of 1970. I was sixteen years old and driving up Highway 1 with some vague idea of being "on the road" in search of hippies and hot tubs. All I knew was that I was supposed to go to Big Sur and, beyond that, I would find San Francisco and the legendary Haight-Ashbury.

My first stop was the Pfeiffer Big Sur campground, where I met my first real hippie. He showed me a great swimming hole up the river, behind the campground, where the assembled tribe was blissfully skinny-dipping. I wasn't sure what I was looking for, but I was starting to find it. I spent a second night at the campground and then gave my new hippie friend a lift to San Francisco. I don't remember his name, but I do remember two things about him—he lived in an apartment on Divisadero Street and he was reading *Island,* Aldous Huxley's last novel.

Within the next few months, I would read Huxley's utopian fantasy and then buy my own paperback copy of *The Doors of Perception*. I was already becoming a high-school stoner, but Huxley's writing would elevate my drug-taking to another level. I was no longer simply getting high. I was on a spiritual search.

It was late in the day when my new friend and I rolled out of Big Sur. It was dark when we approached the city. We went around a curve on the freeway and there was San Francisco—a shining beacon on a foggy summer night. It was a sight I will never forget, and I knew at that moment that I would be back.

According to the conventional wisdom, the scene in San Francisco had already soured. Ken Kesey had declared the death of the hippie. Speed had replaced LSD as the drug of choice in the Haight. That may have been the case, but it all still looked pretty cool to a sixteen-year-old kid fleeing the soulless suburbs of Southern California. My new friend put me up for two nights in his apartment on Divisadero Street. We went over to Marin County for a hike on Mount Tam and then over to Berkeley, and I knew then that was where I would go to college.

By the time I hit town, San Francisco had become the new mecca for the alienated youth of America. We came in droves, a lost army in search of peace, love, and the meaning of life, and if we didn't find that, at least there was lots of sex, drugs, and rock 'n' roll.

I would return to Southern California and finish high school before moving back to the Bay Area the day after graduation. That was the summer of 1972, when I was accepted at summer school to start my freshman studies at the University of California, Berkeley. I was five years late for the Summer of Love, but *c'est la vie*. I've often felt like I was five years late. I'll blame that on my late brother. Alan was born on December 18, 1948, five years before I came into this world. Alan never made it to the Summer of Love, but his imaginary friend would spend much of his life trying to keep the party going as long as possible.

We were still dealing with the divorce fallout in the spring of 1974, when my mother was trying to get control of funds my father had set aside for my college expenses. Another letter I found among my mother's keepsakes was one I wrote during my second year at Berkeley. "I don't like getting mixed up in this alimony crap," I wrote. "Dad is not a rich fat cat trying to give you as little as he can, and you're not a money-hungry ex-wife trying to soak him for all he's got. Too bad you both have that impression. I think it's disgusting and I've told him the same thing, so don't think I'm taking sides."

My brother's death and my father's inability to forgive my mother for letting it happen cast a long shadow over my family, or at least over my perception of it. We never spoke of it. We drank over it. We soothed the pain with another martini—or in my case, a six-pack of beer—chasing cheer to cover sorrow. We moved into another house in another town in another western state. When we got to California, my mother's angry words about not wanting to have another child after Alan died broke the silence. It was the insight that shattered the family myth. My mother's outburst hurt me and haunted me. But in a strange way, it also liberated me.

· · · · ·

Gerald Heard was not a family man, but he would become a firm believer in the family of man. The physical and spiritual abuse he suffered as a child would have a profound effect on the way he viewed "traditional family values." We've already seen that Huxley, a product of Eton, saw great value in the British boarding school system, which separates men of a certain class from their families and—at its best—forces them to think for themselves. Heard, on the other hand, did not leave his school, Sherborne, with a favorable impression of it.

Heard went on to study at Gonville and Caius College in Cambridge, where he graduated in 1911 with a bachelor's degree in history. It was here, writes Alison Falby, his biographer, that Heard first "acquired an Idealist outlook, and sought to integrate history, religion, and the social, physical and biological sciences." His education in the wonders of Bohemian London would begin when he was introduced to the gay painter Glyn Philpot, who painted three portraits of Heard and became a close friend. Philpot was drawn to Heard, at least in part because the painter "shared his religious upbringing, his homosexuality, and his loquaciousness."

They met one evening in 1915 over dinner at the London home of Randall Davies. Heard—who was twenty-five-years old, five years younger than Philpot—would, many years later, recall their first encounter with fondness. "It is now just thirty years since I first met him and it is a decade since I last saw him. Since then one has met a number of people who are considered famous and certainly are remarkable, but I am not sure that any of them have given me quite the sense of uniqueness that Glyn did," Heard wrote. "There were no other guests and, as soon as we were dining, one forgot he was a very successful artist for of course he was as brilliant a talker as he was a painter—indeed he was essentially a personality—one whom if he had no specific art people would have said of him that his character, his style was far more remarkable than anything he did."

Glyn and Gerald talked late into the night, then left to walk back to Philpot's studio in Chelsea, at 33 Tite Street, just up from the bank of the river Thames. "The moment one entered it one saw how perfectly he could make everything he touched reflect him. It was a difficult place to make look comfortable, still more gracious, but he had given it some real beauty. It amused him to take ugliness and, with a brilliant economy of material, to turn the dull thing into an object of peculiar distinctive quality. I stayed with him till one or past and we met very often after that."

Gerald loved many things about Glyn, including the way he would let Gerald watch while Glyn painted his portrait. Heard was a hand-some young man, in a delicate sort of way. He had soft blue eyes and auburn hair parted on the left. He had a reddish moustache trimmed and twisted at the ends over a shaggy goatee. During one of these inti-mate sessions, the artist turned to his subject and said, "The trouble with your face is that at first glance it all seems on a big scale and the more one looks at it, the more one sees that in point of fact everything is really quite small."

The two men talked much about religion. Philpot had been raised as a Baptist but had converted to Roman Catholicism. More than once Philpot had said, "Why don't you become a Catholic?," prompting a theological debate. "We would then enter on those discussions which resemble," Heard said, "the kind of exchanges that would take place between a fish and a bird if they agreed to discuss the advantages and necessities of their respective positions in the world of life. Through him I met a number of people who were actually artists or connoisseurs. . . . I had not seen anything of this world before nor understood its stand-point, and I owe to him the fact that I met the intellectual world."

Were Heard and Philpot lovers? We don't know. But Glyn Philpot did for Heard what Lady Ottoline did for Huxley. He opened the door to another world. Heard walked through that door and met some of London's better-known gay writers and poets, including Lytton Strachey, Duncan Grant, Christopher Isherwood, W. H. Auden, E. M. Forster, and J. R. Ackerley, who worked with Heard at the BBC.

They "formed a raffish and intellectual circle that racketed around London, visiting cinemas, theatres, concerts, the zoo and the Ring in Blackfriars Road." Heard adopted a "slyly exotic" style of dress. He showed up at one dinner party wearing a leopard-skin-collared jacket and purple suede shoes. And they were a notoriously promiscuous lot. Here's how J. R. Ackerley's biographer, Peter Parker, describes Heard's role: "Heard was particularly interested in homosexuality and spent much energy attempting to discover the psychological impulse behind buggery. Homosexual himself, he was also much taken up with the phe-nomenon of promiscuity and carried out an *ad hoc* field study amongst his friends, finding in Ackerley's circle a rich source of primary material. Around this time Heard met a wealthy young dilettante called Christopher Wood."

Wood, who was eleven years younger than Heard, was the heir to the British grocery fortune of Petty, Wood and Co. "Lacking economic urge," Heard wrote in a 1926 letter, his new boyfriend "has nothing to do save play piano." Gerald was fond Christopher's youthful demeanor and found his wavy hair "somehow appealing." In 1929, Heard and Wood moved into an apartment together at 28 Portman Square in London's West End. They were a bit of an odd couple. Heard was interested in ideas and religion. Wood was a materialist and consumer of fine objects. To some, they seemed like two sides of one person, kind of like brothers. Wood would become Heard's longtime companion and traveling partner. In 1937, the couple would come to America on the same ocean liner as Aldous, Maria, and young Matthew Huxley.

Heard had spent a couple of difficult years in the early 1920s working in Dublin as the private secretary of Sir Horace Plunkett, an agricultural reformer and former member of Parliament, as violence was escalating over the issue of Irish nationalism. Civil war erupted, forcing Heard and Plunkett to flee, just before the Irish Republicans burned Plunkett's house to the ground.

They had both returned to London. Sir Horace never married or had children, and he seemed to see Gerald as the son he never had. Plunkett died in 1932, leaving Heard a substantial piece of his estate. Ten years later, Gerald would use that money, together with other funds, to purchase the land and erect the buildings that would become his grand experiment in a new way of living—Trabuco College.

Heard underwent a profound spiritual conversion in the early 1930s that inspired him to chart a new course in life, which included "renouncing sexual interactions," said John Roger Barrie, literary executor of the Heard estate and the adopted son of Jay Michael Barrie. "After the conversion, everything changed. His conversion unfolded over a period of time but stands as a line of demarcation, a watershed point in his life. Heard began reconnecting with his spiritual roots, sans the religious trappings of his family lineage. Heard's whole focus was the evolution of consciousness, and he now passionately sought to attain this for himself. He embraced celibacy. He began practicing spiritual disciplines. His books increasingly emphasized experiential spirituality. He was infused with seemingly unbounded energy from that life-altering event, which reflected the deep spiritual transformation he was undergoing. The Gerald who worked for the BBC was not the same Gerald who would found Trabuco College."

·   ·   ·   ·   ·

The adolescent drama of being a thirteen-year-old schoolboy didn't change all that much from 1902 in England to 1966 in Southern California. I wasn't gay or particularly frail like Gerald Heard, and I wasn't great in sports, but I found power and popularity through story and song. Like Heard, I felt "the heavy pressure of inhibition."

I was shy and self-conscious as a child, perhaps even depressed. I suffered from a relatively minor speech impediment that was never diagnosed or treated because I learned to conceal it at an early age. My mind would be racing, full of feelings and ideas, but the words wouldn't come. When they did, I was so unsure of the sentence I had just articulated that I would silently mouth the words I'd spoken. It wasn't a stutter as much as a silent echo.

Life got better when *Meet the Beatles!* came out. It was early in 1964. I was ten years old and we were still living in Littleton, Colorado. My only real friend, Patty, had already moved to California. My sister had left to go to college. I was now an only child—and a lonely child. I saved up a few weeks of allowance and bought the record. It was the first album I ever bought, and I listened to it over and over again. The lyrics of all the songs are forever etched in my mind. I remember thinking to myself that it can't be that hard to write lines like those.

So I started writing parody lyrics to all the songs on the album. "She was just eighty-three / You know what I mean / And the way she looked was way beyond repair / So how could I dance with her mother? / When I saw her dying there." The girls on the school bus were Beatle-crazy and would sing Beatles songs on the way to school. I got the boys together, and we'd try to drown them out by singing my parody lyrics. One of my fondest childhood memories is climbing onto the school bus one morning and having a bunch of kids—boys and girls—say, "Donnie! Sit with me! Donnie! Sit with me!" That's the day I decided I wanted to be a rock star, or maybe a famous writer. Then we moved to California, and, once again, I had to start all over and try to make new friends.

I was thirteen years old when I got my first electric guitar. I started a band and dedicated myself to living the rock-star lifestyle. This involved two important and intricately connected activities—getting high and getting laid. It took a couple of years to perfect my technique.

Getting high was the easy part. You stood outside the 7-Eleven and found older guys willing to buy you beer, then you hung around the distant edges of other parking lots looking for shadier characters who'd sell you a lid of Mexican grass for ten bucks. The band never really got off the ground. We played at a school assembly and a couple of parties, but it was hard getting my three bandmates together to practice. They were not as dedicated as I was to living the rock-star lifestyle, so I decided to become a solo artist.

Getting laid took a little longer. Lennon and McCartney were two of my early influences. The third was Hugh Hefner. I devoted myself to a careful study of the Playboy philosophy, which brought together three things I truly loved—cool stereo equipment, fast cars, and girls with large breasts. I was now in my freshman year in high school, the season of life when we're forced to join a clique or be labeled a loner or a loser. In Southern California, the cool cliques were the jocks, the surfers, and the stoners.

My best friends from junior high turned out to be jocks. They were great at sports and wound up being the stars of the football team. Since my plans to become a rock star had stalled, I tried to follow them into sports stardom. I went out for football. I spent most of my time on the bench, playing only enough to break an ankle and become a permanent fixture on the sidelines. I didn't have enough of a killer instinct for football, which seemed too much like joining the army, with sadistic coaches acting like drill sergeants at boot camp.

My failure at sports delayed the fulfillment of my immediate goal in life—getting laid. Actually, sex was simply another variety of sport, and it seemed like I was always getting stranded at first base, unable to score. My rock-star roll models were changing. I was becoming a bit of a loner, dark and a little dangerous, kind of a cross between Bob Dylan and Jim Morrison. That was only a cover, of course, a face to show the world. Something else was happening in my life, something deeper, more like a calling.

Beginning in junior high school, the only classes that really spoke to me were English and journalism. I don't think I read anything by Aldous Huxley until high school, but I'd started playing the cynical social observer back in seventh grade. My best friend—the one who became the football star—and I started a mimeographed satirical newspaper where we lampooned the junior high curriculum. It was a middle-school version of the *Harvard Lampoon*, and even the teachers loved it. Later, at Rolling Hills High School and the University of California, the only places I really felt at ease were the offices of the school newspapers—the *Titan* and the *Daily Californian*.

My sexual awakening came a few months before I turned sixteen. She was a girl from school, a few months younger than I. We shared our first kiss and round of heavy petting while on the Snow White's Adventures ride at Disneyland. That's right, my initiation into the wonders of the female form came while I was riding in a car made to resemble one of the beds of the Seven Dwarfs. I can't remember if we were riding with Grumpy, Sleepy, or Happy. The one thing I can say for sure is that we were not in Bashful's car. It was quite a ride and sweet enough that I've always had a soft spot in my heart for the Magic Kingdom.

The consummation of our love—such as it was—came some months later. It was the first time for both of us, and we were nervous about finally "doing it." We settled our nerves with alcohol, way too much alcohol, as in a very large bottle of burgundy wine. We began by sitting around munching on potato chips with onion dip, washing it down with red wine. We made love on my parents' king-size bed. My father had already moved out., and my mother had just started working as a medical receptionist, so I had the house to myself in the late afternoons. It was not exactly the Hugh Hefner moment I had envisioned. I don't remember too many details other than the fact that my first love got sick from all the red wine and the onion dip. I cleaned it up as best I could and carried her out to my car to get her to her parent's house in time for dinner. Her parents were conservative Christians, so I figured that would be the end of our affair. I gently placed her on the front steps of her house and slunk away. Somehow, we survived that fiasco. I think she told them it was food poisoning. Looking back on that afternoon, I now see it as the first of many key moments in my life that would be passed in an alcohol- or drug-induced haze, some of them well remembered, some not.

Having a steady girlfriend allowed me to stop obsessing about getting a girlfriend and start thinking about other things—like what was happening in the world. Evidence of the shift can be found in my little red notebook of songs. As songs, they're still pretty lame, but their focus moves to issues other than my own teenage angst. There are songs about environmentalism ("Daddy, What Is a Tree") and social justice ("The Other Half"). Other lyrics reflect my lifelong reluctance to go out and get a real job ("Nine to Five"), and, interestingly enough, one is a cautionary tale about psychedelic drugs, a caution I would soon ignore, titled "Permanent Trip." There are even a few happy songs, testimony to the love and connection I felt with my first love, the most embarrassing of which I titled "Blond Hair, Bubble Gum, Ice Cream, and Love."

We stayed together for most of the rest of high school, and our two-year partnership was a solid and satisfying one. She helped me through the trauma of my parent's divorce. She let me be a loner without really being alone, a kind of relationship that I would continue to establish—for better or worse—throughout the rest of my life.

.   .   .   .   .

Growing up in a broken home colored my view of love and marriage, and so did the era in which I lived out my teens and twenties. I came of age during the wild abandon of the sexual revolution, which provided an orgy of opportunities for young men like me who were eager to challenge "traditional family values."

Two drugs helped fuel the social, sexual, and spiritual upheaval of the 1960s. The first was the birth control pill, which the Federal Drug Administration approved for use in the spring of 1960. By 1966, six million American women had seized the reins of reproductive freedom, and at least six million men were more than willing to go along for the ride.

Meanwhile, LSD revolutionized the way many of us looked at religion and at reality itself, freeing the mind just as the birth control pill was freeing the body. We embarked on an era of no-fault religion and no-fault divorce. It would be fun while it lasted, but the real children of the sixties, the ones born into the wreckage of the American family, would have another story to tell.

Born in 1953 and coming of age in 1966, I found myself caught in the middle of this extraordinary era of experimentation. As an undergraduate at UC Berkeley in the early 1970s, I lived with the emotional fallout of those social changes, reveled in the sexual freedom they unleashed, and tried to study their cultural effects—all at the same time. I intended, in going to Cal, to major in journalism, but the emotional baggage of my dysfunctional family inspired me to change gears—at least academically—and study the social psychology of the family. My journalism education continued while I served as a reporter and editor at the *Daily Californian,* but I wound up with a bachelor's degree in sociology. It's been decades since I pulled out my old college papers, and doing so brings it all back.

My undergraduate studies included fieldwork as a volunteer counselor at Berkeley Youth Alternatives, also known as the Berkeley Runaway Center. We helped kids who left unhappy homes and wound up on the streets of Berkeley. My work is documented in a term paper I wrote in my sophomore year, "Motive, Myth, and Misunderstanding in Problem Families," a title that points to more than my lifelong love of alliteration. I was twenty years old when I worked at the runaway center—more qualified to be a client than a counselor, but there I was. At the time, I was a big fan of R. D. Laing, the avant-garde psychiatrist and author of *The Divided Self* and *The Politics of the Family.* "A crisis will occur if any member of the family wishes to leave by getting the 'family' out of his system," Laing wrote, "or dissolving the 'family' in himself."

My college paper looked at three families who sought counseling at the runaway center. "There is often more than one family myth with the group," I wrote. "Myth conflict is a frequent cause of aggression and the desire to run away. . . . To maintain the family myth, one must avoid insight." While I didn't say it in my term paper, I was also analyzing my own family of origin, which had always placed a great premium on avoiding insight. My parents were busy buying into the American dream while I was stumbling around the house like a restless sleepwalker. Even as a child, I remember, I felt like a stranger in a strange house. This feeling grew more intense when I was a teenager and it was the 1960s, inspiring me to run off to Big Sur, read books by Aldous Huxley, and start looking for another way.

THREE Revelation

Someone once remarked that pain is the
touchstone of spiritual progress. How heartily
we A.A.s can agree with him, for we know that
the pains of alcoholism had to come before
sobriety, and emotional turmoil before serenity.

Bill Wilson, *Twelve Steps and Twelve Traditions*, 1952

Bill Wilson grew up hearing the story of how alcohol nearly destroyed his grandfather, and he knew from personal experience how it drove his father away. Bill didn't pick up a drink for the first twenty-two years of his life. That changed one night in 1917, the same year that my father was born in New York City to my Grandma Lulu, my earliest known alcoholic ancestor. I never met Bill Wilson, but like millions of other people around the world, I see some of myself in his story.

Wilson was a young second lieutenant in the Sixty-Sixth Coast Artillery Corps ready to be shipped out to France when he first tasted the elixir that nearly destroyed his life. At a dinner party held for young officers in New Bedford, Massachusetts, Wilson was handed a Bronx cocktail, a blend of gin and two kinds of vermouth. He had a second and a third, and before long the awkward soldier was the life of the party.

Pretty young society girls laughed at his jokes. He felt a kind of ecstasy. He would later recall how "that strange barrier that had existed between me and all men and women, even the closest, seemed to instantly go down."

Wilson suffered sporadic bouts of success and failure during the 1920s and early 1930s, when he worked as a stock analyst for various Wall Street speculators. The one constant in his life was his drinking, a progressive disease that took him to the brink of death.

Actually, there was another constant in Wilson's life. Lois Burnham was the daughter of a wealthy New York physician. She first met Bill in the summer of 1914, when the Burnhams were vacationing at one of their summer homes on Emerald Lake in Vermont. Before he met Lois, Bill had become increasingly despondent and neurotic. After he'd flunked out of school, his mother put him in a Vermont military academy, convinced that was what he needed to shape up and get on with his life. But his condition worsened. Bill started having panic attacks. His fingers stiffened up and he couldn't breathe. His heart raced and spasms immobilized his legs. The doctors at the military academy told him there was nothing wrong with him, that it was mental.

Bill and Lois reconnected the following spring, when Bill started hanging around the Burnham property. At first, he thought he'd simply found a friend and a surrogate family. But his feelings for Lois deepened over the summer. Bill found salvation in Lois Burnham. "We fell very deeply in love. And I was cured temporarily of my neurosis," he said. "I loved and was loved and there was hope again." Bill was eighteen years old when he met Lois, who was four and a half years older. They married when Bill returned from the war, and were together until Wilson's death in 1971.

Lois Burnham Wilson would write the book on codependency. She would form Al-Anon, which began as a support group for the wives of alcoholic men. She'd put the "long" in the expression "long-suffering wife." In the fall of 1954, well into their long and turbulent marriage, Bill would sit down with a recording device and try to explain their partnership. He was not a faithful husband. There were other women, younger women, before and after he sobered up. Bill seemed to have persuaded himself that his affairs were psychologically justified because of his wife's maternal bond with him. Even recalling their courtship, he said, "At the unconscious level, I have no doubt she was already becoming my mother, and I haven't any question that that was a very heavy component in her interest in me."

Experts describe alcoholism as a progressive disease, and Bill's problem grew progressively worse through the 1920s and the beginning of the 1930s. He was a binge drinker. He could stop for a while, but would then be off on another spree and be gone for days. Total blackouts and horrific hangovers did not stop his drinking. During the financial boom, Wilson dreamt of becoming the next J.P. Morgan. "I was drinking for paranoid reasons," he said. "I was drinking to dream greater dreams of power, dreams of domination. Money was to me never a symbol of security, it was a symbol of prestige and power."

After the stock market crashed, Wilson found himself sixty thousand dollars in debt. He and Lois were living in a home her parents bought for them in Brooklyn. Every once in a while Wilson would bring in a little money, and then he'd be off on another spree. The hangovers were turning into delirium. He had been a fairly amicable, docile, backslapping kind of drunk who babbled harmlessly before passing out. That was starting to change. "I began to turn violent and talk such gibberish that people about me were frightened to death," he recalled. Lois tried to lock Bill up in the house to keep him out of trouble, but he was a master at hiding the bottle. His wife would be off at her job at a local department store, and Bill would stay home drinking. "It was in this period of enforced idleness that I developed the habit of writing when drunk," he said. "I fancied that maybe I could make a living that way." These drunken screeds would include angry, paranoid letters to Franklin D. Roosevelt, the new president of the United States. Wilson thought the New Deal was a socialist conspiracy, and loved to promulgate that theory while in his cups.

In the early 1930s in New York City, the closest thing to a celebrity rehab center was a Victorian brick building at 293 Central Park West. Towns Hospital was for rich and famous drunks, and Bill Wilson had in-laws with money and a wife with the patience of Job. Some considered its founder, Charles B. Towns, to be something of a quack. Towns formed a partnership with Dr. Alexander Lambert, a professor at Cornell University Medical College, and developed what came to be known as the Towns-Lambert Cure.

Patients who checked in at the end of a spree were given hypnotic drugs to calm them down, then a series of potions to induce the "puking and purging" stage of the Towns treatment. The centerpiece of the regime was known as the Belladonna Cure, a cocktail of herbs, bark, and berries that included two deliriants, *Atropa belladonna* and *Hyoscyamus niger*, also known as deadly nightshade and insane root, respectively. The mixture was given to patients regularly for the first two days and nights of treatment. Towns claimed a 90 percent success rate, which he based on the fact that nine out of ten patients never came back for another treatment.

Bill Wilson came back four times. His last visit was in December 1934. On the way to the hospital, he stopped to pick up four beers. "So I stepped into a grocery store where I had a slim credit. I remember explaining to the clerk that I was an alcoholic on my way to be cured." Wilson drank one beer on the street and another in the subway. He offered the third bottle to another passenger, who declined his offer. He drank that one on the station platform and was waving the fourth beer around when he walked into the hospital.

By this point in his drinking career, Wilson's liver was shot and his brain was pickled with booze. He was told he'd probably die if he didn't sober up this time. Then something amazing happened to this hopeless drunk, a revelation that would come to be seen as the divine spark igniting the most successful spiritual movement in twentieth-century America. "Suddenly, my room blazed with an indescribably white light. I was seized with an ecstasy beyond description. Every joy I had known was pale by comparison. . . . Then, seen in the mind's eye, there was a mountain. I stood upon its summit where a great wind blew. A wind, not of air, but of spirit. In great, clean strength it blew right through me. Then came the blazing thought, 'You are a free man.'"

What happened to Bill Wilson that December night transformed his life and inspired his crusade to free other alcoholics from the demon of addiction. Millions of men and women have passed through the doors of AA since then, but the real story of what happened that night at Towns Hospital—what really fueled the revelation of Bill Wilson and inspired the development of Alcoholics Anonymous—is a more complicated tale.

.   .   .   .   .

Seventy-five years after Bill Wilson's revelation, I find myself in another hospital ward on the other side of the country, in Oakland, California. It's three o'clock in the morning, October 16, 2004. I'm lying in bed— wide awake, mind racing—in my room on the detox/rehab wing of what used to be called Providence Hospital. I'm sharing a room with an East Oakland drug dealer and ex-con who's trying to kick a heroin habit. He spends most of the day and night moaning, talking to himself, scratching the skin off his body and making that gut-retching sound called the dry heaves.

Three days before, I'd checked myself into a twenty-eight-day program designed to let me break free of a decadeslong addiction to alcohol, cocaine, and prescription drugs. I am well into my third night in the ward, but I have yet to get one minute of sleep. I'm staring up at the ceiling, angry at the world and wondering why the hell I can't fall asleep. My main reason for coming here was to kick the coke. I haven't snorted a line for three days. You'd think I'd have trouble waking up, not falling asleep. Of course, I've also stopped my nightly routine of coming down off the coke with a witch's brew of wine, vodka, and Ambien—a sleeping pill that falsely advertises itself as non-habit-forming. My medical overlords on the detox unit have given me a low dose of some useless, rehab-approved sedative.

Suddenly, I have a revelation. Maybe I'm not really an addict. I'm a connoisseur of altered states of consciousness. The junkie moaning in our room, *he's* a drug addict. *He* belongs here. I don't. My life has not completely fallen apart. I have a wife who doesn't think my drinking is *that* bad. I own a house and two cars. I'm a successful journalist with a cushy union job and three well-reviewed works of nonfiction. What the fuck am I doing in this place? This is worse than my worst night as an addict. That's it, I decide. I jump out of bed and march down the hall to the nurse's station.

"Here's the deal," I tell the nurse. "Either you give me something that will put me to sleep right now or I'm outta here!"

These night nurses have seen it all. "Really," this one replies, barely looking up from her paperwork. "You know where the door is. It's unlocked. You can head out that way, or you can sit down, calm down, and wait until I finish this chart."

I sit down, but I don't calm down. I look up at a large poster on the wall, the same poster that greeted me when I checked into the unit three days ago. "The Twelve Steps of Alcoholics Anonymous." This is not why I came here. This is religion. Turn my life over to the care of God? Humbly ask Him to remove my shortcomings? If I had wanted God, I would have gone to church. The first step says, "I came to believe that I was powerless over alcohol and my life had become unmanageable." Sure, I've been trying to stop drinking and using for at least a decade, but I'm not powerless. I was managing my life just fine, thank you.

"What is this, anyway?" I ask the nurse, pointing up at the chart. "I've come to a hospital, not an AA meeting. I've come here to get medical information, medical treatment. If I wanted to find Jesus, I could have gone to AA. Lord knows it's cheaper than this place."

The nurse puts down her pen and looks straight into my bloodshot eyes. By now, she's pulled out my chart and given it the once over. "Let me tell ya something that I probably shouldn't be telling you," she says. "I see this is your first shot at rehab. I've been here a long time, honey, and I've seen a few things. People who come to this place, they either have to really hit bottom, or they have to really find the Lord. Otherwise, you're just wastin' everybody's time."

·   ·   ·   ·   ·

We all have to find our own bottom. I hit mine on a typical Saturday night. It was a few months *before* I went to rehab. My wife wanted to go out to a party at a friend's house, and I didn't feel like going. This was Laura, my second wife, who at this point had no idea how much coke I was snorting.* To get myself motivated, I had several martinis and a bottle of wine with dinner. I went down into the basement and snorted the remnants of my latest stash before we left.

It was a perfectly pleasant party with lots of interesting people, but I simply did not want to be there. I drank another bottle of wine, but still couldn't get into a party mood. I needed to score some coke.

I called one of my connections, but he wasn't answering. I called an old friend whom I'll call "Dean." He had become my secondary dealer. He'd been my main man, but he was more of a user than a dealer and not reliable enough to be my primary connection. He didn't answer either, but I convinced myself that he was home, and had some coke, but wasn't answering the phone because he didn't want to share it with me. Dean lived only a few miles away, so I snuck out of the party without telling my wife I was leaving and headed over to his house. He didn't answer the door, but my drunken brain told me he was really hiding inside. So I broke into his house.

One of Dean's roommates was there. She didn't answer the door because she knew who I was and what I wanted. She told me to get out, and I told her to calm down. Dean wouldn't mind if I went into his room to look for something. She quickly decided the best thing to do was to get out of my way and headed back upstairs. I kicked in Dean's bedroom door and walked across the threshold.

This room was my den of iniquity, my house of the rising sun. I'd been coming here and snorting coke for more years than I wanted to count, sometimes with a couple of other friends, usually with Dean alone. Who knows how many nights I sat in this room, drinking vodka and pontificating while my first wife sat at home wondering if I'd died in a fiery wreck.

It all came rushing back. My simmering rage flared up and I felt a rush of resentment. I thought about the tens of thousands of dollars I'd handed over to Dean in this room. I had been subsidizing his coke habit for years. What a fucking loser! I had a right to whatever I could find. I

---

*My first marriage, of a dozen years, had ended in 1995, in part because of my drinking, drugging, and depression.

tore through his desk. I knew where he hid his grinder, his mirror, his spoon, and his straw. I ripped open a half dozen tiny envelopes he used to dole out the drugs to suckers like me. I scraped together a huge line and snorted it down with righteous indignation.

I stormed out of the house and back to my car. All I wanted, of course, was more. I tried calling two or three other people I thought might have some coke or know how I could get some. No one answered or called me back. I drove over to an Oakland bar where I used to score, but couldn't find a connection there either.

I'd been gone from the party for a couple of hours by now. I drove back in a daze. I sat outside and pounded on the steering wheel until I started to cry. That was it. I was done. I was checking myself into rehab. I'd hit bottom. I still had a house and a car and a wife, but that was it. I was done—or at least I thought I was done.

.   .   .   .   .

The official founders of Alcoholics Anonymous are known to its members as "Bill W. and Dr. Bob," the latter being Dr. Robert Smith of Akron, Ohio, a physician and an alcoholic who played a major role in the development of the organization. But AA would have never gotten off the ground without the work of two other men, Rowland Hazard and Ebby Thatcher. For the real beginning of Alcoholics Anonymous came several years before Bill Wilson checked into Towns Hospital. It began in Zurich, Switzerland, in the late 1920s, in the offices of Dr. Carl Jung, one of the founders of modern psychiatry.

Rowland Hazard was an American businessman. He came from a wealthy Rhode Island family. He had a terrible drinking problem, and he had the money to seek treatment from the celebrated Dr. Jung. Hazard traveled to Zurich and spent a year working with Jung. He thought he was cured, but a couple of weeks after completing his treatment, he was off on another spree. He went back to Jung. "What now?" he said. That's when the famous doctor confessed that he, in fact, had had very poor success with alcoholics, adding that Rowland was one of the worst drunks he'd ever seen. That sent Rowland off on the mother of all binges.

He crawled back to Jung one more time, desperate for some words of encouragement.

"Occasionally," Jung said, "alcoholics have recovered through spiritual experiences, better known as religious conversions."

That got Rowland's attention. "Doctor," he said, "you know I'm a religious man. I used to be a vestryman in the Episcopal Church."

"No, Rowland, that isn't enough," Jung replied. "Faith and good works are good, very good. But by themselves they almost never budge an alcoholic compulsion like yours. I'm talking about the kind of religious experience that reaches into the depths of a man, that changes his whole motivation and outlook and so transforms his life that the impossible becomes possible."

"Well, doctor, if I must have such an experience, where and how do I find it?"

"That's something I can't tell you," Jung replied. "All you can do is place yourself in a religious atmosphere of your own choosing, admit your personal powerlessness to go on living. If under such conditions you seek with all your might, you may then find. But the experience you need is only occasional; here and there, now and then, alcoholics have recovered through them. You can only try."

Hazard returned to New York on a spiritual quest. He started attending meetings at the Calvary Episcopal Church, which were organized by the Oxford Group, an evangelical organization founded in 1908 by a Lutheran minister in Pennsylvania and originally named the "First Century Christian Fellowship" and later "Moral Re-Armament." Leaders of the group—whose influence peaked in the late 1920s and early 1930s—sought out wealthy, prominent members of society with the idea that converting them to the teachings of Jesus Christ would foster the conversion of the entire society. Hazard threw himself into the work of the Oxford Group and, in the summer of 1934, started holding meetings at his summer home at Glastonbury, near Bennington, Vermont.

Ebby Thatcher was one of Bill Wilson's oldest drinking buddies. They originally met when they were students at Burr and Burton Academy, long before Wilson took his first drink. Thatcher's family had a summer home in Vermont. In the summer of 1934 his drinking problem came to the attention of local law enforcement when the drunken Thatcher plunged his father's new Packard off the road and into the side of a neighbor's house. Ebby crawled out of his car, unhurt. Righting himself in his startled neighbor's kitchen, Ebby asked for a cup of coffee so he could sober up. The police were called, and Ebby was almost sent for commitment to Brattleboro Retreat, a Vermont mental hospital. But Thatcher's family had some connections with a local judge, so he was released into the custody of Rowland Hazard, who had started using the Oxford Group's teachings to help drunks of a certain class end their destructive behavior.

This work continued down in New York, where Oxford Group members had begun using the Calvary Church's skid row mission as a kind of Christian treatment center for street drunks. Ebby Thatcher sobered up there—temporarily, it would turn out—and started working with other drunks at the mission.

Thatcher heard that his old drinking buddy, Bill Wilson, was near the end of his rope, a virtual prisoner at his house out in Brooklyn. Ebby called and said he'd like to come by for a visit. Wilson thought they'd spend the afternoon drinking, so for the first time in a couple of days he got dressed, shaved, and brought out a fresh bottle of gin.

Ebby rang the bell at 182 Clinton Street. He walked into the kitchen and spied the bottle of gin on the table, next to a pitcher of pineapple juice. Bill thought Lois would be less upset if she came home and saw that they weren't drinking straight gin. He pushed a glass toward Ebby.

"No, thanks, not now," Ebby said.

"What?! Don't tell me you're on the wagon?"

"No," Ebby replied. "I'm just not drinking now."

They made some small talk, but Bill started to sense his old drinking pal had another agenda.

"What on earth has gotten into you? What's this really about, Ebby?"

Thatcher smiled a half smile and looked Bill straight in the eye.

"Bill," he said, "I've got religion."

"Really," Bill said with a smirk. "What brand?"

"Maybe 'religion' is the wrong word, Bill. Let's just say I met a group of people who showed me a way out. Perhaps you'd like to hear about it."

Bill filled his glass and sat back in his kitchen chair.

Thatcher gave him a quick rundown of the Oxford Group's step-by-step program. It was simply about getting honest with yourself, making restitution where it was owed, and trying to find some connection to God. Ebby was very low key, not like some Christian evangelist. He left Bill with his bottle of gin and something to think about.

.   .   .   .   .

My serious drinking started around the time of my parents' divorce. So much happened in the summer of 1969. A man walked on the moon. Woodstock was happening and the war in Vietnam was raging.

My personal life was just as turbulent. There was the trip to Illinois and the phone call from mother asking why I refused to live with her. I spent part of that same summer staying with my sister and her husband in Wilmington, Delaware. I didn't remember doing a lot of drinking that summer until my sister reminded me that, after I returned to California, she discovered I'd hidden scores of empty beer bottles in a storage area above her garage. Then it started coming back to me. I worked at my brother-in-law's Shell station that summer with a grizzly old navy guy. Larry was really pretty harmless, and he was nice enough to buy me all the beer I wanted, especially when I'd let him keep a few bottles for himself.

My habit of mixing speed and alcohol began during my sophomore year of high school. After school, I'd go to work at a nearby car wash with a crew of Mexican guys who always seemed to have an endless supply of "whites," those tiny tabs of amphetamine that helped us make it through the long afternoons. I soon became the supplier of speed for my friends at school. Then there was the pot. You could find marijuana everywhere, including inside my school locker. You could, at least, until the day I was called into the principal's office, where I was surprised to find my counselor, my father, a policeman, the principal, and an empty chair. "Sit down, Don," my father said.

Sitting there on the principal's desk was a baggie full of joints I'd rolled the night before and had stashed in my school locker. My father had been planning on taking me and three friends over to Catalina Island

that weekend in his sailboat. He was going to stay in a motel on the island and let us sleep on the boat by ourselves. We were getting ready for
the party of the year. For some reason, the whole school seemed to know
about the excellent adventure we had planned, including the location of
our stash. I wound up getting off easy with only a week's suspension
from school. But there was one bit of cruel and unusual punishment.

My father saw a direct connection between the length of my hair and
the type of drugs I was taking, so he took me straight to the barbershop
and ordered a crew cut. "One more stunt like this," he said, "and I'll
throw your ass in a military academy before you know what hit you."
Then he drove me home and walked into the house with me. My mother
was at work, and, because he'd moved out earlier that year, it seemed
strange to see him back in the house. He sat down at the kitchen table
and proceeded to make phone calls to the parents of my three friends. I
can still recall the exact conversation he had with each. "Hello, my name
is Warren Lattin, the father of Don Lattin. I assume you know that your
son was planning a trip to Catalina with us this weekend. Well, the trip
has been cancelled and I think I should tell you why. The boys were
planning on taking a quantity of marijuana with them. Now, I do not
know your son's exact involvement, but I assume they all knew about it."

That's the day I got the reputation as the troubled kid with the divorced parents, an identity that would stay with me for years to come.

Today, when I look back on the beginning of my teenage drinking
and drugging, I see more than adolescent angst and rebellion. My earliest memories of alcohol, including the martini ritual on my father's lap
in the late 1950s, were comforting ones. Many alcoholics tell stories of
drunken, abusive fathers, but my dad was for the most part a mellow
drunk. He was happier, more connected, after a few drinks—as was I
during much of my drinking career.

By the time the 1960s began and we moved from Ohio to Colorado, my
father began to disappear from my life. His sales territory for Thomas
J. Lipton covered a dozen large western states, and he was often out of
town on business during weekday nights. But it wasn't only business
that kept him away from home. I didn't really see it back then, but he was
increasingly estranged from my mother.

When we moved to California, his new sailboat, the *Wanderer*, was his means of escape. My mother was afraid of heading out into the vast Pacific on a twenty-four-foot fiberglass boat—or at least that was the story we were told. But Dad and I had some good times, just the two of us, on the *Wanderer*. As a teenager, before and after the divorce, I was allowed to have a couple of beers when we were out at sea, sailing from the Los Angeles harbor to the island of Catalina for the weekend. I think he hoped that letting me drink with him would keep me off other drugs, illegal drugs.

So much for that theory.

For me, the combination of speed and alcohol was a wondrous elixir, whether it was beer and whites in high school or—later in life, when I had sufficient funds—vodka martinis and cocaine. My drugs of choice made me feel connected to the world and, in a way, to a higher power.

One of the more self-revealing documents I uncovered while researching this book in 2011 was a late-night, cocaine-and-alcohol-fueled letter I'd written to my father twenty-three years earlier, in 1988. It was in a sealed envelope, stamped and addressed to him but never mailed. I have only a vague memory of writing it. But I do recall coming across it several times over the intervening decades and not being able to bring myself to open it—until now. It's a long letter recounting some of the scenes in this book—my brother's death, my obsession over replacing him, my parents' divorce, my father's lack of confidence in me, his prediction that I'd become a drug addict. I even reminded him in the letter of how I used to crawl into his lap when he was reading the evening newspaper and enjoying his martini.

There are several sentences that seem worth quoting in a book about lessons learned from the life of Bill Wilson:

Dear Dad,

I'm very high right now on brandy and cocaine and have learned the importance of speaking from the heart to the people I love (AND I DO LOVE YOU) while I still can. I think one of us will die in the next five or ten years (basically a toss-up as to who), and I know that sounds morbid but I feel it. . . .

I think we get drunk for the exact same reason, which is to get honest and open our hearts. . . .

I think you have a lesson to teach me about alcohol and drug addiction, and I want you to teach it to me before you or I die from it. I think this problem (which is also a blessing because I wouldn't be writing this if I were sober) was passed on from your mother to you and then to me. I could speculate what the lesson is, but I won't. You tell me. . . .

It's 2:55 A.M., Friday, December 23, 1988, and I'm going to print this out and mail it before I go to sleep, or else I probably won't.

> I love you,
> Don

My father died seven years later. After he passed away I learned that he was forced to go to a few AA meetings over the years, once after getting a DUI. He didn't like all the God talk, so he stopped going. If he were alive today I'd tell him that one of the things I learned from AA is that many of us drink in a misguided effort to quench a religious thirst. It's how we get some temporary relief from the spiritual emptiness.

And now, I wouldn't have to get drunk and coked-up to tell him that.

. . . . .

Bill Wilson watched Ebby Thatcher walk out of his kitchen. "Religion," he muttered, reaching for the half-empty bottle of gin. "Ebby Thatcher found religion! Right!" Bill thought to himself. "He's just trading one kind of insanity for another—alcoholic insanity for religious insanity!" But Wilson couldn't shake that image of his old pal turning down a drink and doing so with a smile. Ebby Thatcher had been a hopeless drunk, institutionalized for a time. He was even worse than Bill. But there he was, sitting in Wilson's kitchen, sober and exuding such hope and confidence.

Wilson kept drinking for another week but couldn't stop thinking about Ebby. Lois thought she'd noticed a change in Bill that day. It *was* a miracle that Ebby Thatcher was sober. Bill told Lois what Ebby had said about the Oxford Group. She saw a ray of hope, but she had heard this so many times before. Her husband would get enthusiastic about some cure, some great realization he'd had about his drinking, but it always turned into false hope.

They'd tried religion. A friend who was a Christian Scientist had suggested they explore the teachings of Mary Baker Eddy. Lois had bought a copy of Eddy's book *Science and Health*, and she and Bill had taken turns reading it aloud. But Bill couldn't swallow it. You had to *believe*, and he did not believe.

Their marriage had reached the breaking point, and not only because of Bill's drinking. Lois had survived three ectopic pregnancies, leaving her unable to bear a child. She had just started a new job as a salesclerk on the furniture floor of a Brooklyn department store, nineteen bucks a week, plus a 4 percent commission. Her parents had given them the house on Clinton Street, the house where she grew up, but still they could barely pay their other bills.

Bill sat at home all day, going out only to buy more gin. Then Lois came home one day and Bill was gone. He wasn't sitting in his favorite kitchen chair writing angry letters to the president of the United States. Maybe he was off on another spree. It turned out that he was, but this time it was different. It was the last spree.

Bill had decided to go find Ebby at the Calvary Church mission on East Twenty-Third Street. Of course, he stopped in a few bars along the way to fortify himself for his coming confrontation with God. Feeling a nice buzz, he climbed down into the subway and rode into Manhattan. On the way from the subway stop to the mission, he popped into another bar and started drinking with a Finnish guy, a fisherman named Alec. After a couple of drinks he convinced Alec to go with him to the mission.

They walked in and found Ebby Thatcher, who saw how drunk they were. Ebby poured strong black coffee into them and forced them to eat two plates of baked beans. Then he led them into an evangelistic service that was just starting.

Bill sat back and watched a ragged collection of bums and winos walk up to the altar and offer themselves to God. He started to follow them to the front of the chapel. At first, Ebby was afraid his old friend was too drunk, terrified that he'd launch into some angry speech about the foolishness of religion. He pulled the coattails of Bill's overcoat to keep him from stepping forward, but Bill could not be stopped. Wilson would not remember what he said that day. But to Ebby's surprise, his friend calmed down and gave a heartfelt little speech about his fruitless search for permanent sobriety.

Bill kept drinking for a couple more days, but then he decided to give Towns Hospital one last try. He fell into a deep depression at the hospital, deeper than usual. He was falling into the abyss. His obstinacy was finally crumbling, as was the wall around his heart. "Anything," he cried out. "I'll do anything. If there be a God, let Him show Himself!" That's when the room filled with light. Bill felt a breeze. He felt freedom. He felt an ecstasy greater than any fueled by alcohol, followed by a great peace. "So this," he thought, "is the God of the preachers."

·   ·   ·   ·   ·

Bill Wilson and I have a few things in common. We were damaged by a bitter parental divorce. We both turned our back on God at age twelve. We had marriages marred by substance abuse. Lois and my first wife were both long-suffering and had medical problems that left them unable to have children.

Bill and I both struggled with depression and spent years self-medicating with alcohol and other drugs. We got high to feel connected. We were at times painfully shy and insecure, but also prone to grandiosity and egomania and angry outbursts. Bill wanted to be J. P. Morgan, and I wanted to be Bob Dylan—or at least Bob Woodward.

We both had a long, stormy affair with God. I never wanted to admit it to myself or anyone else, but my decision to become a religion reporter was a cover story for my longing for some kind of spiritual connection. It was a way for me to be cynical and spiritual at the same time. Sure, I'll go to church, but only if you pay me.

Like Bill, I would have to hit bottom to find a higher power. That no-nonsense nurse who lectured me on my dark night of the soul—the one who told me against her better judgment that I had to hit bottom or find Jesus—was right on both counts. It was the worst and best thing to say to a guy like me. I wasn't looking for Jesus and—at least compared to Bill Wilson or the junkie back in my room—I had not really hit bottom, at least not in my mind. That turned out to be a misunderstanding that kept me using for another year.

There's more than one way to stop abusing alcohol and other drugs, but the journey starts with the realization "Yes, I *do* have a problem." I was in my thirties the first time I took one of those self-help quizzes designed to help you figure out whether you're an alcoholic or a drug addict. Do you drink to overcome shyness? Check. Have you missed work because of your drinking? Check. Have you been arrested because of your drug or alcohol use? Check.

By the time I was in my forties, I had to admit to myself that I was an alcoholic and that I was addicted to cocaine. But I was the kind of alcoholic who could hold my liquor. I could have three martinis and feel only a pleasant buzz, especially after I started adding cocaine to my daily cocktail; then I could drink all night and still drive home.

I was, like my father, a "functioning alcoholic." We both had jobs where drinking was just part of the job. He was a business executive back in the days of the three-martini lunch. I was a newspaper reporter. We saw ourselves as a different breed, especially back in the proverbial good old days. We wrote, we drank, we wrote, and then we drank some more. When I started working at the newspaper, there were still lots of colorful and cranky old characters in the business. We still batted out our stories on typewriters and yelled, "Copy!" when we were done.

.   .   .   .   .

For as long as anyone can remember, the offices of San Francisco's premiere newspapers have been conveniently located only one block from Skid Row. Today, the *Chronicle* is at Fifth and Mission Streets, a block from Sixth Street, the current boulevard of bad luck. Back in the old days, long before I hit town, the *Examiner* and *Chronicle* offices were near the corner of Market and Third Streets, a block from the old dive bars and flophouses of "Three Street."

One of the last of the really seedy dives to close down on Three Street was called Jerry and Johnny's. It was an old newspaper tavern. By the time I started working at the *Examiner* in the 1970s, the newspaper had moved to Fifth Street, but Jerry and Johnny's was still open over on Third. The wall behind the bar was covered with ancient black-and-white photos of all the old guys I was just getting to know, taken back in the day before they were old, bald, fat, or almost dead from drink.

Most of the buildings around the bar had been abandoned, awaiting a redevelopment project that would eventually turn the neighborhood into a glitzy convention center with luxury hotels and expensive restaurants, but Jerry and Johnny's hung on until the last wrecking ball swung its way. By then, the *Chronicle* had been over at Fifth and Mission for decades, and the *Examiner* had been there for fifteen years.

One of my first assignments at the *Examiner* was to go collect the newspaper's three top editors over at Jerry and Johnny's and bring them back to the city room. It seemed they were too plastered to make it on their own. They still preferred Jerry and Johnny's on Third Street to the M&M Tavern on Fifth Street, which had become the favorite watering hole for most *Examiner* staffers. I was in my early twenties and working as the Berkeley stringer, a part-time job covering news from across the bay. But I happened to be in the main office that day, so I was dispatched to go pick up this trio of missing editors. There was, after all, a newspaper to put out.

They were so drunk and disorderly that they couldn't be trusted to walk two blocks, so I drove my old VW bus over to Third Street, rounded them up at Jerry and Johnny's, and gently shepherded them into the back of the bus. Then I drove two blocks and poured them out onto the sidewalk near the Fifth Street entrance to the *Examiner*. It was my introduction to big-time journalism in San Francisco, and I loved it. In a few weeks, one of the editors I'd rounded up at the bar offered me a full-time job.

There were still guys around with flasks in their pocket and bottles in their desk. One reporter carried a .45-caliber Colt pistol around with him. He was a decorated Korean War vet who'd worked a few years as a vice cop in L.A. He'd swagger into the newsroom in the morning, pull the .45 from his waistcoat and drop it into his desk drawer with a loud "clank." Adding to the Wild West feel were a few spittoons that had yet to be removed from the city room. A thick cloud of cigarette smoke hung over the room.

At times, the place seemed more like a frat house than a newsroom. Back in the 1960s and 1970s, the *Chronicle* was infamous for its stable of freewheeling, hard-drinking columnists. One of them, a rock music and pop culture critic named John Wasserman, had a series of run-ins with my predecessor on the religion beat, the Reverend Lester Kinsolving. Lester was a conservative Episcopal priest who wore his collar in the office and took it upon himself to enforce religious orthodoxy in San Francisco—not an easy job. The Reverend Kinsolving didn't drink, but he could be as exuberant and abrasive as the rest of the gang.

One day, Kinsolving came back from an assignment to find that the entire contents of his desk, along with his telephone and typewriter, had disappeared. He immediately suspected Wasserman, who sat next to him in the city room and did not exactly share the values held by the religion editor. John was a popular staffer remembered for, among other things, inviting a squad of strippers from a North Beach nightclub to a *Chronicle* Christmas party. Lester's suspicions about Wasserman were confirmed when the Right Reverend waited for the rock critic to go out on assignment and did the same to his desk. Yes, it turned out, Wasserman was the rascal who'd cleaned out the priest's desk.

Kinsolving would go on to make a name for himself as a right-wing commentator and radio talk-show host in the Washington, D.C., area, where he achieved some infamy asking provocative questions at White House news conferences. Wasserman would die in the winter of 1979 in a horrendous car wreck on a rainy night in South San Francisco. He was forty years old. John was driving the wrong way on Interstate 280 when his silver Volkswagen Rabbit collided head-on with a bright red Karmann Ghia. The two occupants in the other car also died. Wasserman, who'd just left a party, reportedly had a blood alcohol level that was nearly three times the legal limit.

There but for the grace of God . . . Over the next twenty years, God knows how many times I drove home drunk across the San Francisco–Oakland Bay Bridge. Through sheer luck, I never killed anyone and never got a DUI.

One of our rituals at the *San Francisco Examiner* was "the shirtsleever." We would get up from our desks and, without putting on our coats, like we were simply heading to the men's room or the coffeepot, proceed to the M&M, located just a quick stumble down the sidewalk. Some memories of those days are forever lost, but I do recall tripping down the sidewalk one afternoon and being stopped by an old *Examiner* photographer, one of the guys who still wore a hat whenever he left the office. Looking back on it, I'll bet he was a recovering alcoholic, a "friend of Bill." He gave me a steely look and said, "Watch out for yourself down there, kid. Those stories don't always have happy endings." I didn't realize it at the time, but he was warning me about my habit of hanging out with the old drunks at the M&M, where I loved listening to their stories about the good old days almost as much as they loved telling them.

San Francisco newspaper lore is full of stories about drunks who missed the big story, or more triumphant tales about rummies that got totally shit-faced yet still got the job done. When I first started working at the paper, it seemed to me that some of the biggest drunks were also some of the best reporters.

George Murphy was by his own description "the world's best rewrite man." That's a key player in a deadline-driven newsroom, the one who takes notes over the phone from various reporters out on some big story, simultaneously weaving all these feeds into one fine story. Murphy was also one of the better reporters at the *Chronicle,* with one notable exception. On the afternoon of September 22, 1975, Murphy was supposed to be at a Union Square hotel covering a speech by President Gerald Ford. A few hours later, red of face after a few drinks, Murphy breezed back into the city room like a man without a care in the world. He walked up over to the city desk to check in with Carl Nolte, one of the editors working the desk that day—and one of my main drinking buddies at the *Chronicle.*

"Hello, George," said Nolte, his voice dripping with sarcasm. "As you know, someone tried to assassinate the president of the United States while you were covering him at the St. Francis Hotel. I assume you are all over this story."

Murphy stood at the desk in stunned silence.

"No?" Nolte asked. "No? Jesus fucking Christ! Well, don't you worry, George. We're all over it—even if *you* are not."

Murphy was not on the scene when a woman named Sara Jane Moore fired a revolver at the president as he was leaving the hotel, missing Ford but nevertheless making news. The unlucky newsman had headed straight over to the M&M as soon as Ford ended his speech, missing all the action.

Earlier that month, Murphy had been on the ball when Lynette "Squeaky" Fromme, a follower of Charlie Manson, tried to shoot President Ford in Sacramento. Murphy later explained how he let himself miss this second assassination attempt on the president, asking, "Who would have thought lightning would strike twice?"

Murphy stopped drinking before he died, but not long before. His passing came at one of his favorite North Beach watering holes one day in 1980. He sat down at the bar and ordered a bottle of mineral water. He laughed at someone's joke, then quietly laid his head down in his arms and passed away.

Carl Nolte wrote the obit, calling Murphy "one of the best of the old-time San Francisco newspapermen . . . a reporter of the old school—smart, witty, hard drinking, self assured." He was fifty-two.

Cocaine appeared in the newsroom in the late 1970s and became popular with a relatively small group of editors and reporters, myself included. In the mid-1980s, when I was working in the *Examiner* city room, a veteran reporter named Paul Avery was assigned to sit next to me. Avery had been one of the hotshots at the *Chronicle* in the 1960s and 1970s and was attempting a career comeback at the *Examiner*. He was most famous for his earlier reporting on the Zodiac case—a series of still-unsolved murders that terrorized Northern California in the 1960s. His stories got the attention of the Zodiac killer himself, who sent a letter to Avery warning, "You are doomed." That missive inspired everyone at the *Chronicle* office—including Avery—to start wearing campaign-style buttons with the words "I am Not Paul Avery" printed on them. Paul would later be immortalized in the 2007 movie *Zodiac*, in which actor Robert Downey Jr. depicts both Avery's doggedness as a reporter and his love of cocaine. (Downey was perfect for the part, having had his own real-life struggles with the seductive nose powder.)

By the time I met Paul, his love affair with cocaine had become a nightmare. Paul was one of the first guys I knew with a serious coke problem. We sat in the back row of the *Examiner* city room. Avery would come into the office reeking of booze and looking like he hadn't slept all night. There was a small private bathroom near our desks where you could lock the door behind you. A wide stainless steel shelf was attached to the wall below the mirror and above the sink. Over the years, I took drugs in countless bathrooms, but this one was the perfect place to snort coke. Paul was a frequent visitor to that little room, and he'd snort so much coke that I could sometimes sneak in behind him, pull out a credit card, and scrape together a decent line from his leavings.

It took me many years to get to Paul's level of abuse. By then, he was dead from pulmonary emphysema. My last memories of Avery are of drinking with him at the M&M, watching with alarm as he'd take a hit from his oxygen tank, then light up another cigarette. Paul died in 2000. He was sixty-six.

· · · · ·

You might think that seeing the decline of a fellow journalist would scare me away from cocaine. You might, but that's because you don't understand the mind of an addict. I used to tell myself, "You have to be smart to be a drug addict," and I came up with all kinds of smart ways to control my daily allotment of cocaine. There's an old saying about cocaine being "God's way of telling you you're making too much money." Well, God must have had a plan for my life. He convinced HarperCollins to pay me way too much money as an advance on my second book.

Great writers from Hemingway to Hunter Thompson consumed copious amounts of drugs and alcohol while they worked. Hemingway and Thompson also blew their brains out, literally, but I preferred to not remember that part of the story.

My coke problem started getting out of control around the dawn of the new millennium. I was between wives. I was working on my second book, home alone, with a pile of cocaine at my side. But, like I say, you have to be smart to be a drug addict. The piles of cocaine kept getting bigger and disappearing faster. One of my brilliant strategies was to buy a very strong lockbox. I'd go out and score an eightball (an eighth of an ounce) of coke. To make it last more than one night, I would neatly divide the white powder into two piles, lock half of it in the lockbox, and then mail myself the key. That way, a day or two later, I could open the box and enjoy the rest of my little treat. It worked for a while, but they just don't make lockboxes like they used to.

It took a long time, but I finally realized that the drugs and alcohol weren't working anymore. One of the countless clichés that you hear at AA meetings is: "My worst day sober was better than my best day drunk." Not for me. I had a great time getting high. It worked for many years, but at a certain point it stopped working.

Getting loaded began as a way to get out of the house and onto the dance floor. It made me the life of the party, the funniest guy in the room. In the end, getting loaded was about hiding in my basement with a bottle of vodka and a pile of coke, hoping no one would bother me. It wasn't fun anymore. It hadn't been fun for years, but I kept doing it over and over and over and over . . .

.   .   .   .   .

Bill Wilson hit bottom in Towns Hospital on that December night in 1934, and what happened next, on the morning after his ecstasy, helped set the course of Alcoholics Anonymous and, to a lesser extent, the direction of American religion in the last half of the twentieth century.

What happened was, Ebby Thatcher came by Wilson's room that morning with a gift—a copy of a book by William James titled *The Varieties of Religious Experience*. To Wilson, the book was something of a revelation. It revealed a new way of looking at religion, not as a collection of rigid dogmas and tired doctrines, but as a vehicle for personal and enlivening spiritual experience.

James says he wrote *Varieties* in reaction to "all that absolutism and one-sided dogmatism by which both philosophy and religion have been infested." James was interested in the *essence* of religion. How important was William James to the founding of AA? Here's how Wilson later explained it when looking back on the day after his revelation at Towns Hospital. "By nightfall, this Harvard professor, long in his grave, had, without anyone knowing it, become the founder of Alcoholics Anonymous."

James, the father of American psychology, and his brother, Henry James, the novelist, are the famous sons of Henry James Sr., who turned away from *his* father's stern Presbyterianism and toward Swedenborgianism, a mystical religious movement founded in the eighteenth century by Emanuel Swedenborg, a Swedish scientist. This is the same spiritual tradition in which Lois Wilson was raised, so Bill Wilson already had some knowledge of it. Bill was, after all, living in the same Brooklyn home where Lois grew up.

It's not hard to find William James and Emanuel Swedenborg in the teachings of Alcoholics Anonymous. Martin Marty, the noted scholar of American religion, says of Henry, the father of William: "With the aid of Swedenborg and his own instinctive talent, the elder James fused old religion and new into a private blend that suited only his own soul." Henry and William James were, in other words, suggesting that spiritual seekers connect with "God as we understand him."

William James based *The Varieties of Religious Experience* on a series of lectures he delivered in Edinburgh, Scotland, in the spring of 1901, at the dawn of the twentieth century. A little more than three decades later, Bill Wilson opened his new copy of *Varieties* in his room at Towns Hospital. We can be fairly certain that he underlined the following passage. "Sobriety diminishes, discriminates, and says no; drunkenness expands, unites, and says yes. It is, in fact, the great exciter of the YES function in man. . . . To the poor and the unlettered it stands in the place of symphony concerts and of literature. . . . The drunken consciousness is one bit of the mystic consciousness, and our total opinion of it must find its place in our opinion of that larger whole."

Elsewhere, James writes that the only cure for "dipsomania is religio-mania." Bill Wilson agreed. Alcoholism was a misguided search for spiritual connection. William James and Carl Jung—who would meet at Clark University in Worcester, Massachusetts, in 1909, a year before James's death—had the same diagnosis. Alcoholism could be overcome by a powerful religious conversion. There is a solution, Jung wrote in his letter to Wilson, for alcoholics or any others struggling to free themselves from their demons. They must find a spiritual connection without the assistance of distilled spirits. And the way to do so, Jung wrote, was to seek solace and healing "by real religious insight or by the protective wall of human community."

Bill Wilson, Aldous Huxley, and Gerald Heard would devote the rest of their lives to both cultivating the awareness and creating the conditions that would allow us—if we so choose—to do just that.

FOUR

Abroad

> Democracy's future is dark. . . . Our goal is
> then neither the reaction of dictatorship nor the
> blind, material progress of the present inorganic
> democracies. . . . The way out and forward is
> through the evolution of consciousness.
>
> Gerald Heard, *Man the Master*, 1941

Some young men join the navy to see the world. Aldous Huxley and I found another way out. We were both able to persuade newspaper editors that it would be a great idea to send us on trips around the world. We were young men, white Anglo-Saxons of a certain class, born with considerable privilege but poor enough that we had to work for a living. "Seeing that one practices a profession that does not tie one down," Huxley observed, "I feel that one ought to see as much of this planet as possible."

Huxley's journey around the world began in the fall of 1925, when he and Maria sailed from Genoa, bound for the Suez Canal, and then to Bombay. He was already a famous enough author and journalist that he was paid in advance for a series of travel articles to cover most of his expenses. The stories were later compiled in a book titled *Jesting Pilate.* My circumnavigation of the planet came decades later, when I landed a

Chronicle assignment that took me to Mexico, Africa, Russia, and Japan for a series of articles exploring how the Mormon Church had grown from a persecuted American cult to a major world religion.

India was still a British colony when Aldous and Maria set sail. Four decades later, in the 1960s, thousands of American seekers—some of them inspired by Huxley's writings—would travel to India in search of ecstasy or enlightenment. But they were inspired by Huxley's *later* writings. What's most extraordinary about his early accounts of India is his dismissal of that nation's rich spiritual heritage. What we find in these writings is the young, cynical Aldous, the Huxley who was still a few years away from his encounter with Gerald Heard. Huxley's early trip to India was more of an ordeal than a pilgrimage. "India is depressing as no other country I have ever known," he wrote. "One breathes in it, not air, but dust and hopelessness." He went on to call Hindu spirituality "the primal curse of India and the cause of all her misfortunes."

"It is this preoccupation with 'spiritual' realities, different from the actual historical realities of common life, that has kept millions upon millions of men and women content, through centuries, with a lot unworthy of human beings," he wrote. "A little less spirituality, and the Indians would now be free—free from foreign domination and from the tyranny of their own prejudices and traditions. There would be less dirt and more food. There would be fewer Maharajas with Rolls Royces and more schools."

As a young journalist, Huxley worshipped at the altar of H. L. Mencken, a curmudgeonly newsman who spun cynicism into high art. "Mr. Mencken turns a pair of very civilized eyes on the extraordinary and fantastic spectacle which is contemporary American life," Huxley wrote. "We should welcome his appearance among us here; for we have sore need of critics who hate humbug, who are not afraid of putting out their tongues at pretentiousness however noble an aspect it may wear, who do not mind being vulgar at need, and who, finally, know not only how to make us think, but how to make us laugh as well."

One of the highlights—or perhaps lowlights—of Huxley's round-the-world trip was a summer night spent with Mencken in Manhattan. Here's how Huxley began his letter of introduction:

Dear H. L. Mencken,

I am entering the U.S.A. by the back door—tho' I suppose they call it the front door in California—from the Orient, where I have been spending some months to satisfy myself empirically that all this rigmarole of Light from the East, etc. is genuine nonsense. Having done so, I am now on my way home . . . and passing through your continent. Will there be a hope of seeing you? My wife and I will be spending some three weeks or so in New York from about mid-May onwards. . . . It will be a great delight if you're visible.

How could any curmudgeon resist a letter like that, especially from the grandson of T. H. Huxley, the man who coined the word *agnostic*? Mencken invited the Huxleys to dine with him at Moneta's restaurant in New York. "Mencken gave us so much to drink," Maria recalled. ."I felt so sick I enjoyed it less than I might have."

Before their encounter with Mencken, Aldous and Maria had left India after a four-month stay, confessing that they were "rather glad to escape." From there they sailed to Burma, Malaysia, Java, and the Philippines. They couldn't wait to get back to Western civilization. On April 7, 1926, they boarded a comfortable Dutch ocean liner in Manila, breathing a sign of relief, and set sail for Japan, their last stop before continuing across the North Pacific to San Francisco.

The Huxleys sailed through the Golden Gate aboard the ocean liner *President Cleveland* on May 5, 1926. Curious as to whether Huxley's first visit to the United States received any notice in the local press, I headed over to the San Francisco History Center, which maintains an extensive newspaper archive on the top floor of the city's main public library. I didn't expect to find much. This visit to San Francisco was six years before Huxley published *Brave New World*, the novel that would make him a household name, and three years before his best-known book of the 1920s, *Point Counter Point*, came out.

I was wrong. One of the first newspaper clippings I found was an impressive three-column feature display with a large photo of young Aldous standing on the deck of the *President Cleveland* with binoculars around his neck and a walking stick in his left hand. He's standing behind Maria, who is lazily draped over a folding wooden deck chair.

She has mink stole around her neck and a stylish bowler hat pulled low across her brow. She's a flapper girl, but one with a certain touch of class. Pictured to the Huxleys' right is Henrietta Sava-Goiu, a French poet who happened to arrive on the same ship. "They Land in California on Globe-Trotting Tour," the *San Francisco Chronicle* headline of May 6, 1926, proclaims. "Authors on World Cruise Visitors to San Francisco." Aldous is described as "grandson of the famous English philosopher of that name and a novelist of note."

This was back in the days when packs of newspapermen routinely boarded arriving ships in search of famous people to interview. But before these reporters could ask Huxley a question, he interrupted them to ask, "What is the news from home?"

At the time, England was in the grip of a militant general strike. One of the reporters handed Huxley a newspaper with an account warning that civil war or revolution could be in the offing. "This situation is amazing to me," said Huxley, who went on to reassure the local press that "British conservatism and clear thinking will re-assert itself and the present political strife will find solution."

These old newspaper stories were not found in some sterile database or a book of compiled essays. They were from the actual newspaper clippings, brittle yellow pieces of newsprint neatly folded and packed into long brown envelopes. The newspaper morgue that these clippings came from, formerly that of the old *San Francisco Examiner* and now maintained by the San Francisco History Center, is the same one I first explored as a young reporter back in the 1970s. Touching the newspaper, seeing how these stories were laid out on pages that people actually read back in the day, brought them alive. It also reminded me that I'm part of this city's rich history, or at least it was another reminder that I am, in fact, getting old.

The first big-city newspaper I worked for was the *Examiner*, once the proud flagship of the Hearst empire. It effectively died in 1999, when the Hearst Corporation bought the larger and more prosperous *San Francisco Chronicle* from the descendents of its nineteenth-century founders, Charles and M. H. de Young, and, soon after, shut down the *Examiner*. (It exists today in name only as a thin, free tabloid and a Website filled with amateur bloggers promoting an assortment of products and causes.) The entire *Examiner* morgue was acquired lock, stock, and barrel by the San Francisco Public Library. Its staff now maintains the old steel cabinets stuffed with thousands of envelopes and hundreds of thousands of newspaper clippings, the same cabinets that used to be at the *Examiner* offices near the intersection of Fifth and Mission and, before that, at the old Hearst building at Third and Market.

Sitting at one of the long library tables, I started daydreaming about what I would have asked Aldous Huxley if I'd been one of those reporters standing on the deck of the *President Cleveland* back in the spring of 1926. Knowing myself—and knowing what I know about how to get on the front pages of San Francisco newspapers—I probably would have ignored the growing British labor unrest and asked Mr. and Mrs. Huxley to share a few tidbits about the libertine sexual habits of those freethinking Bloomsbury bohemians back in London.

My reverie was interrupted when I realized that the next three envelopes on the table before me were stuffed with clippings filed under Huxley's *byline*. Only then did I realize that Aldous Huxley—like myself—once had a regular column in the *San Francisco Examiner*. Our stories are tucked away in the same brown envelopes in the same ancient steel cabinets.

Huxley wrote about all sorts of things in his columns, which were syndicated by the Hearst chain in the 1930s and which appeared in newspapers across the United States. Some of these short pieces eerily predict events in his life, as well as in the lives of the rest of us. Many futurists writing in the early twentieth century failed to anticipate the revolutionary role computers would play in our lives. Not Huxley. One of his columns from 1934 (before the word *computer* came into fashion) is headlined "Adding Machine—More Important Socially Than Aeroplane." Huxley begins by reminding us that he was born in the days of the horse and buggy. "Today, at forty," he writes, "I inhabit a world where men can fly from England to Australia in less than three days." But what most intrigued Huxley back in 1934 was the fact that "machines can now undertake the simpler forms of thinking and artistic creation." They are "destined to perform these functions to an ever greater extent," he writes, calling this "a fact whose significance cannot be exaggerated. . . . Our thinking and creating machines do much more than throw people out of work—they raise problems of individual psychology as well as of social organization. For what they do is to make men and women seem useless in their own eyes. . . . They thus tend to put an ever higher premium on men of exceptional talents and to make the ordinary person increasingly superfluous."

This is exactly what happened at the *Examiner*, the *Chronicle*, and hundreds of other newspapers across the United States. The computer's first victims were the printers in the back shop, followed by the press operators and the truck drivers. Content and delivery migrated to the Internet, where newspapers made the disastrous decision to start giving away their product for free. Circulation of the print edition plummeted, along with advertising revenue, so the people who sold the ads were let go and, finally, the already decimated staffs of reporters, photographers, and editors were slashed in an endless series of layoffs and buyouts.

Our industry was history, and so were we. Journalism was our currency, and it was ruthlessly devalued in the new lean, mean economy. Real reporting is expensive and time-consuming. Fewer and fewer companies were willing to pay for it. Some of us reinvented ourselves as freelance journalists or authors of narrative nonfiction, usually at steep pay cuts. Others sought refuge in public relations and other varieties of product promotion, which seems to constitute much of what now passes as journalism. Newspapers began to be called "legacy media," and our work wound up where I found myself looking over these old clippings—in the history room of the public library.

Another Huxley column that nearly jumped out of its envelope was simply headlined "Faith," a quality the young Aldous Huxley did not seem to possess in large measure. Here, in a column written in the fall of 1932, Huxley bemoans the decline of faith, not only religious faith but also "secular faiths that impelled [our] fathers to political and economic action—the faith in democracy and individualism and personal liberty, the faith in *laissez-faire* capitalism and unlimited competition." In an observation that seems partly aimed at himself, Huxley worries about "a new kind of knowingly cynical journalism." "People with a faith feel

impelled to do something about the horrors and scandals of social life,"
he writes. "To be content to do nothing but make a joke about them is a
sign that faith in the possibility of some higher form of living has disappeared. Cynicism is acceptance."

Huxley's columns from the 1930s also reveal an early interest in drugs
that provide their user with an altered state of consciousness, from caf-
feine to cocaine, beer to opium. "Why do human beings make use of
these pick-me-ups and stupefacients? For two reasons: because they are
bored with their surroundings and because they are bored with themselves." In this 1934 piece headlined "Stimulants," Huxley writes: "There
is not one of us, I imagine, who has not at some time felt the desire to
transcend himself, to take a holiday from all his habits of thought and
feeling, to change his character and become, if only for a moment, somebody else."

In an article titled "A Treatise on Drugs," Huxley notes that people have been consuming mind-altering plants and liquids for all of
recorded history. The way to stop people from abusing drugs, he says,
is not by passing laws against them. "The way to prevent people from
drinking too much alcohol, or becoming addicts to morphia or cocaine,
is to give them an efficient but wholesome substitute for these poisons,"
Huxley wrote in the fall of 1931. "The man who invents such a substance
will be counted among the greatest benefactors of suffering humanity."

Seven years later, in the fall of 1938, a Swiss chemist looking for new
medical uses for ergot would synthesize a substance he would call lysergic acid diethylamide-25. Dr. Albert Hofmann would place his vial of
LSD on a shelf at Sandoz Laboratories, unaware that he had invented
the most powerful mind-altering drug in history. Hofmann would discover the power of this substance when he accidentally dosed himself in
the spring of 1943. Ten years later, Aldous Huxley would have his own
psychedelic baptism and emerge as the leading spokesman for a generation of seekers moving into the fast lane on the highway to self-transcendence. He would show us that we don't even have to leave home to take
the ultimate trip.

Many of my newspaper-funded travels would not have been possible without the help of another man who refused to stay home and quietly do his job. His name was Karol Joseph Wojtyla, but you may remember him as Pope John Paul II, the wildly popular, globe-trotting pontiff of the late twentieth century. My tenure as a writer of religion stories roughly coincides with the pope's twenty-six-year reign. In the two-thousand-year history of the church, only one man occupied the throne of Peter longer than John Paul, and none of them so artfully used the media to take his message to every corner of the world. While I did not become a full-time religion writer until the early 1980s, I wrote my first story about religion for the *Examiner* in 1978, the same year that Wojtyla, the archbishop of Kraków, was elected pope. My last major articles for the *Chronicle* were about the death of John Paul in the spring of 2005 and about the Vatican conclave that elected Cardinal Joseph Ratzinger to replace him as Pope Benedict XVI.

Covering a papal pilgrimage is a bit like covering the campaign of a successful presidential candidate, or like being on tour with the Rolling Stones, or perhaps a combination of the two. Barack Obama had lots of reporters covering him when he was running for president, but not as many as John Paul did at the height of his papacy. Lots of people came out to see Mick Jagger prance across a sprawling stage; but those arena events were intimate affairs compared to the services where hundreds of thousands of people flocked to share communion with the Polish pope.

When the pope would visit a city, especially in places like Catholic-dominated Latin America, it was not uncommon for him to attract the largest crowd ever assembled in that city. And the pope did this day after day on these tours—presiding over hundreds of thousands of worshippers gathered on some open field, then climbing into his pope-mobile for a tour through packed city streets, and then celebrating another regal mass at the city's cathedral.

For a reporter, it's impossible to keep up with the guy. You're moving so quickly and filing stories so fast that you forget what city or even what country you're in. When people tell me they're planning a vacation in a place like Buenos Aires or Santiago or Quebec, one of my standard lines is: "I was there with the pope." I was there, and I wasn't there. I traveled the length and breadth of South America with His Holiness, but don't ask me what any particular place looks like. I was not really there. I was in the papal bubble. And, if I'm honest with myself, I must admit that there are some other reasons for my foggy memory.

My tenure as a religion writer for San Francisco newspapers also coincides with my career as a high-functioning alcoholic and cocaine addict. My drinking and drugging didn't stop when I got on an airplane to cover the pope. Quite the opposite. Getting high at high altitudes was one of my favorite pastimes. The wine may not have been consecrated on Shepherd One, the chartered Alitalia jet that carried the pope and the press on these trips aboard, but it certainly flowed freely.

Some of my fondest memories as a religion reporter are a string of long, wine-soaked, expense-account dinners in little restaurants near the Vatican. And, yes, I think I do remember most of them. We were a mix of American religion reporters and other journalists in Rome who covered news across southern Europe, including stories out of the Vatican. One of these nights is chronicled in a series of photos I discovered while doing research for this book. I do remember the dinner on the outskirts of Rome around a table literally covered with bottles of wine and liquor. I must admit, though, that I have only the foggiest memory of dancing my ass off at some discotheque on the outskirts of Rome. But I do have the photo.

One of the wonderful things about flying around with the pope was you got *two trips* to Rome out of the deal. First, you flew to Rome to hook up with His Holiness. Reporters flew on the same plane as the pope only during the initial outgoing leg of the journey, in this case from Rome to Miami. Then the pope and his ecclesial entourage flew in their own plane, hopping across the country, while the now-larger press corps followed in a separate, chartered jetliner, landing first at each stop so reporters were in place when the pope disembarked. The only time Pope John Paul II ever took questions from journalists was on the first leg of a trip abroad and on the flight back to Rome, when reporters were allowed back onto Shepherd One. He did not hold press conferences or subject himself to interviews at the Vatican, so if you wanted to talk to the pope you had to buy a ticket to fly on his plane. The tickets were not cheap and they were not easy to get. The Vatican allowed only several dozen journalists on the plane. We each had two or three seats to ourselves back in the coach section. The pope was in a special chamber built for him at the front of the plane, where the first-class passengers normally sit.

There was a catch to this arrangement. There was no guarantee that the pope would wander back to the coach section for interviews. He usually did, but not always. In fact, on the last leg of the 1987 American tour, from Detroit back to Rome, the pope never appeared. For a while, it looked like the pope was going to keep to himself on the first leg of the journey too. It was a long flight from Rome to Miami, but the male stewards on Shepherd One kept the press well fed and lubricated. They came down the aisle with silver carts of roasted meat, carving off a slice at your seat. The bottles of wine miraculously multiplied, just like with Jesus at that wedding at Cana. Our hosts passed out fine leather shaving kits and other souvenirs embossed with the pope's insignia. They also revealed a sly sense of humor in the selection of the film for a flight taking the pope to the New World. They choose *The Mission*, the 1986 Robert De Niro movie about eighteenth-century Spanish Jesuits in South America.

I was sitting next to an old friend and colleague, Diane Winston, then the religion writer for the *Dallas Times Herald*. Each journalist was supposedly allowed to ask one question of the pope, and Diane and I were kidding around about what we'd *really* like to ask the spiritual leader of the world's 1.1 billion Roman Catholics. She came up with a great question, but lost her nerve when the moment arrived. "Boxers or briefs? What are you wearing under those robes, Your Holiness? Boxers or briefs?"

It was an eleven-hour flight from Rome to Miami. We were making our descent and the pope had yet to appear in the press section. Suddenly, a door popped open and the pope stepped through it. About four dozen reporters and photographers sprang from their seats and started jumping over each other to be the first one to get to the pontiff. "Calm down. Everyone will get a chance to ask His Holiness a question," one of his handlers assured us. The papal press corps was a truly international entourage, so the questions were asked in six different languages, most of which the pope himself spoke. I started to worry, since I speak only English. No one was translating the questions or the answers. I realized that I would have no idea which answer was going to be the one that made the news. There would be no time to translate all this when we hit the ground and ran to telephones to call in our stories. I'd have about half an hour before the final afternoon deadline at the *Examiner.*

Thank God the answer to the question I asked turned out to be the big story from the plane, or at least the big story in San Francisco. Pope John Paul II was heading there, and massive demonstrations were planned by gay rights activists enraged over a recent church statement about homosexuality being an "intrinsic moral evil." At the same time, San Francisco was in the early throes of the AIDS epidemic, and the pope had yet to say anything about the connection between homosexuality and the spread of the AIDS virus. The head of the Southern Baptist Convention, the nation's largest Protestant denomination, had made news by saying AIDS was God's wrath against homosexuality.

By the time I got to the pope, the Alitalia 747 was making its final descent into Miami. The plane was rocking from side to side. On a normal flight the passengers would all be sitting down with their seat belts fastened and their seats in the full upright position. The pope and I were standing in the aisle bumping into each other. I stuck my tape recorder in the pontiff's face and said, "Your Holiness. Many homosexuals in San Francisco are dying of AIDS—"

"Terrible. Terrible," the pope said. "I will visit a group of AIDS victims in the basilica in San Francisco. The church is doing all that is possible to heal and especially to prevent the disease with its moral teachings."

It was hard to hear over the roar of the plane.

"Some religious leaders," I yelled, "think God is punishing homosexuals with AIDS. How do you see the hand of God in this terrible plague?"

The pope fingered the golden crucifix dangling over his white robes. "It is not easy to know the intentions of God himself," he said. "He is a great mystery. We know that he is justice, he is mercy, and he is love."

"Then why do gay people feel like they are outcasts in the church?"

"They are not outcasts," the pope replied. "The homosexual, like all people who suffer, are inside the church. No, not inside the church. In the heart of the church."

We soon landed in Miami, and I elbowed my way past a gaggle of Italian reporters (no small feat) to get to a telephone before the deadline for the final edition of that day's *Examiner*. "Pontiff Says Gays in 'Heart of Church,'" the headline proclaimed on page 1, over the fold. "Today's News Today," as we used to say in the waning days of the afternoon newspaper.

One week later, after stops across the southern United States, the Papal Express finally pulled into San Francisco. The signature moment came when the pope walked into the Mission Dolores Basilica to meet with a group of sixty gay and straight people afflicted with AIDS. Among them were a Catholic priest with AIDS and a four-year-old boy who had contracted the disease from a blood transfusion. The photo everyone remembers from that day shows the pope cradling four-year-old Brendan O'Rourke in his arms, a compassionate gesture coming at a time when many people mistakenly feared that AIDS could be contracted through casual contact. "God loves you all without distinction," the pope said, "with an unconditional, ever-lasting love."

·   ·   ·   ·   ·

There were no jetliners or globe-trotting popes when Aldous Huxley and Gerald Heard came to the United States on a trip that would turn out to be a one-way journey to the New World. Huxley and Heard sailed out of Southampton aboard the *Normandie* on April 7, 1937, accompanied by their respective partners, Maria Huxley and Christopher Wood,* along with the Huxleys' sixteen-year-old son, Matthew. The Huxleys would not only change their address. They would change their whole outlook on life.

Back in London, Aldous and Maria had been going through a difficult period. On the surface, everything was fine. *Point Counter Point* was

---

*Heard's companion, the independently wealthy Christopher Wood, should not be confused with Christopher Isherwood, the well-known writer and one of Heard's closest friends. Isherwood described Wood as "the spoilt, wayward younger son, with his airplane, his musical boxes, his superbicycle and all his other dangerous or expensive amusements and toys." Isherwood 1997, p. 21.

published in 1928, followed four years later by *Brave New World*, making Huxley one of England's most successful writers. He and Maria had an apartment in Paris and a shiny red Bugatti, an Italian touring car, one specially modified for Huxley's long legs. They had a villa in Sanary, a literary enclave on the southern coast of France, their retreat whenever life in England became too depressing.

Aldous's physical health was never robust, but now Huxley was battling psychological demons. He was struggling with insomnia. He was depressed. His old friends, skepticism and cynicism, were coming back to haunt him. And so was the political situation in Europe. Hitler was on the rise, a nightmare whose dimensions Huxley began to envision after happening upon a London rally featuring the head of the British Union of Fascists and a violent gang of Blackshirt thugs. Huxley felt a sense of gloom about the world, along with "a considerable gloom about myself."

Gerald Heard and Aldous Huxley were a few years into their lifelong friendship. Heard had a suggestion, a long-term treatment for Huxley's gloom and society's doom. The only way out was a psychological, spiritual transformation for mankind, individually and collectively. Huxley began warming to this idea and started reading books with titles like *Yoga and Western Psychology*. When Huxley's depression failed to lift, Heard recommended a regime of breathing exercises to help his friend manage his anxiety. At the same time, Heard and Huxley realized that the crisis facing Europe needed a social solution. It was not *just* a question of individual transformation. They became outspoken supporters and activists in the Peace Pledge Union, a British pacifist group that attracted more than a hundred thousand members in the mid-1930s. In fact, Heard and Huxley's pacifist campaign was one of the main reasons for their 1937 visit to the United States. They planned to continue that crusade with a U.S. lecture tour later in the year. They would come under rising pressure to rethink their ideological vision, return to England, and join the battle against Adolf Hitler and the specter of Nazi aggression. But they would stay in the United States throughout the war and for the rest of their lives.

Heard and Huxley had begun their collaboration before setting sail for America. They became commentators on BBC radio, where Heard had a regular program about advances in science and religion. Some sound recordings of the Aldous Huxley and Gerald Heard show give us a taste of what it was like to listen to their conversations. One of their 1932 radio programs followed a BBC News report in which the German foreign minister announced that Germany would no longer pay war reparations from World War I, warning that trying to force such political payments "is bound to lead to trouble not only for Germany but for the whole world."

"Well," Heard says, "that was a depressing news bulletin."

Thus begins a conversation that quickly jumps from the current political situation to theological explorations to philosophical musings about capital punishment to a cross-cultural analysis of social attitudes about violence and cruelty to animals. From there it's on to a riff about the French Revolution and how political rulers are coming to understand that propaganda can be a more effective means of social control than the use of force. That, in turn, inspires the dynamic radio duo to go off into a discussion about martyrdom in the early Christian Church. "It only cost some three or four thousand martyrdoms before the Roman Empire capitulated and Christianity, which had been a capital offense, became first tolerated and then, quite quickly, the state religion," Heard says. "If only the church had learned that lesson! Instead of that, it forgot the power of passive resistance as soon as it won its victory, and took to violence."

"That's the trouble with organized religion," Huxley replies. "It provides so many justifications for violence. It is interesting to reflect that, as a matter of historical fact, humanitarianism has increased as organized religion has declined. For when you think you know what absolute truth is, you feel justified in forcing other people to agree with you."

This was the kind of repartee Heard and Huxley planned for their American tour, which was to begin in late 1937, following a working vacation and two-month road trip across the United States. The vacation would include an extended stay at the remote New Mexico ranch of Frieda Lawrence, the widow of Huxley's dear and departed friend, the novelist D. H. Lawrence. Huxley also wanted to investigate the possibility of making some quick money writing screenplays in Hollywood, while Heard was looking to sell off properties in Nebraska and Wyoming that he'd inherited from his old patron, Sir Horace Plunkett.

Heard first raised the idea of fleeing Europe in the fall of 1933 during a ten-day stay with the Huxleys at Sanary. In a letter to his brother, Julian, Aldous reports that Heard was "advising us all to clear out to some safe spot in South America or the Pacific islands before it's too late. He [Heard] enjoys his glooms: but the fact does not necessarily mean that the glooms are unfounded. The German spectacle is really too frightening."

Upon arriving in the United States, the entourage spent a few days at the Rhinebeck, New York, home of an old friend before buying a shiny new Ford and heading out on their road trip across America. It was an interesting choice of car, given that Henry Ford had been depicted as the Antichrist in *Brave New World*. But the sedan was big enough to contain the Huxleys, their teenage son, Gerald Heard, and all the luggage they'd brought with them for an extended stay in the United States. (Christopher Wood did not accompany them on the road trip.) They headed south out of New York and, after brief stops in Philadelphia and Washington, D.C., pulled into Durham, North Carolina, on May 4. Maria was at the wheel. Heard, an avid follower of the latest research into psychic phenomena, wanted to visit the Duke University parapsychology lab of Professor J. H. Rhine, who was conducting eyebrow-raising experiments in telepathy and extrasensory perception.

Huxley was shocked to discover how famous he was in the United States. He'd wanted to lay low that spring, but word got out that he was planning on visiting Duke. Professor Jay Hubbell, a noted scholar of American literature, begged him to give a talk to students in the Duke English department. "The undergraduates who are interested in writing seem to me more interested in your work than in that of any other living novelist," Hubbell wrote in a letter mailed to Huxley's London address. Huxley, who was thinking about enrolling his son at Duke, agreed to the engagement in a telegram sent from New York. Then, in a note sent from the Albemarle Hotel in Charlottesville, Virginia, a few days before his arrival in Durham, Huxley added, "I am writing to explain that we are traveling very light in a car and that I have no evening clothes with me; therefore must make my appearance, in the words of the hymn, 'just as I am, without one plea.' About speaking, I am a very bad after-dinner speaker but on the other hand I like conversation and the exchange of ideas. . . . I get much more out of a two-way traffic of ideas than out of a one-way speech—especially if the speech happens to be my own."

But it was too late for low-key. By the time Hubbell got the letter, he'd already sold 250 tickets to a May 4 dinner to honor the famous English writer. Meanwhile, Heard had long been scheduled to give a formal address, "An Anthropologist Looks at International Relations," only hours before the Huxley dinner. Despite advance notice in two Durham newspapers, only a dozen people—including the Huxleys and the sponsoring Duke professor—showed up for Heard's lecture. But he did get a nice write-up in the next morning's edition of the *Durham Morning Herald* under the headline "Psychological Origin for World Crisis." The reporter, who was kind enough to not mention the small turnout, provides a concise summary of Heard's worldview: "Dr. Heard declared that the crisis follows man's attempt to overcome his environment and the subsequent unbalance that was brought within himself. We must have the same power over the inner world as we have over the outer, said the speaker. . . . There must be a revolution in thinking, he said, as radical as that of Copernicus."

At the time, Heard was under consideration for a teaching post in the Duke anthropology department. According to Hubble, "Duke did not offer Heard a professorship." It's not clear whether that "pitifully small audience," as Hubble described it, was a factor in that decision. Heard's interest in spiritualism and the academically suspect field of parapsychology may have worked against him, or perhaps there were rumors about his sexual orientation. In a letter withdrawing his name from formal consideration, Heard acknowledged that there were candidates with more "academic status" who truly needed the position. "About the value of my own contribution to academic anthropology," he wrote, "I had had considerable doubt."

Huxley's evening address at the Duke dinner is described in a separate article on the same page of the morning newspaper. Speaking to the English department faculty and the Undergraduate Writers Club, Huxley advised the assembled professors against forcing too much reading on their students, suggesting that they might spend less time reading and more time contemplating. "Indiscriminate reading, said Mr. Huxley, becomes a matter of 'keeping up with the Joneses and is an escape from reality. It is harmful because it keeps the reading addict from being alone, and prevents capable, serious reading of quality material. . . . Leisurely reading of carefully selected material, with periods of reflection, will produce free minds that are able to withstand the propagandistic onslaughts such as dictators are making against the European people, Mr. Huxley declared."

Huxley was pleasantly surprised by the academic program and the curious architecture at Duke, a university that owes its modern existence to one of the twentieth century's most successfully marketed addictive drugs—Lucky Strike cigarettes. At the time of Huxley's visit, the university was in the midst of a major expansion funded by its primary patron, James D. Duke, whose American Tobacco Company had come to dominate the tobacco industry by acquiring the Lucky Strike Company and some two hundred other cigar and cigarette makers. Duke favored a nostalgic neo-Gothic architecture, or as some critics have dubbed it, "Gothic Wonderland." The university completed its soaring Duke Chapel in 1935, only two years before Heard and Huxley's visit. At first, the English visitors found it odd to have twentieth-century American students housed in buildings made to resemble medieval cloisters. "Perhaps," Huxley would later write, "medieval clerics were not so different from today's undergraduates." He was intrigued by how the campus reflected no exact epoch yet projected "a certain composite and synthetic Gothieness." "The purist in one's bosom is indignant; and yet these buildings are genuinely beautiful. Yes, genuinely beautiful," Huxley observed. "Indeed, I prefer the towers and quadrangles of Duke to many of the genuinely antique buildings of our university towns."

After two days in Durham, the entourage was back on the road, with Maria in the driver's seat again. Aldous sat next to her, gazing out at a rolling country of indeterminate contour—miles of tobacco fields and pine forests that succeeded one another interminably. The sun was shining on a brilliant spring day. Huxley turned toward Heard and Matthew, who were sitting in the backseat of the Ford. "It's a pleasant, but not exciting place," Huxley would later recall. "It is a place where one would never expect anything in particular to happen."

They were heading deeper into the mountains of western North Carolina and their next stop on the great American road trip. Heard and Huxley had an invitation to speak at Black Mountain College, an innovative liberal arts college that operated from 1933 to 1957. The school was—like Huxley and Heard—a bit ahead of its time. Inspired by John Dewey's principles of progressive education, Black Mountain focused on the idea that the arts are central to the experience of learning. In its early years, the democratically run college attracted a number of European artists and intellectuals fleeing Nazi persecution. Its later faculty included Buckminster Fuller, John Cage, Arthur Penn, Willem de Kooning, and Robert Creeley. Huxley came to Black Mountain to discuss "the limitations of the novel" with Theodore Dreiser, the noted American writer, and John Andrew Rice, a mercurial scholar who founded the college after a falling out with another North Carolina school. Here, Huxley faced a more critical audience than the fawning undergraduates at Duke.

At the time, Huxley was one of the best-known writers in England and the United States, but his work was not critically acclaimed. Critics ravaged *Brave New World,* published in the United States only five years earlier by Harper and Brothers. It was dismissed as "a thin little joke" by one reviewer and as "a lugubrious and heavy-handed piece of propaganda" by another. Other critics were put off by Huxley's preoccupation with sex and by the emotionless promiscuity of the characters in the book, which envisions a nightmarish future in which Henry Ford is worshipped as God and his assembly-line innovations are used to produce test-tube babies programmed for the seamless operation of an authoritarian state. Any hints of social dissent or spiritual exploration are kept in check by sexual freedom, hypnotic drugs, and mindless entertainment.

Throughout his career, Huxley's critics accused him of being more interested in ideas than in plot or character development. His characters can come across as lifeless and heavy-handed as they express their thoughts and desires. Huxley's early novels won praise but also sparked extraordinary condemnation. Literary gatekeepers like James Douglas, editor of London's *Sunday Express*, predicted Huxley would inspire "a popular cult of blasphemy and a profitable school of nameless innuendo. The novel will creep and crawl with the vermin of diseased imaginations." Conrad Aiken, the poet, novelist, and Pulitzer Prize winner, grouped Huxley with a school of young writers "concerned with satire, with burlesque, and, in the absence of any stable convictions concerning art or morals, with the breakdown of forms." André Gide, the famed French novelist, called *Point Counter Point* "illegible." Ernest Hemingway was annoyed by Huxley's habit of putting "his own intellectual musings" into "the mouths of artificially constructed characters." Other famous writers were kinder. Rebecca West, writing in the *Daily Telegraph* in early 1932, called *Brave New World* "a serious religious work" and "one of the half-dozen most important books that have been published since the war."

The passage of time would not find greater appreciation of Huxley's literary worth. I revisited some of the novels that I read with wonder in my teens and early twenties and came away less inspired. Many of the ideas are still thought-provoking, but the stories are often convoluted or contrived. I am not alone in that perception. On the fortieth anniversary of Huxley's death, the literary critic Harold Bloom introduced a retrospective on Huxley's work by saying that his best novels, *Antic Hay* and *Point Counter Point*, survive as quaint "period pieces," while *Brave New World* "seems strained and even silly." I have to agree with Bloom's conclusion that Huxley's lasting literary legacy is found in such works as *Music at Night*, his 1932 collection of essays.

Huxley always said he was a better essayist than novelist, and he began his remarks at Black Mountain in anticipation of that critique. "I am interested in putting ideas across, and I think I have made a certain technical progress in the art," he said. "I think I should say that I have learned the art of embodying the thing more into the substance of the novel."

The students asked Huxley about his impressions of the United States. "The longer I stay in this country, the less I understand its politics," he replied. "Although people live in a democratic country, many of them actually live in a dictatorship, the dictatorship of their bosses. The problem is how to get self-government down into industry." America was still in the bowels of the Great Depression when Huxley and Heard made their way across the country. "I had no idea that there were such depths of poverty in the Deep South," he told the students at Black Mountain. "Yet the thing that strikes me most about this country is its hopefulness. In spite of the depression, in spite of everything, I find an extraordinary hopefulness running through people. It is this hopefulness that distinguishes your continent from Europe, where there is a hopeless depression and fear."

It was that sense of hopefulness—that essential American optimism— that would inspire Aldous Huxley and Gerald Heard to turn their backs on the Old World and live out the rest of their lives in the United States. And it should come as no surprise that they would pick the part of the country where anything was possible, where all things are new. They would—like so many of us—come to California and start over.

·   ·   ·   ·   ·

My airborne interview with the pope on his way to California was one of the highlights of my career as a religion reporter. But my favorite alcohol-fueled papal adventure was on an earlier, even longer journey that took us back and forth across the breadth of Canada. That twelve-day pilgrimage stretched all the way from remote Flatrock, Newfoundland, where the pope blessed a small fleet of fishing boats, to bustling downtown Vancouver, with an ill-fated detour to visit a gathering of Catholic Eskimos up in the Northwest Territories.

One of the wonderful diversions of that tour was a special train that took the pope on a slow ride through the heart of French-Catholic Canada, from Quebec City to Montreal. Thousands of the faithful lined the railroad tracks to wave to the pope, who was placed behind a large window of the illuminated caboose. Reporters covering the trip rode in a press compartment two cars before the papal caboose. There was nothing for us to do for hours and hours, but the kind folks at Rail Canada were thoughtful enough to provide an open bar to keep us entertained.

After a few drinks, we noticed that a Polish photographer from one of the Toronto papers, named Boris, bore a striking resemblance to His Holiness. By now, night had fallen, so we turned off the lights in our car. We draped a sheet over the shoulders of Pope Boris and placed him in a center window, which we illuminated with television lights. We fashioned a miter out of a pillow, painted a yellow cross on it with a highlighter pen, and placed it on the head of our newly crowned pontiff. We made a silver staff from a sound boom and, to finish it off, gave Boris a fresh can of Molson Ale to proudly display to the faithful. We finally lost it and fell down laughing when Boris pulled his American Express card out of his wallet, pressed it against the window, and proclaimed, "Don't leave home without it!"

Pope Boris was hard to beat, but there was one equally memorable moment on the pope's long Canadian tour. John Paul II always went out of his way to meet with the indigenous peoples in the nation that hosted him. Besides, it was always a good photo op, and the pope knew a good photo op when he saw one. The Indian tribes from Canada's frozen north, many of whom were converted by Catholic missionaries, wanted to meet the pope on their own turf, a traditional native meeting ground in the Northwest Territories where two great rivers, the Mackenzie and the Liard, converge. The pope honored their request even though his handlers had warned him that his plane, and the press plane following him, might not be able to land at the tiny airport in Fort Simpson. When it was foggy, as it often was, there was no way planes could land there.

The pope may have divine connections, but he was not able to use them that day to make the fog lift over Fort Simpson. Both planes made the trek north and started circling while the pope sat in his compartment and prayed for improved weather. The pope is a stubborn man and agreed to give up only when told that the planes were running low on fuel and would have to make an unexpected stop at the nearest real airport, in Yellowknife.

Papal visits are carefully choreographed events. There is not much room for whimsy or improvisation. Papal speeches and sermons are written and reviewed months ahead of time and rarely contain anything resembling actual news. They are much like the stump speeches politicians make when they are running for president of the United States. It's not easy squeezing a news story out of the pope reiterating centuries-old church teachings everywhere he goes.

Yellowknife, on the other hand, was an unexpected stop. There was no script. The pope just happened to drop into town. The pope, his entourage, and the press crowded into the small airport waiting room at Yellowknife while our planes refueled and the pope prayed for the fog to lift over Fort Simpson.

A local radio station announced that the pope had unexpectedly landed in Yellowknife, and a small band of the frozen faithful soon gathered outside the airport hoping to catch a glimpse of their spiritual leader. The pope had nothing else to do, so he decided to go out and give *an impromptu speech.* I turned to Bruce Buursma, the religion writer from the *Chicago Tribune* and one of my pals on the Godbeat. "This is going to be good," I said as we followed the pope out onto a cold, windy airport parking lot.

There was no sound system set up to address the Catholic Eskimos, but someone found an old bullhorn for the pope to use. John Paul was standing next to a Canadian cardinal, who handed the bullhorn to His Holiness. There was a little red button that you squeeze to activate the device, but the pope couldn't get the bullhorn to work. He was speaking, but no one could hear a word over the howling wind. The cardinal reached over to help the pope hold down the little red button. Suddenly, the bullhorn went on, and the first thing we all heard was the cardinal saying, "Let me squeeze it for you, Holy Father," and then the sound once again went dead.

Buursma and I started laughing and we couldn't stop. Yes, we both have sick minds, but there was more to it than that. We had spent the last week journalistically squeezing it for the Holy Father, trying to squeeze news stories from boring papal sermons.

Then the bullhorn started working again.

"Canada," the pope said in his thick Polish accent, "big country. Sometimes rainy. Sometimes foggy. Sometimes windy. But the pope thanks you peoples for finding the pope in . . . in . . . "

The pope had forgotten where he was, and so had the cardinal standing next to them.

" . . . in dis place."

Over the years, I heard dozens of the pope's speeches and sermons, and read more than a few pastoral letters and papal encyclicals, but the address at Yellowknife will always have a special place in my heart. Pope John Paul II has died and gone to heaven. He is well on his way to sainthood. But whenever I'm feeling down, all I have to do is think back on the hallowed words of that Canadian cardinal and all seems right in the world.

"Let me squeeze it for you, Holy Father."

·   ·   ·   ·   ·

There would be one more stop on the Huxley pilgrimage across the southern United States, a visit to the Lawrence ranch in the mountains of New Mexico. Heard left the Huxleys in Atlanta to hook up with his partner, Christopher Wood, who accompanied him on a side trip to visit Heard's inherited properties in Nebraska and Wyoming. Fifteen years later, the proceeds from the sale of that property—along with money inherited from his father—would allow Heard to buy a large parcel of land in the Santa Ana Mountains of Southern California and build Trabuco College.

Heard would rejoin the Huxleys in New Mexico, but his diversion allowed him to miss a thousand-mile trek across Texas. This was in 1937, before the completion of the interstate highway system. Even famous Route 66, which wandered from Chicago to LA, had not yet been fully paved. Heard's departure gave Aldous a bit more room to squeeze his lanky frame into the boxy brown Ford they'd bought back in New York, and which had lost its showroom gleam. Mud was baked on the wheels, and the windshield and grill were covered with the remains of strange, giant insects. Maria, the intrepid driver, was starting to lose it. "By the time we got to Texas," she wrote to a friend, "the desert grew more desertic, the roads dustier, and the sun more and more vicious." Here's how Aldous described the first part of the road trip in a May 20 letter from the

Alamo Hotel in Colorado Springs to his editor at Harper and Brothers in New York:

We've had a most interesting trip—marred only by a heat wave in the deserts of Texas, which were consequently like hell. However, we ultimately reached paradise in the form of an air-conditioned hotel in El Paso. The truth about this country is that nature never intended human beings to inhabit it—but put every obstacle in men's way, heat, parching drought, arctic winters, flood, gigantic mountains, swamps. The only part where man seems to be really welcome is the middle south—from Maryland to North Carolina. For the rest he seems to be there on sufferance and at the cost, on his part, of enormous efforts, pains and privations.

After a stop at the Carlsbad Caverns, the Huxleys began the long climb up to Santa Fe and Frieda Lawrence's ranch on Lobo Mountain, north of Taos. When Lady Ottoline Morrell had first brought Huxley and Frieda's husband together back in 1915, Lawrence was intent on starting a utopian colony in Florida and persuaded young Aldous to join him on the project. Lawrence later talked about starting a colony on his 165-acre property in New Mexico, which had been given to him and Frieda by the American arts patron Mabel Dodge Luhan. D. H. Lawrence lived on the ranch for only a few years during the 1920s, but Frieda spent the rest of her long life in the mountains outside Taos.

Aldous, Maria, and Matthew arrived at the ranch after being on the road for nearly a month. Maria was exhausted. She'd been doing too much driving and not enough eating. She weighed herself on a scale she stumbled across at a drugstore in Taos. She'd always been thin, but she was now down to ninety-eight pounds. In letters home she complains about "the mad situation I have gone and put myself into." She and Aldous happily accepted Frieda's offer to spend the rest of the summer on the ranch.

They settled into a three-room log cabin alongside a babbling brook. It was a big improvement from life on the road, but still too primitive for Maria's tastes. "I am not very pleased with all this," she writes. There was so much work cleaning and repairing the cabin that she became "very rattled underneath" and so tired that she didn't know "how much longer I can carry on." She complains about having to live without servants, and how, after dinner parties with Frieda and her new Italian lover "it is taken for granted that I do the washing up."

Gerald Heard rejoined the entourage and was given a little hut across the stream from the Huxley cabin. He was around for a while, but soon took off to Hollywood to stay with Christopher Wood. Heard had grown a little beard in New Mexico, but according to Maria it "had to come off when he went out to Chris." In her letters, Maria always shows a soft spot in her heart for Gerald, whom she refers to as "his ghostliness, who comes and goes." She writes that "he is very precious to us all in a different way, and we miss him" whenever he left. "There is an art of accepting things from people which I feel I shall never acquire," Maria says. "I suffer a great deal when Gerald tries, and succeeds, in doing my housework."

Aldous Huxley shows in his letters a love/hate affair with the American landscape and the American people. Looking over his writing from the summer and fall of 1937, I see a shift in his attitude toward the States, but also a change in his feelings toward himself. He was getting lots of work done during his time on Lobo Mountain—something that always lifted his spirits. "I am greatly enjoying America, which, I now realize, I simply hadn't seen before this occasion. What an extraordinary, queer, fascinating country!" He describes New Mexico as "this astonishing country of huge mountains, dry plateau, Indians, Mexicans, and also, alas, of artists—for they abound in Santa Fe and Taos. However, we're far away on a mountain and take great pains to see as few of them as possible."

His writings from this three-room cabin, eight thousand feet above sea level, reveal the shift from Huxley the cynic to Huxley the mystic. He was finishing what he called "my sociologico-philosophical book." It was titled *Ends and Means: An Enquiry into the Nature of Ideals and into the Methods Employed for Their Realization.* Huxley begins by asking one of his trademark big questions—perhaps the biggest. Across the centuries and across culture, he writes, from Isaiah to Karl Marx, prophets and politicians have proposed various schemes to realize a common goal of liberty, peace, justice, and brotherly love. Which of them offers the correct path? None of them, Huxley answers. The way forward is for man to free himself from all the old philosophies and political ideas. "The ideal man is the non-attached man," Huxley asserts. "Non-attached to his bodily sensations and lusts. Non-attached to his craving for power and possessions. Non-attached to the objects of these various desires. Non-attached to his anger and hatred; non-attached to his exclusive loves. Non-attached to wealth, fame, social position."

"Liberation from prevailing conventions of thought, feeling and behavior is accomplished most effectively by the practice of disinterested virtues and through direct insight into the real nature of ultimate reality," Huxley asserts, suggesting (like Heard) that his readers begin a serious meditation practice as the best way to achieve that insight.

Most of *Ends and Means* is a detached, intellectual exposition on Huxley's thoughts on how to achieve various social reforms. But toward the end of the book, in a chapter titled "Beliefs," he changes voice in a few self-revealing paragraphs. "For myself, as no doubt, for most of my contemporaries, the philosophy of meaninglessness was essentially an instrument of liberation," he writes. "The liberation we desired was simultaneously liberation from a certain system of morality. We objected to the morality because it interfered with our sexual freedom; we objected to the political and economic system because it was unjust."

Huxley wrote that in 1937, but it sounds to me like something we could say about those of us who came of age in the counterculture and sexual revolution of the 1960s and 1970s.

In an apparent reference to the Bloomsbury circle, Huxley confesses, "The chief reason for being 'philosophical' was that one might be free from prejudices—above all, prejudices of a sexual nature." Huxley concedes that "the desire to justify a certain sexual looseness played a part in the popularization of meaninglessness."

Times had changed, and so had the philosophy of Aldous Huxley.

"After the [First World] War the philosophy of meaninglessness came once more triumphantly into fashion," he writes. "By the end of the twenties a reaction had begun to set in—away from the easy-going philosophy of general meaninglessness toward the hard, ferocious theologies of nationalistic and revolutionary idolatry. Meaning was reintroduced into the world, but only in patches. . . . This can have only evil and disastrous results."

Does that sound a bit like what happened during the backlash against the liberation movements of the 1960s or 1970s, most clearly seen in the rise of Ronald Reagan as the governor of California and president of the United States? It does to me.

Then, and now, another war always seems inevitable. The one facing Huxley and the rest of the world was with Germany. Hitler had assumed total control over that war-torn nation and pushed through racial purity laws to persecute and isolate German Jews. Dachau, the prison labor camp outside Munich, was already open for business. Other leading pacifists were beginning to see that an exception to nonviolence had to be made in the face of Adolf Hitler. But Heard and Huxley maintained their pacifist stance to the end. Theirs was more of a philosophical pacifism than a political position. They would continue their analysis of the root causes of militarism in Germany but also in Britain, Russia, and the United States. Huxley writes, "We have thought of ourselves as members of supremely meaningful and valuable communities—deified nations, divine classes and what not—existing in a meaningless universe. And because we have thought like this, rearmament is in full swing, economic nationalism becomes ever more intense, the battle of rival propagandas grows ever fiercer, and general war becomes increasingly probable." He also observes, "Our European admiration for military heroism and martyrdom has tended to make men believe that a good death is more important than a good life. . . . War is not a law of nature, nor even a law of human nature. It exists because men wish it to exist."

Ends and Means was published in England on November 8, 1937, a few months after Maria finished typing the manuscript in the mountains of New Mexico. That same week, Hitler convened a secret meeting of his top generals and revealed his plan to conquer Europe.

Nothing would stop Hitler, certainly not a series of lectures by Gerald Heard and Aldous Huxley. Heard and Huxley would come down from the mountaintop and give the cause of peace one last try with an American lecture tour. They would fail miserably, and their disillusionment with the world would soon force them to turn their back on Europe and turn inward.

They were bound for the Golden State, which would offer some shelter from the storm. There they would find another retreat, this time in the Santa Ana Mountains, where they would begin their most serious effort to embody the enlightened philosophy they sought to promote. They would discover that those teachings were much easier to preach than to practice. But it was still only 1937. There were still a few good years left to ignore the obvious signs of doom, to distract themselves in a wondrous world of fantasy and illusion. They were headed for Hollywood.

FIVE

Hollywood

The cause of drunkenness and drug-taking is to be
found in the general dissatisfaction with reality. . . .
Alcohol and drugs offer means of escape from the
prison of the world and the personality. . . . The
only rational way of dealing with the drug and
drink problem is, first, to make reality so decent
that human beings will not be perpetually desiring
to escape from it.

Aldous Huxley, "Poppy Juice," 1932

By the fall of 1937, the Huxleys had moved into a home at 1425½ North
Crescent Heights in Hollywood. Aldous was showing signs that this trip
might be more than an extended vacation and lecture tour. He wrote to
friends in England that he was finding California "very agreeable and
amusing and fantastic and interesting. A place of virtualities, where
absolutely anything might happen. Meanwhile, almost everything is
happening—movies, astronomy, sweated labour in the fields, philan-
thropy, scholarship, phony religions, real religions, all stirred together in
a vast chaos in the midst of the most astonishing scenery, ranging from
giant sequoias and rock peaks to date palms and red hot deserts."

Huxley and Heard rolled into Los Angeles just as a very different
class of migrants was westward bound. During the 1930s, depression
and Dust Bowl refugees came to California in search of work or at least

better weather. They were, of course, in straits more dire than those of the traveling party crammed into Huxley's boxy brown Ford. Those Midwestern migrants were only the first waves of a tsunami of soldiers, sailors, and shipyard workers who would pass through California during the coming war years. Many of them, like Huxley and Heard, would find new opportunities in the Golden State. They would stay in California, and they would forever change the wondrous place Huxley described in his early letters home.

In one long missive to Mary Hutchinson, the Bloomsbury siren who shared her love with both Aldous and Maria, Huxley describes California as a multitudinous land of "endless forests" and "red-hot mountains like those of Arabia." He marvels at the giant sequoias, which had stood in those forests for more than two thousand years. "They are the most impressive natural objects I have ever seen, with a strange character of their own, a kind of aged serenity immensely impressive and moving." There were "orange groves—hundreds of miles of them, alternating with avocados, pears, persimmons, walnuts, peaches, cotton and fields of lettuce and artichokes as large as English ducal estates."

"Then of course there's the sea coast—barren in the southern part of the state where the land is almost a desert except where irrigated, when it takes on the extravagant fertility of an oasis—green further north, where you can have bits of country like Devonshire, and then the really fabulous spectacle of San Francisco."

Huxley was equally fascinated with the Southern California social scene. "Going out to dinner, one constantly has to travel thirty miles each way and frequently the house one goes to turns out to be perched on the top of a mountain with terraces and gardens and swimming pools scooped out of the slope and the most spectacular panoramas in every direction. And then the strangest variety of people—the movie world in its own little suburb of Hollywood ... with its fearful Jewish directors, and the actors, and the film writers, who make more money than any other kind of author and are generally speaking not authors at all."

His connection and consultant on how to profit from the mighty Hollywood studios of the 1930s was Anita Loos, the trail-blazing woman screenwriter. Huxley originally met Loos on his earlier trip to the United

States. In a May 14, 1926, letter he wrote to Loos from the Congress Hotel in Chicago, not long after he sailed into San Francisco on his maiden voyage to America, Huxley introduced himself by telling Anita how "enraptured" he was by her novel, *Gentlemen Prefer Blondes*, a wildly successful book that had come out the previous year. The story, a satire of flappers and the changing sexual mores of the Roaring Twenties, was based on a series of sketches Loos first penned for *Harper's Bazaar*. The book would later form the basis of an equally successful 1953 film starring Jane Russell and Marilyn Monroe.

As social satirists, Loos and Huxley were very much on the same page. Huxley's early novels *Crome Yellow* and *Antic Hay* satirized the breakdown of post-Victorian British morality. So it was no surprise that these two thoroughly modern writers became lifelong friends. "My wife and I are to be in New York for about a fortnight," Huxley wrote in 1926. "It would be a very great pleasure—for us at any rate—if we could arrange a meeting with you during that time."

Aldous and Maria were invited to come by Loos's New York apartment for afternoon tea. While they would become good friends and creative soul mates, Aldous and Anita were an extraordinarily odd-looking couple. Standing face-to-face, the petite Loos came up to the bellybutton of the towering Huxley. She was struck by the man's enormous majesty. "He was a giant in height with the look of an archangel drawn by William Blake," she recalled. "And his myopic eyes made him appear to be focusing on things above and beyond what ordinary mortals saw."

A decade later, Loos introduced Aldous and Maria to such Hollywood celebrities as Charlie Chaplin and Greta Garbo. Chaplin became a fairly close friend, Garbo a fascinating acquaintance. Back in England, Mary Hutchinson got the latest Hollywood gossip in her letters from Aldous. "We even had a glimpse," Huxley wrote, "of the ordinarily invisible Garbo, whom we met at Anita Loos' [home] looking infinitely ninetyish [as in the 1890s] and perverse, in a very sporty Lesbian tailor-made. Not that she is exclusively a lesb. Rather omnifutuent—her present boyfriend being [Leopold] Stokowski the conductor."

Loos, meanwhile, had begun her own study of the unusual marriage of Mr. and Mrs. Huxley. "Maria Huxley was the living definition of the word 'fey.' Her existence sparkled with fascinating idiocies," Loos recalled. One day, after the Huxleys had settled into their Hollywood home, Loos was invited over for dinner. The meal consisted of a platter of string beans, served at room temperature and surrounded by cold sliced bananas. On another visit, some of Matthew's teenage friends had come over to celebrate his seventeenth birthday. Maria served the famished teenagers tiny portions of roasted chicken. Aldous noticed that Maria had thrown out most of the dark meat. "But Sweetins," said Aldous, using the Elizabethan pet name they favored for each other, "why don't you cook the drumsticks?" Maria replied, "Because, Sweetins, they looked so gross in comparison with their dainty little wings."

"Along with her eccentricities," Loos recalled. "Maria had virtues that made her a true helpmate. She was Aldous' best-loved companion, his secretary-typist, and in Hollywood she drove the family car. Best of all, she protected Aldous from the swarms of pests and ridiculous disciples that attach themselves to a great man."

Loos helped set up Huxley's first meeting with a studio executive at MGM. Of course, the famous English writer needed no introduction. At the time, Hollywood studios were offering contracts to many well-known authors; two who had already signed were F. Scott Fitzgerald and Dorothy Parker. Huxley was signed, but he soon found that he was not the sort of writer who could easily turn out compelling screenplays. Not that it really mattered. More than anything else, Hollywood was buying the Huxley name, and Aldous and Maria were happy to sell it in the form of an initial contract that brought in eighteen hundred dollars a week—an incredible salary in 1938. They made some calculations and realized that, in only eight weeks, they'd make more money than Huxley had made on his last two books.

Huxley was teamed up with another writer to work out a film treatment for *Madame Curie*, a memoir written by the daughter of the Polish-born scientist and two-time Nobel Prize winner best known for her research into medical uses for radioactivity. It seemed like the perfect project for a man with known talent for writing about science for a popular audience. To top it off, the luminous Greta Garbo was slated to star in the film.

Nevertheless, Huxley was hesitant. "But how can I? And what can Garbo do in it?" he complained to Maria. "And anyhow I wouldn't be able to please them." Anita Loos persuaded him to take the assignment. "You'll make enough to set you up for life," she told Aldous. "And I will protect you from the studio."

Huxley agreed. Garbo was in Paris, where director George Cukor cabled her the good news about Huxley joining the project. "He is an inspiration and a godsend," Cukor wrote. "He will make Curie human and important." Garbo was thrilled. It was the summer of 1938. She was getting tired of, and a bit old for, the role of seductress, a role that had made her a silent-film star in such movies as *The Temptress* and *Flesh and the Devil*. Garbo now wanted meatier, more mature roles. "Wonderful plans," she cabled back.

But by the time Garbo returned to California in October 1938, the project was falling apart. Huxley's 145-page treatment was considered too literary. According to one account, MGM producer Bernie Hyman, who had struggled to get the rights to the story, didn't even bother to read Huxley's lengthy treatment after his secretary told him: "It stinks." Cukor dropped the project to direct another film that seemed to have good prospects—something called *Gone with the Wind*.

Huxley did not take the rejection lightly. "Anita couldn't understand why he was so upset," recalled Christopher Isherwood, the British writer, who moved to Southern California shortly after Heard and Huxley arrived. "She didn't understand that we thought writing something for Greta Garbo was more glamorous than winning a Pulitzer. She had been around the magic [Hollywood] held for outsiders like Aldous and me. She thought Hollywood had failed Huxley where I'm pretty sure that Huxley felt he had failed Greta Garbo."

Another director would pick up *Madame Curie* with a rewritten script. Greer Garson wound up playing the starring role, and Huxley's name was not mentioned in the credits when the film was finally released in late 1943. Huxley ended up with one screen credit at MGM, for cowriting a screenplay based on the Jane Austen novel *Pride and Prejudice*. It was released in 1940 with a cast that included Greer Garson and Laurence Olivier.

Huxley tried his hand over at Twentieth Century-Fox, where he worked with Robert Stevenson and John Houseman on a screenplay of the Charlotte Brontë novel *Jane Eyre*. The film, released in 1944, starred Orson Wells, Joan Fontaine, Elizabeth Taylor, and Agnes Moorehead. Huxley's final screen credit was for writing the screenplay for the 1948 Universal-International film *A Woman's Vengeance*, based on his own 1922 story "The Gioconda Smile."*

Greta Garbo held on to the idea of making a movie with Aldous Huxley. They spent one memorable afternoon together at the home of the famously reclusive star. Huxley described Garbo's palace as "silent as a grave" and giving "absolutely no indication that it might be occupied." He was about to leave when a servant finally answered his knock and led him into a large, dark, sparsely furnished room. He saw a small woman sitting on a very large couch, who turned out to be Garbo's lover, Mercedes de Acosta. Huxley sat down and made small talk until Garbo made her entrance. "She was dressed like a boy," Huxley recalled, "a very beautiful boy." Garbo told Aldous that she wanted him to write a screenplay about Saint Francis of Assisi. Huxley was warming up to the idea when Garbo mentioned that *she* would play the role of the popular Italian saint. Huxley was never sure how serious Garbo was about the idea, but nothing ever came of it.

Someone still *should* make a film about one Huxley-Garbo encounter. Garbo, who once expressed a desire "to travel to India and become wise," wanted to meet J. Krishnamurti, a famous Indian philosopher who had installed himself at a retreat center in Ojai, about an hour north of Hollywood. Garbo had been attending lectures by an Indian swami at a temple in the hills above Glendale. "She was drawn to prophets—genuine and otherwise," recalled Christopher Isherwood. "But she wanted to learn the meaning in life in one easy lesson . . . before her butterfly attention wandered away again." Since Aldous and Anita both loved picnics, they decided that a Garbo-Krishnamurti rendezvous would be a great excuse for one.

---

*For the complete story of Huxley's years as a screenwriter, see David King Dunaway's book *Huxley in Hollywood*.

Krishnamurti was a fourteen-year-old boy growing up in India when he was "discovered," in 1909, by the leaders of the Theosophical Society and anointed as the messiah of the coming New Age. In the summer of 1929, an adult Krishnamurti made headlines around the world by renouncing that role and telling his devotees: "I do not want followers, and I mean this. The moment you follow someone you cease to follow truth. . . . Look within yourselves for enlightenment." Yet he continued to lecture, suggesting a "think for yourself" philosophy that would resonate with many spiritual seekers.

Krishnamurti was born in South India in the summer of 1895, making him only ten months younger than Huxley. They first met at Huxley's home in Hollywood in the spring of 1938, and Huxley began visiting the famed Indian philosopher at his Ojai retreat center. At the time, Huxley was suffering from a bad case of bronchial pneumonia, which had put him in the hospital for a while, but the meeting with Krishnamurti—which had been arranged by Heard—helped lift the sick man's spirits.

Krishnamurti could see that Huxley was an intellectual, but also sensed a deeper spirit, one that resonated with his own. They talked about all kinds of things—the difficulty in communicating without falling into propaganda, the various ways of practicing yoga, the problem of organizing spiritual groups without vested interests. Krishnamurti immediately took to both Aldous and his wife. "He is so charming and amusing and so simple," Maria said after one visit. "How he must suffer when he's treated as a prophet."

Krishnamurti looked forward to Huxley's visits to the Ojai Valley, where they would go off on long walks in the woods. Krishnamurti normally didn't like to converse during these outings. It distracted him from experiencing nature. But being with Huxley was different. They talked about music, classical and modern. They talked about the latest scientific developments and their effects on society. Huxley was always in tune with their natural surroundings. "To go for a walk with him was a delight," Krishnamurti recalled. "He would discourse on the wayside flowers and, though he couldn't see properly, whenever we passed in the hills in California and saw an animal close by, he would name it." A deep affection between the two men developed—to the point that they didn't really have to speak to communicate. They would often sit together for long periods without saying a word.

As Huxley and Krishnamurti came together, the world was falling apart. World War I was still a relatively fresh memory, and now Europe once again faced the eve of destruction. Pacifism ran deep in Huxley's and Krishnamurti's souls, so deep that even forces as evil as Nazi Germany would not inspire them to renounce pacifism and join the call to arms. On their walks, they talked about the coming war and their despair at the state of the world. At Ojai, the questioners at Krishnamurti's public talks were becoming incredulous over his philosophical refusal to fight even those who were urging the United States to enter the fight. "We are in imminent danger of being involved in the war," one man said. "Why not give us some concrete suggestions of how to fight against it?"

"War is only an outward manifestation of inward confusion and the struggle with hate and antagonism," Krishnamurti replied. "There is really only one war, the war within ourselves. . . . Merely to have suggestions or instructions given by another—what you should do under this or that circumstance—does not bring peace."

Huxley took to the airwaves to encourage the British people to think deeper about the psychological causes of war in all of us—not just among the Nazis. In an lecture broadcast on BBC radio, Huxley said:

For noncombatants, war actually makes life seem *more* worth living. To some extent this is true of the peacetime preliminaries and conditions of war. The first condition of war is that the population of the planet should be divided into organized groups, and that each individual should be conscious of his own group's separateness from and superiority to all other groups.

Today these potentially war-making groups are nations. Nationalism can be made to yield the individual immense psychological satisfaction. There is the satisfaction, to begin with, of feeling yourself at one with your fellows. This is intensified almost to ecstasy during war. By means of propaganda and patriotic display, it can be kept at a very high pitch even in times of peace.

The dictators of modern Europe are all past masters at keeping it perpetually simmering, almost at boiling point. But, of course, this feeling of solidarity is not the only one they encourage. Nor indeed, is it the only one that their subjects love to experience. Like war itself, nationalism justifies the individual in giving expression to those antisocial impulses and emotions which he has always been taught to repress. The patriot is allowed to indulge with a good conscience in vanity and hatred. Vanity in regard to his own group, hatred in regard to all other groups.

On one of their walks, Huxley suggested a picnic with Garbo and Krishnamurti. The Indian sage was more interested in talking to the philosopher Bertrand Russell, who was in town for an extended visit. But they found a date that would work for everyone and compiled a guest list that turned into a Hollywood who's who.

By the fall of 1939, Garbo and Krishnamurti had both grown tired of their celebrity status as superstars of the silver screen and the spiritual scene, respectively. Garbo knew she wasn't "the Divine One," as she'd become known. It had been nearly a decade since Krishnamurti had renounced his messianic role. They had a few things in common. They'd both been robbed of their childhoods and turned into someone else's fantasy, one sacred and one profane. Garbo had been plucked out of her native Sweden and sent to Hollywood to be molded into the sultry vamp of silent film, while Krishnamurti was plucked to fulfill the Theosophists' messianic dreams.*

On the appointed day of the picnic, Krishnamurti drove down from Ojai with an entourage of attendants and Indian ladies in colorful saris. They were all strict vegetarians, forbidden to eat from cooking vessels contaminated by the flesh of animals, so they brought along their own set of pots, pans, and utensils. Garbo—always afraid of being recognized in public—appeared wearing a beat-up pair of men's trousers and a battered floppy hat pulled over her face. She was also on a strict vegetarian diet and came with a bunch of raw carrots tied to her waist.

---

*Krishnamurti had been hobnobbing with Hollywood stars since the 1920s. One day he visited the set of Cecil B. DeMille's opus on the life of Christ, *The King of Kings.* Krishnamurti later recalled a moment when a photographer took a picture of him standing between DeMille and actor H. B. Warner, who was playing the role of Christ. "I left soon afterward," Krishnamurti said. "I thought three saviors on the same set was perhaps a little bit too much." John Kobler, *Damned in Paradise: The Life of John Barrymore* (New York: Athenaeum, 1977), p. 229.

Other guests included Charlie Chaplin and his wife, Paulette Goddard, who brought a generous supply of champagne and caviar. Goddard had donned a Mexican peasant outfit and woven colored yarn into her braids. Rounding out the picnic party were Loos, Aldous, Maria, and the teenage Matthew, along with Bertrand Russell and Christopher Isherwood.

They rendezvoused on Sunset Boulevard and set off in a caravan of cars looking for a safe place to build a campfire. They wound up heading into Tujunga Canyon, about thirty miles north of Hollywood, stopping after the road narrowed and finally ended. There, the guests hauled their picnic supplies out of the cars and carried them down to a stony riverbed. It was a beautiful spot surrounded with forested precipices. It reminded Isherwood of a scene in the lower Alps.

After lunch, the entourage hiked farther into the canyon until they reached a spot where a high wire fence had been strung across the riverbed and marked with No Trespassing signs. Somebody said it looked a bit like a concentration camp. Loos spotted a place where they could burrow under the fence. "Come on. It will be an adventure," she said. "We'll be like escaping refugees."

At first, it seemed too sick a joke, but Loos and Chaplin crawled down to the spot and started digging with their hands, pulling out rocks and scooping up dirt. Huxley and Russell had been walking along, engaged in a philosophical debate about whether one could continue to be a pacifist with Hitler on the march. It was October 1939. Hitler had just invaded Poland, and World War II seemed inevitable. They continued the debate as they got down on their knees and joined the excavation, laughing like kids playing out a wartime fantasy. Before long, the party had dug out a large, shallow pit. One by one they got down on their bellies and wriggled under the fence.

Once they were on the other side of the fence, the laughter seemed a bit forced and the playful mood faded. Having returned to adulthood, the party strolled off in twos and threes, with Huxley and Russell continuing their discussions about the coming war and the future of England. Krishnamurti may have wandered off with Rosalind Williams Rajogopal, a young Ojai attendant who had just begun a long, romantic affair with the would-be messiah.

Isherwood, who'd drunk too much beer at the picnic, stayed back long enough so that he could walk with Garbo. He tried to start a conversation, but couldn't breach the famous reserve. "If she weren't Garbo, I could be great friends with her," he later told his mother, "but she is so terribly isolated; always having to cover her face with her hand or hat when we pass anyone, for fear of being recognized. It's like going around with someone who is wanted for murder."

As they strolled farther into the canyon, Garbo began to warm up to Isherwood. She wanted to keep the playful mood alive. "As long as we're on this side of the fence," she said, "let's pretend we're two other people—quite, quite different."

"You know," Isherwood replied. "I really wish you *weren't* Garbo. I like you. I think we could have been great friends."

"But we *are* friends!" Garbo replied, laughing. "You are my dear little brother."

Isherwood almost blushed. "Oh, shut up!" he exclaimed.

The next day, Isherwood reflected on his Garbo encounter in his diary. "I suppose everybody who meets Garbo dreams of saving her," he wrote, "either from herself, or from Metro-Goldwyn-Mayer, or from some friend or lover. And she always eludes them by going into an act. This is what has made her a universal figure. She is the woman everyone wants to interfere with." As it turned out, Garbo and Krishnamurti never got much of a chance to talk. They had been put next to each other for the picnic, but had hardly said a word. "I think they were both scared," Isherwood wrote in his diary.

Isherwood and Garbo headed back down to the fence, just as Loos, Chaplin, and Huxley were encountering a sheriff's deputy, as Loos later noted. As they were walking up, they heard the officer say in a loud, gruff voice, "What the hell's going on here?"

He'd spotted the fire from the Indian ladies' cooking pots and figured he'd stumbled upon a camp of hobos. It was the end of the fire season and the authorities were on high alert. Huxley noticed that the deputy had a pistol in his hand. "Don't anybody in this gang know how to read?" the cop said, pointing to a nearby No Trespassing sign.

"Yes, officer, I can read," Huxley politely replied. "We are so sorry. We did not see the sign. But let me assure you that we have no intention of desecrating the river."

Loos couldn't keep a smile off her face. When they got there, the river bottom was already strewn with rusty cans, pop bottles, and other rubbish. Huxley offered to clean it all up if the deputy would simply let them finish their lunch.

The cop wouldn't hear it. "Get going," he yelled. "And that means *now!*"

"Of course, officer," Huxley replied, deciding that it was time to play his celebrity trump card. By then, Aldous had enjoyed a few glasses of champagne, which had loosened his tongue. "But first, sir, would you care to meet Mr. Charlie Chaplin, or perhaps Miss Greta Garbo," he said, pointing over to the shady figure in the floppy hat and torn men's trousers.

"Don't give me that line! I've seen their movies and they certainly don't belong in this outfit. Now get out of here before I arrest the slew of you."

With that, the party gathered up their belongings and guiltily headed back up to their cars.

·   ·   ·   ·   ·

No transcript exists of the conversation Garbo had with Krishnamurti that October afternoon, assuming they ever got a chance to have one. The last surviving member of the picnic party, Matthew Huxley, died in 2005.* Unfortunately, I failed to take advantage of the one opportunity I had to hear a firsthand account of the day the "Reluctant Messiah" met "the Divine One." That was in the spring of 1983, when I interviewed Jiddu Krishnamurti in his room at the Huntington Hotel in San Francisco, high atop posh Nob Hill. But it's still a story worth telling—especially in a book that relates the misadventures of a religion writer on drugs.

Krishnamurti was the closest thing I ever had to a guru. Leave it to

---

*After finishing high school in Colorado, Matthew Huxley earned degrees at the University of California, Berkeley, and Harvard University before beginning a long career in public health, including many years spent as an epidemiologist at the National Institute of Mental Health. He died of a heart attack on February 10, 2005. He was eighty-four and was survived by two children, Trevenen and Tessa Huxley of New York City.

me to pick a spiritual leader with no interest in telling me how to live my life. I was in my early twenties when I discovered his writings. He questioned everything. He encouraged doubt, and I reveled in doubt. In 1929, when he dissolved the religious organization that had been set up to promote him as the New World Messiah, he renounced all efforts to organize belief. He did not want to start "a creed, a sect, a religion, to be imposed on others," he said. "This is what everyone throughout the world is attempting to do. Truth is narrowed down and made a plaything for those who are weak, for those who are only momentarily discontented. Truth cannot be brought down, rather the individual must make the effort to ascend to it."

I started reading Krishnamurti's books during my junior year of college in England, at the University of Birmingham. It was around the time I was getting deeper into Huxley's novels and essays, although I had no idea back then that my two heroes had been such close friends for much of their lives.

Krishnamurti was in San Francisco in April 1983 to give two talks at the Masonic Auditorium; these were among his last major public addresses prior to his death the following February. Before taking the cable car up Nob Hill from Powell and Market Streets to meet him, I spent the morning looking through the old *Examiner* clips on Krishnamurti— through those same steel cabinets that wound up in the history room at the public library.

The old news clippings were fascinating. Normally skeptical newsmen wrote breathlessly about the coming of the sixteen-year-old "Hindoo boy." "Youth Is Hailed By Mystics as Divine," proclaims one five-column headline over a huge photograph of the Brahman boy with the dark piercing eyes. "Some Already Call Him the Messiah."

In 1925, only a year before he began renouncing the spiritualism and the messianic mythmaking of the Theosophists, Krishnamurti was in San Francisco. "Hindu 'Messiah' Decries American Jazz," one headline reads. "Flapperism Laid to U.S. Lack of Repose." On that visit, thirty-year-old Krishnamurti met a group of reporters in his room at the Fairmont Hotel with his discoverer, seventy-nine-year-old Annie Besant, at his side. She told the press that the voice of Christ entered the young

Indian's body for the first time during a recent address to devotees in India. His voice changed entirely as he suddenly "spoke as the Savior himself." Besant added, "I feel sure as time goes on that these manifestations will become increasingly frequent."

Krishnamurti assured the wide-eyed reporters that he was very much like mortal men. "I play golf, and I enjoy other athletic games," he explained, "not because they are fashionable but because they seem to purify and strengthen the body." Too many Americans, he said, waste their time on emotional distractions. "They get this through the cinema, through nauseating plays and through such manifestations as flapperism."

Fifty-eight years later, I sat down with Krishnamurti at another Nob Hill hotel. This time, I was the thirty-year-old know-it-all, and Krishnamurti was two weeks away from his eighty-eighth birthday. His jet-black hair had turned to gray. His eyes, now more tired than penetrating, looked out from a deeply lined, sagging face. He was wearing a fine, tailored suit and staying in one of the finer suites in this old-money hotel. I pulled out my microcassette recorder, pressed "Record," and laid it down on the coffee table between us.

"Back in the 1920s," I asked, "did you really believe that you were the 'Messiah,' as promoted by the Theosophical Society?"

Krishnamurti gave me a look that said the question really annoyed him. "God knows," he said. "That was about fifty years ago, sir."

"I realize that," I said. "But I'm just wondering what you were really thinking at the time."

"What I was thinking at the time was that all this had nothing to do with truth. It was a circus. They found my brother and me in 1909. We were young and innocent."

"Why do you think they chose you?"

"I don't know why," he said, shaking his head like he couldn't stand the question. "You'd have to ask them—but they're all dead."

One of Krishnamurti's most popular books, *The First and Final Freedom*, was published in 1954 with an introduction by Aldous Huxley. "There is a transcendent spontaneity of life, a 'creative reality,' as Krishnamurti calls it, which reveals itself as immanent only when the perceiver's mind is in a state of 'alert passivity,' of 'choiceless awareness,'"

Huxley writes. "This choiceless awareness—in every moment and in all circumstances of life—is the only effective meditation."

Perhaps this was something I could get my disgruntled interview subject to discuss. "What do you mean by 'choiceless awareness?'" I asked.

"Just being aware of that curtain, aware of that pullover you're wearing, aware of what is happening in the world—the brutality, murder, and corruption—aware of what is happening inside you."

"How is that different from ordinary awareness, the awareness of someone walking down the street?"

Krishnamurti replied, "People walking down the street aren't aware of what is happening around them."

"Why not?" I asked.

"Because they are self-centered. They are absorbed with their own problems and their own selfish motives, so they are unaware of what is happening in the world."

"Do you advocate—"

"I don't advocate," Krishnamurti replied.

"Do you have any suggestions as to how we can be less self-centered?" I asked, restating the question.

"That's a tremendously long process. First, just observe what is happening in the world. Observe human behavior. That's the standard by which you judge. Human behavior has produced the world. Look at your conditioning and see if it is reasonable, whether that conditioning has any intelligence behind it, or is it purely action/reaction."

Krishnamurti and I spent an hour together in his room at the Huntington Hotel. It was a tough interview, but he warmed up a bit at the end. It was 3:30 P.M. when I got back to the *Examiner* city room. My deadline wasn't until noon the next day, which seems far off to a reporter working on an afternoon newspaper with four deadlines a day. But I got straight to work. This was a story I really cared about, and those didn't come along that often. I pulled my headphones out of my desk and started going through the audiotape, pulling out the best quotes. About an hour later, the phone rang.

"Hey, Don," the voice said. "It's Dick."

"What's happening?"

"Not much. I'm calling to see if you're up for a party. A friend of mine is opening up a new restaurant in Berkeley. Free food. Free drinks. Wild women."

"I don't know. I got a good story here. You'll never guess who I just interviewed."

"Jesus Christ?"

"Close," I said. "J. Krishnamurti."

"Really. I want to hear about that. What's your deadline?"

"Not 'til tomorrow."

"Then come on over, man. It starts in half an hour, at five. Donovan Bess will be there. He'd love to hear about Krishnamurti."

"Hmmm. Sounds tempting . . . What the fuck. I'll be right over. But I'm only going to stay for an hour or so because I need to get back here and work on this story."

Famous last words.

Under normal circumstances, the promise of free food, free drink, and wild women was all I needed to put off finishing a newspaper story. This time, it took more. It took the promise of meeting Donovan Bess, a retired *Chronicle* reporter who wrote some of the smartest stories about the spiritual seekers of the 1960s. Donovan was an old friend of Dick Hallgren, the guy who'd just tempted me to skip out of work early and head across the Bay Bridge for a party over in Berkeley.

Dick and Donovan were the only reporters at the *Chronicle* who really understood what was going on in San Francisco during the early years of the psychedelic sixties. The *Examiner* was clueless. It thought the Summer of Love was a police story. Dick and Donovan left the *Chronicle* in the early 1970s, a few years before I started at the *Examiner*. Donovan had retired and Dick had been fired for doing what I was about to do—caring more about getting high than getting the story. Back in Dick and Donovan's day, getting fired from the *Chronicle* for drinking was quite an accomplishment, since some of the best reporters on the paper were alcoholics. Dick would eventually quit drinking in the mid-1980s, setting an example I would choose to ignore until 2003, when my own drinking and drugging would nearly get me fired from the *Chronicle*, or at least get me forewarned about cleaning up my act.

Donovan was born in Iowa in 1909, the son of a Presbyterian preacher man. He wrote two novels before celebrating his twenty-fifth birthday and joining the *Chronicle* staff in 1942. Later, Donovan provided some of the most intelligent coverage anywhere of the human potential movement. Doing background research for my stories in the 1970s and 1980s, I'd often come across his work and was always impressed. I'd read so many of his old stories that I felt like I knew him, but we didn't actually meet until this day in 1983, the same day I met Krishnamurti.

Donovan had been living in London, where he'd become the disciple of a eccentric Sufi teacher known as Mrs. Tweedy. I'd get to know him over the next few years, visit him in London, and wind up being the reporter who wrote his obit for the *Chronicle* when he died in 1990, in Luxor, Egypt. He and a lady friend had been off riding camels in the desert the day before he died.

Dick and Donovan were in fine form when I found them at the party. I headed straight for the bar, immediately forgetting the promise I'd made to myself to take it easy so I could get back to the newspaper that evening and finish the story. Donovan too was an admirer of Krishnamurti, so he wanted to hear all about my encounter that afternoon. At some point, we started talking about the stories Donovan had written back in the day about the psychedelic scene of the sixties.

"Do you still trip?" I asked.

"Every now and then," Donovan replied, "just for old times' sake."

"I think I'm done with LSD," I said. "Too intense. The only psychedelic drug I'd take now—other than mushrooms—is MDA. That is one amazing drug. Have you tried it?"

Donovan laughed. "Have I tried it? Let's see," he said, reaching into his coat pocket, "I think I have three hits right here. Why don't we take it, go back to the newspaper, and write your story together."

It was an offer I couldn't refuse. I suggested that, rather than drive back into the city, we head over to my house in nearby Oakland. I had my tape recorder with me. We could listen to the interview and write up the story on a laptop computer I had at home. "Sounds like a plan," Donovan said.

Dick, Donovan, and I dropped the MDA, climbed into my car, and headed for my house. We were coming on to the drug and feeling fine when we burst through the door. We fell onto the couch. Of all the mind-altering substances I ingested over the years, MDA was my favorite. It produces a subtle, yet at the same time powerful, feeling of contentment. It's not a head trip. There are no hallucinations. You feel incredible waves of empathy, love, and compassion toward all and everything. You feel it more in your heart than your head. It's the sensual psychedelic. You want to hug everything and anything—the dog, the couch, the guy sitting next to you. You feel like moving, stretching, dancing. About the only thing you don't feel like doing is writing a newspaper story, not even one about Krishnamurti.

We tried. I got out my tape recorder. I brought out my laptop, one of those old Radio Shack TRS-80 models we used in the early days of computers, the ones with the tiny screen and enough memory to hold two or three short newspaper stories. We started listening to the tape. The interview seemed stupid, superficial. I could barely stand to hear it. "It's only words," I said. "Let's listen to some music."

MDA's effects are wonderful, but as with all drugs there's a price to pay. It's speedy and can keep you up most of the night. The *A* stands for *amphetamine*. It works its wonder by messing around with serotonin and other brain chemicals. Its sister drug, MDMA, later known as "Ecstasy," became popular in the rave scene of the 1990s. It remains a popular party drug, even though recent studies indicate that heavy use may contribute to depression, confusion, and memory loss.

For me, depression was a common side effect the morning after an MDA trip. And not only the morning after. I've struggled with depression much of my life, and with memory loss in more recent times. It's impossible to say how much of that comes from getting old and how much stems from decades of pouring alcohol and other drugs into my body and brain. The good news is my memory started to come back after a year or two of sobriety. Nevertheless, I still can't quite remember what happened the morning after my encounter with J. Krishnamurti and Donovan Bess.

All that's left is a yellowed newspaper clipping headlined "Former 'Messiah' Now Extolling a 'Think for Yourself' Philosophy." That evidence indicates that I must have been pretty wasted the next morning, for I took the easy way out and filed little more than an edited question-and-answer transcript of my interview. It's a thin piece of journalism, and the story certainly was not enlivened by whatever insight and wonder we may have felt the night before.

Now, the whole Krishnamurti incident strikes me more as sad than funny. It reminds me of how getting high used to be the most important thing in my life, more important than doing a decent job on a story about someone I really cared about interviewing and understanding.

Krishnamurti would not have been pleased to read this account of what happened after our interview. In the 1960s, he was often asked what he thought of the psychedelic drug culture. "It came to the point that I couldn't mention young people without his thinking about drugs, and being carried away into tirades," said William Quinn, who was close to Krishnamurti in the 1960s. According to Quinn, Krishnamurti thought Aldous Huxley and Alan Watts, the popular British author and lecturer, bore primary responsibility for the "drug plague" that struck the country not long after Huxley's death in 1963. "Like Pied Pipers they had used their prestige to convert the young to their belief in this magical short cut to religious reality," Quinn said. "Krishnamurti felt that a religious mind has to flower in a humble, unconscious, organic way, and that drugs were an illusory short cut, smashing through complex and delicate psycho-physical structures. He said the use of drugs by would-be holy men had been observed for centuries in India, and was known there to be a complete dead end."

Perhaps, but it was a road that many of us—including Aldous Huxley, Gerald Heard, and Bill Wilson—would have to go down ourselves. That trip was coming, but in late 1939, it was still nearly two decades away.

．　　．　　．　　．　　．

Gerald Heard missed the big picnic with Greta Garbo and J. Krishnamurti, and I wondered why. It seemed like he should have been there. But at that moment in his life, Heard didn't feel like socializing with the superstars of the silver screen and the human spirit.

In the late 1930s and early 1940s, in the period leading up to the founding of Trabuco College, Heard became increasingly isolated from the Huxleys and other close friends. To become a true pacifist, Heard concluded, he must first find peace within himself. He began meditating in two-hour sessions, three times a day—in the early morning, around noon, and then in the early evening. His friends started to worry about the austerity Heard was imposing on himself. His life had been reduced to a single bed and a tiny bathroom behind a house in Laurel Canyon. His meditation practice had turned into an obsession. He wasn't merely celibate; he was cutting himself off from the rest of the world. He was living on a diet of raw carrots, raisins, eggs, and tea.

One day, Christopher Isherwood came by to check up on him and was shocked by what he found. Back in his Bohemian days in London, Heard had been known for his dapper dress, his fetish for fine suits. Now he was dragging about in jackets with ragged cuffs and jeans with holes and patches in the knees. "The London Gerald had struck me as being temperamentally agnostic, with a dry wit and primly skeptical smile," Isherwood recalled. "The Los Angeles Gerald was witty, too, but he had the quick eager speech and the decisive gestures of a believer."

Gerald Heard and Chris Wood were the first two people Isherwood looked up when he arrived in Los Angeles that summer. Isherwood and his longtime friend W. H. Auden, the English poet and playwright, had sailed from Southampton aboard the French liner *Champlain* on January 19, 1939, bound for New York. Auden had introduced Isherwood to Heard in London in 1932, when Gerald was working as a science commentator for BBC radio. Isherwood visited Heard in his cottage at 8766 Arlene Terrace, which was behind the main house Wood rented at that Laurel Canyon address.

"Here was a new Gerald—disconcertingly, almost theatrically Christlike, with his beautiful little pointed beard which tilted the whole face to an upward, heaven-seeking thrust," Isherwood wrote in his diary. "When I came to know Gerald's habits and ways of life, I suspected that they formed a deliberate, or subconsciously intended, picture of himself as a mendicant, an Irish 'poor relation.' If Gerald invited you to dinner, he took the most exaggerated precautions not to disturb Chris. You couldn't go into the kitchen until Chris had driven down the hill for his evening meal in Hollywood. As the sound of the car died away, Gerald would stage-whisper, 'Himself has gone away now. The coast is clear.'"

Isherwood fell away from Heard in the early 1940s, in part because one of Isherwood's companions "couldn't resist challenging Gerald's authority as a [spiritual] teacher and mocking his old-maidish fastidiousness, his affectations of speech, his evasiveness, his Irish blarney. Gerald, who was extremely sensitive to any hint of criticism, began to withdraw, injured," Isherwood writes in one of his memoirs. "I stopped seeing him unless it was absolutely necessary."

Maria and Aldous Huxley were also losing touch with Heard. Maria had gotten used to her role as Heard's de facto secretary and chauffeur. Maria's wifely duties already included driving her nearly blind husband to his various appointments. But Heard's vision was fine; he simply refused to drive or buy a car. He also declined to own a telephone.

Maria had to arrange her schedule to coordinate with Heard's ascetic lifestyle, delivering him messages and driving him here and there. She told a friend that Heard's monastic existence was an extraordinary indulgence, but one she was willing to put up with because he'd always been so close to Aldous. Yet they would soon learn to live without him. Huxley lost his patience for his friend's mystical indulgences. Months passed between visits. "Poor Gerald," Maria wrote to a friend. "He is profoundly sad. He feels he muddled many of his friendships and does not understand how."

Maria complained in another letter that Heard was becoming rigid and priestly in his views. He was losing his sense of humor. "He can't see us for more than two hours at a time because of his meditations," Maria wrote. "Meditation takes for him the place of drugs. When it's time [to meditate] he throws us out."

In the time leading up to his extreme monasticism, Heard had become increasingly involved with the religious life of the Vedanta Society, a Hindu missionary organization that would inspire Heard, Huxley, and Isherwood to look deeper in the mystical traditions of the Orient and begin a long association with the guru of Hollywood, Swami Prabhavananda. This charismatic, cigarette-smoking swami would have a defining impact on Heard, Huxley, and the metaphysical intelligentsia gathering around them in Hollywood and, later, out in Trabuco Canyon.

.   .   .   .   .

Prabhavananda was a young missionary when he came to California in 1923 to begin work that would soon lead to the founding of the Vedanta Society of Southern California. But the organization really began to take off in the 1940s, when Heard, Huxley, and Isherwood began writing for Vedanta publications and speaking at the Vedanta Temple in the Hollywood Hills.

The Vedanta story begins in India with the life of Ramakrishna Paramahamsa, a famous Bengali mystic. He was born into a poor Brahman family in 1836 and given the name Gadadhar Chatterji. At the age of seventeen, he moved to Calcutta, where he worked as a temple priest. But his spiritual quest soon took him beyond the Vedas, the ancient Indian scriptures that form the basis of the religion the West knows as Hinduism and its followers call the Sanatana Dharma, or the "eternal law."

Ramakrishna was a bit like the spiritual seekers of today—like American Jews who turn to Buddhist meditation or Catholics who fall under the sway of a Sufi teacher. His spiritual search went beyond his own tradition as he sought to understand the teachings of Islam and Christianity, to taste the mystical ecstasy that lies beyond the doctrine and dogma of all religion.

One of Ramakrishna's disciples was a young Calcutta student with the given name Narendranath Dutta. He became a follower of Ramakrishna in 1884, two years before his guru's death. Dutta took the name Swami Vivekananda and quickly became the Apostle Paul of the religious movement that had started to form around Ramakrishna—who might have otherwise become only a footnote in the encyclopedia of Hindu holy men. In 1893, Vivekananda sailed to America to be a delegate representing the Hindu faith at the World's Parliament of Religions in Chicago, one of the watershed events in American religious history. This was the first organized gathering of religious leaders from Eastern and Western traditions, and it attracted extensive coverage by newspapers across the United States. The convention, part of the large World's Columbian Exposition, was the first time many Americans saw exotic spiritual teachers from the East or heard words like *yoga* and *Zen* and *nirvana*.

Swami Vivekananda was one of the stars of the show. He stood before thousands of delegates and guests in an orange robe, his turban wrapped around his head and spilling down like a scarf over his left shoulder. He was greeted with a standing ovation. "Sectarianism, bigotry, and its horrible descendant, fanaticism, have long possessed this beautiful Earth," he said in his address. "They have filled the earth with violence, drenched it often with human blood, destroyed civilization, and sent whole nations to despair. Had it not been for these horrible demons, human society would be far more advanced than it is now."

Wars of religion would, of course, continue in the twentieth century and into the twenty-first in places like India, Ireland, and the Middle East. Fanaticism and fundamentalism would continue to scar the religious landscape. Americans were reminded of that violence by the horrific events of September 11, 2001. In fact, the timing of that terrorist attack has prompted some Vivekananda devotees to point out that the swami delivered his famous address on September 11, 1893, exactly 108 years before that dreadful day.* That may be a sign of Vivekananda's prophetic power, or it may be an eerie coincidence, but either way Vivekananda pointed toward another approach. .

He pointed toward a religious practice that encourages tolerance and respect, an approach that highlights, not the differences that divide, but the common moral and mystical teachings that run through all the world's religions. It was a path that would appeal not to those who had found the one true way but to seekers looking to deepen their understanding of ways to live together with more awareness and compassion.

After the convention, Vivekananda spent three years touring and lecturing in the United States, planting seeds that would grow into a net-

---

*For a variety of reasons, the number 108 has religious significance in India, and there are 108 beads on the necklaces worn by monks.

work of Vedanta centers across the country. He returned to the United States from India in 1900, when he spent six weeks as a guest in the South Pasadena home of one of his first American disciples, Carrie Mead Wyckoff, who was later given the name Sister Lalita. Vivekananda died in 1902, but Sister Lalita would remain for decades a leading disciple and patron of the Vedanta movement in Southern California. Her association with the Vedanta missionary Swami Prabhavananda would set the stage for the portentous arrival of Gerald Heard and Aldous Huxley in Southern California.

Prabhavananda was born in a village northwest of Calcutta in 1893, the same year Vivekananda addressed the World's Parliament of Religions. His given name was Abanindra Nath Ghosh. By the time he reached his teenage years, Abanindra had read accounts of the life of Ramakrishna, who had been born in a village not far from his own and was considered by many to be an avatar, which in the Hindu tradition means a manifestation of God on earth. When he was eighteen, the young man came across Ramakrishna's widow, the "Holy Mother." Abanindra was not yet ready to join the order and become a monk. Instead, he devoted himself to the growing nationalist movement against British occupation of India, but only for a few years. He returned to the monastery and, in the autumn of 1921, took his vows and became Swami Prabhavananda.*

He was first assigned to the Vedanta Society outpost in San Francisco, where they needed an assistant swami. Prabhavananda was soon sent up to Portland, Oregon, to open a mission, and it was there that he met Sister Lalita, the American woman who had hosted Vivekananda in Southern California more than two decades earlier. By now, Lalita was a widow. She'd also lost her only son. So the aging woman became a kind of adopted mother to the young swami, offering him her Hollywood home to use as the headquarters for his new Vedanta Society of Southern California.

At first, the Hollywood swami was something of a curiosity. People would show up at his home at the base of the Hollywood Hills in search

---

*The name means "one who finds bliss within the Source of all creation." The suffix *ananda* means "bliss" or "peace" and is given to swamis in the Vedanta order.

of a horoscope or a psychic reading. But over the next few years Prab-havananda slowly came into his own as a lecturer capable of explain-ing Indian philosophy to audiences of Southern California seekers. The crowds grew larger, as did the donations. Plans were made for the con-struction of a temple, a kind of miniature version of the famous Taj Mahal. It was dedicated in the summer of 1938, just as Heard and Hux-ley were settling into their new lives as the leading members of the Brit-ish mystical expatriates.

Heard and Huxley heard about Prabhavananda and went to check out the new Hollywood temple. Over the next decade, the teaching of Vedanta would become one of the major elements in Heard and Huxley's eclectic philosophy. At the center of Vedanta is Brahman, a "Supreme Reality" beyond all definition yet unifying the world. It cannot be felt by the senses or understood by the intellect, but can be approached by quieting the mind and the ego, usually through some kind of medita-tion practice.

Heard threw himself into the devotions and spiritual discipline that Prabhavananda taught. Huxley took the teachings seriously but did not devote himself to them. Both were initiated into the sect, but neither Heard nor Huxley really became a dedicated disciple of "Swami P." The three men were roughly the same age, all in their mid- to late forties, and Heard and Huxley came to the table with their own share of wisdom to impart.

Christopher Isherwood was another story. He, like Huxley, had been introduced to Prabhavananda through Heard, but Isherwood would be-come a dedicated, lifelong disciple. "Both of them were eclectics," Isher-wood would later say of Huxley and Heard, "continually on the lookout for fresh formulations of ideas, new items of information which they could fit into their complex individual world picture. Neither of them could have put himself unreservedly under the direction of a single teacher."

As a gay man, Isherwood was attracted to the body and soul of Prab-havananda. The swami was a small man and exhibited a lack of self-consciousness that was almost childlike. Isherwood noticed that the teacher had very wide nostrils and wondered if that was due to the deep breathing he recommended during meditation. His broad, smooth fore-head and golden skin radiated serenity, yet he looked somewhat comic when he spoke, as two large front teeth poked out of large, lush lips, almost rabbitlike.

"As a youth he must have had a lithe, athletic body which I would no doubt have found sexually attractive," Isherwood observed. "I was aware of a strong sexuality in him which seemed to be controlled, rather than repressed or concealed. He would remark, quite often and without embarrassment, that some girl or woman was beautiful. His honest rec-ognition of the power of sex attraction and his lack of prudery in speak-ing of it was a constant corrective to my inherited puritanism."

Huxley and Heard both lectured at the Vedanta center, lending their names to the cause and giving the movement a significant boost in Los Angeles and beyond. But Huxley was drawn more to Krishnamurti, who, like Huxley, was an iconoclast, deeply suspicious of the whole idea of a guru-disciple relationship. Krishnamurti meditated but refused to recommend any particular spiritual discipline to his nonfollowers. "Meditation is one of the greatest arts of life—perhaps the greatest, and one cannot possibly learn it from anybody," he said. "That is the beauty of it. It has no technique and therefore no authority."

Huxley found real truth in the story of Krishnamurti's life—that of a Hindu who broke away from Hinduism, rejecting the rites and rituals of devotional religion. This also explains why he kept his distance from the folks at the Vedanta Temple in Hollywood. "Aldous and Prabhava-nanda," Isherwood observed, "were temperamentally far apart."

.   .   .   .   .

Meanwhile, another Englishman with eclectic interests was about to make his California debut. He was a young man destined to extend and expand the work of Huxley and Heard into the sexually and spiritually liberated world of the 1960s and 1970s.

Alan Watts was coming to town.

Huxley would die before what we think of as "the sixties" had really begun, and Heard would soon be forgotten. But Watts would wind up

having an enormous impact on the spiritual proclivities of my generation. The *New York Times* would call him "perhaps the foremost Western
interpreter of Eastern thought for the modern world."

Born in England in 1915, Watts was twenty years younger than Huxley and twenty-six years younger than Heard. He came to the United
States in 1937, the same year Heard and Huxley steamed into New York
on the *Normandie*. Watts came as the twenty-two-year-old husband-to-be
of a young American woman he'd met in England. Twenty years later,
his best-selling book *The Way of Zen*, published in 1957, would help make
Buddhism one of the central elements of the coming counterculture.

Watts's interest in Buddhism, Hinduism, and Taoism began during
his teenage years in England, and, like many spiritual seekers of the
1930s and 1940s, he briefly passed through the Vedanta Society on this
journey to the East. He did not meet Huxley until an encounter with
him in New York. Watts was fascinated by the work of his fellow British
expatriates—Huxley, Heard, and Isherwood—and wanted to learn more
about their synthesis of Christian and Oriental mysticism out on the
West Coast.

Watts had been reading Huxley's books and essays for years, so he
expected to be confronted with the cold, mordant wit of a seasoned cynic,
but what he found was "a kind, sensitive . . . man whose wit expressed
genuine astonishment at the wondrous enormities of human folly. To get
its full flavor you had to hear the essential which books can never con-
vey, the sound of lilting, aristocratic King's English, with its tone of gentle, scholarly detachment and benevolent amusement," Watts recalled.
"It was difficult for me to be with him for much more than half an hour
without starting to imitate the rhythm of his speech."

Watts headed out to California to spend more time with Huxley and
get a firsthand look at how his fellow Brits were gathering around some
Indian swami named Prabhavananda. Watts had been active in Theosophy circles back in England and was a great admirer of Krishnamurti.
Upon his arrival in Los Angeles he was invited to lecture to a group of
like-minded Southern Californians. In his talk, he made a remark about
the similarities between the ecstasy of *samadhi*, or mystical experience,
and sexual orgasm. The remark sparked a debate at the lecture that soon

spread through the incestuous circle of spiritual seekers in the City of Angels. The question became: "Can you be an enlightened, realized, and liberated being and still engage in sexual intercourse?"

Here's how Watts would later describe the sudden controversy over sexuality and spirituality in Southern California:

> Swami Prabhavananda and his Vedanists were all for asceticism and sexual abstinence. . . . Gerald Heard was of approximately the same opinion. . . . The Krishnamurti people were vaguely embarrassed by sex, yet held that asceticism and spiritual disciplines were fraudulent, being ways of exalting egoism by denying it. Aldous Huxley, with his infinitely curious and open mind, was wobbling on the edge of decision. The Zen contingent had no qualms about sex, but went full tilt for tough discipline in meditation. . . . The psychotherapeutic clan, as good Freudians and Jungians, were all for healthy sex and self-acceptance, with some subtle accommodation to social convention.

Against this backdrop, Alan Watts and Aldous Huxley were invited to tea at Swami Prabhavananda's apartment at the Vedanta Temple in Hollywood. It was a room, as Watts recalled, "which had so many doors that it seemed like the setting for a French farce." The subject quickly turned to the iconoclastic teachings of J. Krishnamurti.

"Krishnamurti is a very fine man," the swami said. "I don't think any of us can doubt the greatness of his character. But his teaching is very misleading. I mean, he seems to be saying that one can attain realization without any kind of yoga or spiritual method, and of course that isn't true."

Watts politely reminded the swami that his tradition states that people are already enlightened. They just don't realize it. "As far as I can see," Watts said, "the more people consider themselves to have made progress in such work [yoga and mediation], the greater their spiritual pride. They are putting legs on a snake—congratulating themselves for bringing about, by their own efforts, a state of affairs which already *is*."

Then Huxley chimed in. "Isn't it rather curious that there has always been a school of thought in religion which attributes salvation or realization to an unmerited gift of divine grace rather than personal effort?"

Prabhavananda conceded that this might be true in exceptional cases, but expressed shock that Watts seemed to be saying "an ordinary ignorant and deluded person is just as good, or just as realized, as an advanced yogi."

"Exactly," Watts replied.

· · · · ·

Meanwhile, other divisions were emerging among the band of British mystics in Southern California. There had always been some distance between Isherwood and Huxley, who rejected the whole disciple-guru relationship that Isherwood had with his swami. Isherwood recalled a conversation he'd had with Huxley one day in the summer of 1940. He'd told Huxley about Prabhavananda's latest meditation instructions, prompting a sharp rebuke from Huxley. "Krishnamurti never meditates on 'objects,'" Huxley said. "He believes that doing so might lead to insanity."

Isherwood regretted bringing the matter up. He should have known that Huxley would instill doubt about his newfound faith in Vedanta. "This conversation disturbed me very much," Isherwood wrote that night in his diary. "But I'm also aware that these doubts are not quite candid; they are being prompted by the Ego as part of its sabotage effort."

Christopher Isherwood had followed Heard to Hollywood, but with no intention of going on a spiritual search. He wanted to get away from the coming war—and get a piece of the screenwriting action. Back in London, Isherwood had heard rumors that Heard and Huxley had gotten mixed up in the cult of yoga. "To me, all this Oriental stuff was distasteful in the extreme," he'd later recall. "I saw the Hindus as stridently emotional mystery mongers whose mumbo jumbo was ridiculous rather than sinister. That Heard and Huxley could have been impressed by such nonsense was regrettable."

In the end, Isherwood would become a most devoted Vedanta disciple. Heard seemed to be positioning himself as, if anything, a rival guru. Huxley had pulled away from the Hindu piety of the Vedanta monks. He was also pulling away from Heard. Sybille Bedford, Huxley's lifelong friend and biographer, attributes their "intangible rift" to differences in spiritual temperament. "Aldous would not go along with Gerald's personal involvement in the religious life—the preaching in temples, the assumption of spiritual directorships; Aldous, to put it very bluntly, could neither believe in nor approve of Gerald as a guru figure."

Heard was a regular speaker at the little temple overlooking Hollywood Boulevard, always filling the small sanctuary with around 150 congregants. Heard edited the Vedanta Society's journals, the *Voice of India* and *Vedanta and the West*. At the same time, he was having doubts about the personal holiness of the Hollywood swami. There was a certain lack of austerity at the temple. The swami enjoyed his tobacco and his fine *nonvegetarian* meals a bit too much. The ladies of the society waited on him hand and foot. Heard wrote a letter of resignation. It was politely worded, but Heard clearly suggested that the swami was not living a proper life of renunciation. "Gerald's dislike of the atmosphere at the Vedanta Center was an expression of his own very different temperament," Isherwood explained. "He recoiled from the women, with their chatter and laughter and bustle, because they were lively and vital and he was a life-hater."

Heard had begun thinking about setting up his own ashram, a spiritual commune where he could gather a band of like-minded seekers and put his eclectic religious philosophy into practice. He was on the verge of founding Trabuco College, where the lives of Heard, Huxley, and Bill Wilson would all finally intersect.

SIX

Trabuco

> The chief activator of our defects has been self-
> centered fear—primarily fear that we would lose
> something we already possessed or would fail to
> get something we demanded. . . . No peace was to
> be had unless we could find a means of reducing
> these demands.
>
> Bill Wilson, *Twelve Steps and Twelve Traditions*, 1952

Bill Wilson rolled down the car window and felt a cool Pacific breeze wash over his face. He smiled that self-satisfied smile that his wife, sitting next to him in the backseat, knew so well. More than a thousand people had just come out to hear him speak at an event in Los Angeles. He and Lois had been given a private tour of Universal Studios by an AA member in Hollywood, where they visited the sets and had lunch in the commissary. Wilson was starting to feel like a celebrity himself, which, according to the teachings of Alcoholics Anonymous, is not such a good thing. AA warns its members against grandiose thinking, in part because of Wilson's propensity—drunk or sober—to see himself as the center of the universe.

It was early January 1944, and Wilson was having a good day. The world was at war, but Bill Wilson felt at peace, at least for today. Who knew how he'd feel tomorrow? But that would be tomorrow. Like they say in AA, "one day at a time."

It had been just over nine years since Wilson's revelation at Towns Hospital in New York in December 1934. As an organization, Alcoholics Anonymous considers itself to have been founded on June 10, 1935, when Dr. Robert Smith took his last drink. AA members consider "Dr. Bob," an active member of the Oxford Group in Akron, to be Wilson's first disciple and AA's cofounder. The organization got its start during that first summer that Bill W. and Dr. Bob began visiting drunks at an Akron hospital and started building their fellowship. At first, they were known as the "Alcoholic Squad" of the Oxford Group.

By 1938, they had split off from that evangelical movement. Forcing drunks to accept Jesus Christ as their personal Lord and savior was not working. They needed an open-ended approach. God would be soft peddled. Drunks needed only to find a higher power, a goal designed to simply make them start to realize that *they* were not the center of the universe. Individual members could design their vision of the divine. God "as we understand him" turned out to be the successful formula. In the spring of 1939, the fledging fellowship published its founding text, *Alcoholics Anonymous*, known by AA members as "the Big Book."

Sales were slow the first two years, and so was membership growth. AA members were mostly clustered in Akron and New York, where Wilson lived and worked, and in Cleveland, where a man who sobered up with the help of Dr. Bob started his own chapter. Cleveland emerged as a major center of AA's early work following a glowing five-part series published in the *Cleveland Plain Dealer* in October 1939. The reporter spent Thursday evenings with a group of forty to fifty "former hopeless rummies." He also went to parties they held on Saturday nights that were "just as gay as any other party held that evening despite the fact that there is nothing alcoholic to drink." The reporter concluded that this band of drunks "cured each other" by understanding each other's twisted state of mind. They completely understood why someone would go out "and get drunk at the gates of an insane asylum where he has just visited an old friend, a hopeless victim of 'wet brain.'"

But the newsman uncovered something else in his investigation of

Alcoholics Anonymous. He ended the first part of his series by noting that these men "have an equally simple, if unorthodox, conception of God." In the second part of the series, the reporter tells how the AA cure is based on religious *experience*. It can come from "the Thomism of the Roman Catholic Church. Or the stern Father of the Calvinist. Or the Great Manitou of the American Indian. Or the Implicit Good assumed in the logical morality of Confucius. Or Allah, or Buddha, or the Jehovah of the Jews." He tells of one AA member who decided that "God" is found in "Nature," while others "simply cogitate about 'It' in the silence of their minds."

It's important to remember that this was all happening not at an Esalen retreat in California in the summer of 1968 but in Cleveland in the fall of 1938.

Bill Wilson saw what happened in Cleveland and started looking for a way to score another publicity coup, this time in New York or nationally. His break came in early 1941, when the *Saturday Evening Post*, which had a national circulation of three million, assigned one of its top investigative reporters, Jack Alexander, to look into Alcoholics Anonymous. Wilson and three other AA leaders met the journalist at his New York apartment. They told him amazing stories and cited unbelievable success rates. Alexander was not impressed. "The stories sounded spurious," he later recalled. "I had a strong suspicion that my leg was being pulled. They had behaved like a bunch of actors sent out by some Broadway casting agency." He found Wilson to be "a very disarming guy and an expert at indoctrinating the stranger into the psychology, psychiatry, physiology, pharmacology and folklore of alcoholism."

Alexander knew he had a story, perhaps even an exposé of a con man making a buck off other people's misery. But then he started going to AA meetings and hospitals in New York and Philadelphia. He went to check out the AA chapter in Chicago, where he met some reporters who'd joined AA and quit drinking. "I'd spent most of my working life on newspapers and I could really talk to these men," he recalled. "The real clincher came in St. Louis, which is my hometown. Here I met a number of my own friends who were A.A.s, and the last remnants of skepticism vanished. Once rollicking rum pots, they were now sober. It didn't seem possible, but there it was."

Alexander's glowing, seventy-five-hundred-word piece appeared in the *Saturday Evening Post* on March 1, 1941. The response was overwhelming. More than six thousand letters poured into the magazine's offices, many of them from desperate alcoholics. Alexander forwarded them to the small AA office in New York, which in turn sent them to AA chapters around the country. It was finally happening. Alcoholics Anonymous had become a thriving nationwide movement. Suddenly, AA was popping up everywhere as individuals who read the Big Book started meeting together in small groups. Between 1941 and 1945, the ranks of Alcoholics Anonymous grew from two thousand to fifteen thousand members.

This was just what Bill Wilson wanted, and it overwhelmed him. Bill and Lois began their trip to California in late 1943. One reason for the trip was their desire to visit the AA community that had blossomed in and around Los Angeles. But they also needed a vacation. Bill Wilson had suffered from depression his entire life—during his drinking days and his sober years. He'd have a productive month and then fall into an extended depression where he couldn't find the strength to crawl out of bed. AA was booming, but Bill still found himself falling into the abyss. Lois persuaded him that a road trip across America would revive his spirits, and the deal was sealed when AA members in California offered to pay for the journey.

Bill's depression seemed to lift when the couple got away from New York City and the burden of spearheading their fast-growing movement. On the way out to the West Coast, they visited AA chapters in Chicago, Omaha, and Denver. They stopped at the Grand Canyon. Bill got squeamish when he stood at the brim and looked down into the void. Lois, standing next to him, gazed down with perfect equanimity. At the bottom of the canyon, the couple opened their picnic basket and lay back in the tall green grass along the Colorado River. They felt at peace.

The feeling reminded them of their camping trips back in the 1920s, when Bill was still drinking and working as a field agent for Wall Street investors, trying to get inside information about the health of various American corporations. Wilson had carved out a sometimes-profitable niche for himself during the boom times of the Roaring Twenties. He'd hit the road to inspect manufacturing plants and talk to the workers. It could have been a lucrative gig, if not for the binge drinking.

Lois would sometimes accompany Bill on these trips, partly to keep an eye on him. They were so broke that they had to travel on an old motorcycle with a sidecar and sleep by the side of the road in a patched-together canvas tent. Bill tended to drink less when he was away from his favorite Manhattan bars. Even though they had been desperately poor then, Bill and Lois fondly recalled the freedom they felt on those trips, especially when Bill would get a week or two of sobriety under his belt.

Their lives were different now, in these first few weeks of 1944. Bill had been sober for more than a decade. They had money. They stayed in hotels or with AA members who welcomed Wilson into their homes as "a living saint." Wilson and his wife were about sixty miles south of Los Angeles when they saw the expected turnoff for El Toro Road. They headed up the windy road into the foothills of the Santa Ana Mountains for an encounter that would, once again, transform Wilson's life. He and Dr. Bob had been reading the works of Gerald Heard. Dave D., an AA member from Palo Alto, had been to Trabuco and offered to take Bill and Lois to the retreat center and introduce Wilson to Heard. Now Wilson was about to meet the man he would later call "the best example of spirituality" that he ever knew.

·   ·   ·   ·   ·

The idea for Trabuco College came out of a meditation seminar organized by the Quakers' American Friends Service Committee at a small college in La Verne, a town east of Los Angeles. Those at the seminar included Heard, Isherwood, and Isherwood's cousin, Felix Greene, who would provide the organizational expertise needed to obtain building supplies and get the project off the ground—not an easy task as the United States was preparing to enter World War II. Greene, who would later work as a foreign correspondent covering China and Vietnam for the *San Francisco Chronicle*, had worked with Heard at BBC radio in London. Using the money he'd inherited from Plunkett and his own family, Heard spent around one hundred thousand dollars to buy a three-hundred-acre parcel overlooking the Pacific and build the college.

"Trabuco will be a college in the sense of the Latin word *collegium*, a community," predicted Christopher Isherwood. "It will be a club for mystics, non-sectarian, non-dogmatic—a clearinghouse for individual religious experiences and ideas." Isherwood could as easily have said that Trabuco College would be a place where people could be "spiritual but not religious." Heard described his project as "un-denominational."

"Trabuco hopes to grow, spiritually and organically, as the growth of its members progresses," Heard wrote in a prospectus. "The founders do not regard themselves as possessed of any special message or esoteric 'revelation.' Trabuco begins its work in a spirit of humble and openminded enquiry. There are no 'prophets' among us."

Maybe not, but Trabuco did have Gerald Heard.

Heard originally had a modest conception of the place, but Greene expanded it into a much larger undertaking. Heard's friends were amazed at the speed at which the college took form. Greene hired California architect Garret Van Pelt to design a small campus of buildings with red tile roofs, ringed with cloisters, giving the college the feel of a Spanish mission or perhaps a rural Italian monastery. Trabuco, in Heard's original vision, would operate like a sort of spiritual commune, combining manual labor and household work with meditation, interfaith study, and psychological practice.

Isherwood said Trabuco College was mostly Felix Greene's creation. "Gerald went along with all this, a little dazed, a little unwilling, but tremendously impressed and excited. It seemed to me that a new cult, Heardism, was being born, with Felix, a sunburnt and smiling Eminence, holding the real power behind the throne."

In the spring of 1942, just as the first college buildings were going up, Heard wrote to his friend the novelist E. M. Forster. In his letter he envisioned Trabuco as a religious community that would forge "a new syncretism of Vedanta, Buddhism and some elements of Christianity."

For the first few years, Trabuco seemed to flourish. Twenty-five men and women gathered together in Trabuco Canyon to live under Heard's spiritual direction, strangely isolated in a world that seemed to be tearing itself apart. Heard was convinced that the only way to save civilization was for humanity to spiritually evolve, one soul at a time. "Humanity is failing," he preached. "We are starving—many of us physically, all of us spiritually—in the midst of plenty. Our shame and our failure are being blatantly advertised, every minute of every day, by the crash of explosives and the flare of burning towns." At the root of the war was a civilization sick with "diseased egotism" and individualism. "Greed and fear are the compelling motives of man," he said. "Our choice is to go on to a new state of being—or to end."

"Gerald had this nightmare of a dream," recalled William Forthman, who spent about a year at Trabuco College and later lived on the same Santa Monica estate that served as Heard's home during much of the 1950s. "He thought the Second World War was going to be terribly destructive, even more than it was. When he left England in 1937 he knew Europe was in for a really bad time. He said it would be like the Dark Ages after the fall of Rome. Like then, we would need remote monasteries to keep learning alive. He was thinking of Trabuco as the place where a small group would survive in a dark world. The world got dark, but not as dark as Gerald thought it would."

Forthman was a great source of information about life at Trabuco and life with Gerald Heard. I tracked him down in Southern California, where he had retired after teaching philosophy at Cal State Northridge. Forthman was twelve years old when he first met Heard in the late 1930s. His parents were Quaker pacifists and members of the Mount Hollywood Congregational Church, where Heard delivered a monthly guest sermon. "I was very impressed by Heard," Forthman recalled. "He was such an erudite, scintillating person—a real font of knowledge. And he treated young people with respect. He did most of the talking, of course, but he'd also take the time to listen to us."

Heard laid out his spiritual solution in a small book published in 1941, *Training for the Life of the Spirit*. It outlines a rigorous program of meditation and self-improvement designed to cultivate a state of "alert passivity." Through deep reflection and detached awareness, students at the college would seek a profound state of spiritual comprehension. Heard believed that with proper training, human intelligence could evolve in such a way as to achieve "the conscious realization of union with That from which it has sprung." Buddhists called it enlightenment. Heard called it "the Invisible Reality which we so glibly call God."

Heard's monastery was sometimes called the Trabuco College of Prayer, but he was not talking about "prayer" in the conventional sense of the word. This was no Christian college. "You must become Godlike," he said. "You will evolve into that divine manhood which is the purpose of life and the only hope of mankind." Petitionary prayer—asking God for something—is a useless exercise of the ego. "It [the ego] can only ask effectively for what it wants and its asking keeps it therefore as and what it is." That's not transformation. It's a vicious cycle leading nowhere. Heard proposed another kind of meditation and contemplation. He called it a "delicate technique whereby the spirit may be lifted out of that otherwise closed circle and brought out onto the upward grade of evolution, spiritual evolution."

In Isherwood's opinion, Heard was passing through "an anti-Christian phase." He loved reading Meister Eckhart and Saint John of the Cross, but was moving toward Indian philosophy. "Several times," Isherwood wrote in his diary, "he told me that he could never become a Christian, as long as the Church claimed for itself a monopoly of divine inspiration—which Hindus and Buddhists don't—and as long as the crucifixion was presented as the inevitable and crowning triumph of Christ's life."

In the years between the two world wars, Heard had emerged as one of the leading intellectuals in England and, later, in the United States. He was an amazingly prolific writer, issuing major works every two or three years. His books were taken seriously, reviewed by the *New York Times.* Heard was seen as a man who could help society find a way between the certainties of science and the mystery of religion.

He was also something of a heretic. *Commonweal,* one of the leading Roman Catholic journals of the era, dispatched a correspondent to Trabuco Canyon to investigate the latest project of the mysterious Mr. Heard. "Mr. Heard," the correspondent reported, "is leading a sect, a group, one of the many sprouted by the mystically fertile soil of California, and seems to be, perhaps unconsciously, founding, if not a new religion, then a new, modern brand of Gnosticism." Gerald Heard's religion was never easy to categorize, but Anne Fremantle, the *Commonweal* correspondent, gave it her best shot. She found a pantheist running a Buddhist ashram—or maybe the place was more like a Quaker meeting with yoga classes.

"Mr. Heard has always had a following. His two most famous friends,

Aldous Huxley, the novelist-philosopher, and Wystan Auden, the poet, stand out amongst many hundreds who studied with Mr. Heard, and learnt much from him," Fremantle wrote. "Mr. Heard's importance is that of an instrument, through which certain melodies have been, and are being, played. Messrs. Huxley and Auden have already outdistanced him in their spiritual progress. It may be that Mr. Heard's value lies uniquely in the message and the music he has already relayed."

That would turn out to be a prophetic assessment. Gerald Heard probably did peak at Trabuco in the 1940s, but the disciples he attracted during that decade and in the 1950s and 1960s would continue his influence for decades to come.

Miriam King, a student at Stanford University, had been thinking about entering a Catholic convent in Carmel, three hundred miles up the coast from Trabuco, when she encountered Gerald Heard. It was the summer of 1944. King had been part of a small group studying the life and teachings of Jesus; the leader of that group, a Stanford law professor, was a big fan of Gerald Heard's writings. He organized a field trip to Trabuco College. King sat enthralled during Heard's lecture, then had a private audience with the man, who talked her out of entering the Carmelite convent—at least for the time being. King returned to her classes at Stanford in the fall, but began a correspondence with Heard that lasted over the next several months. The young woman was captivated by her new tutor's brilliance and flattered by the attention he devoted to her and her efforts to cultivate her spiritual life.

King returned to become a novice at Trabuco. At the time, Heard was leading a course of study on Dionysian spirituality. King recalled that she listened to Heard talk about God as the "tremendous and fascinating mystery" and the "awe-filled and spellbinding wonder." Heard introduced her to the world of medieval Christian mysticism; to the writings of Meister Eckhart, the German Dominican; and to the teachings of *The Cloud of Unknowing*, an anonymous fourteenth-century English work.

King looked forward to the times when Aldous Huxley would visit and she could simply sit there, rapturously listening to his brilliant interchange with Heard. "Gerald was more than a guru," King recalled. "He possessed amazing knowledge, yet was devoid of pretension. We saw him once a week in his room for spiritual instruction and could talk with him any other time. Once I told Gerald that the behavior of a woman there had begun to annoy me after many months of her coming to my room every morning and giving me my instructions for the day while striding up and down, reading from her list. He said to try to see the poignancy of human beings, which solved the problem for me. That's something I've always at least tried to practice."

Another young seeker who passed through Trabuco during the war was Marvin Barrett, who later became a magazine editor and longtime lecturer at the Columbia School of Journalism, and who early in his life took Heard on as "my reluctant spiritual director." Heard was "God-intoxicated," Barrett recalled, "and I became tipsy myself. . . . Perhaps it was because he had fought so hard for his belief in God, against family, the received wisdom of the academy and the laboratory, and his brilliant smart-aleck chums, that he was so singularly convincing. The layers left by the struggle made a firm foundation for his conviction and my conversion."

There was something magical about the life in Trabuco Canyon, with its stunning silence. The monastery had no electricity, and at night the oil burning in the Aladdin lamps gave a soft, sweet glow to the cloisters.

Word of the experimental community out in California spread across the country during the war, especially through the network of conscientious objectors who knew and respected Heard and Huxley's work as leading pacifists in the 1930s. Physical work was part of the daily routine, but it didn't seem the same as chores back home. "When we took Aldous Huxley out to collect cow pies in the pasture, he would pick up a dry one and say, 'Ah, a treasure!' His eyesight was very, very poor. He could not tell peaches from apricots at the table," King recalled.

Trabuco initiates rose every morning at six and filed into a round, windowless building called the Oratory. After a period of meditation they would gather in the kitchen for breakfast and the first of Heard's two daily lectures. They drank their coffee and ate their oatmeal as Heard, sitting above them on a high stool, gave his morning lecture. "There were wonderful teachings," King said. "He'd talk about the Christian mystics, all kinds of things."

Heard's regime of meditation, prayer, and study was designed "to rouse ourselves into silence, into alert passivity." Trabuco was a place where one could be free of life's distractions. "Most people cannot concentrate when they wish to, because most of the time they want to be distracted; they have cultivated distraction as a drug, and the habit cannot be broken."

Not many of the Trabuco novices had the discipline or the dedication to follow the path of Gerald Heard. The intensity of Heard's vision and the rigor of his program help explain why Trabuco College never really got off the ground. He claimed he did not want to become the guru of Trabuco, but kept approaching that role, then fading into the background. His magnetism came through most powerfully in his lectures, not his books, which can be turgid if not downright unintelligible. He was never really comfortable as a leader, especially to the women who came to live in the canyon.

Heard's views and sexuality and spirituality would cause problems at Trabuco. Gerald and Chris Wood had lived together in an apartment in London and lived in separate buildings on Wood's estate in Laurel Canyon. "Gerald was very attached to Chris. They were a real couple," Forthman said. "Before coming to California, Gerald had become celibate. Chris had a series of boyfriends. Some of these young men were not very reputable, but Gerald still had this great affection for Christopher. It was like having a relative you love but are always trying to reform."

Over the years, Heard had developed a negative view of human sexuality. "Sexual appetite will not check itself and having given us pleasure leave us at ease," he wrote. "It will become an addiction, a feverish dream, a restless habit out of which no pleasure is any longer derived but the repetition of which cannot be checked." According to John Roger Barrie, Heard embraced celibacy in 1934, when he began to practice meditation and ended his sexual relationship with Christopher Wood. "Heard maintained unbroken celibacy throughout the remainder of his life," Barrie said. "His relationship henceforth with Wood was platonic."

Why did Heard become celibate? Was he struggling with his homosexuality? Barrie said the purpose was to "sublimate the sexual drive toward spiritual ends." "It was not in the form of a torturous repression but rather a joyous sublimation. Heard had read books on Hinduism,

Buddhism, and Taoism in 1934. He thereafter dedicated his body as an experimental laboratory to verify the yogic principle of harnessing sexual energy to attain spiritual illumination. He had an almost super-human output during the 1940s—eighteen books, a series of lectures, articles, and appearances, along with his Trabuco duties. Added to these secular activities was his daily regimen of meditation for six hours each day. Gerald was a sincere and intense spiritual aspirant."

Barrie's father, Jay Michael Barrie, had been a conscientious objector during World War II. He met Heard at Trabuco in late 1944. "At this first meeting an instant rapport was mutually recognized, and three weeks later I went back to stay," the elder Barrie would later recall. "From that time until his death twenty-seven years later, despite the fact that there were many ups and downs in our relationship, he was the closest and most influential human being in my life." John Roger Barrie said his father worked as Heard's researcher, editor, and business manager. He was also his traveling companion, close friend, and caregiver, Barrie said, but the two men were never "lovers."

Heard's esoteric view of sexuality was outlined in his 1939 book *Pain, Sex and Time*, where he explores why people have such a low tolerance for pain and such a high tendency to be driven by lust. By controlling and channeling these lustful energies, men, and presumably women, can use techniques to arrest their orgasm, alter their consciousness, and transcend time. "Tantric Asia," writes Jeffrey Kripal, an authority on the transmission of esoteric Indian philosophy from East to West, "func-tioned as something of an archetypal model for Heard in his search for a type of asceticism that was not life-denying but consciously erotic, a lifestyle that could embrace the evolutionary energies sparkling in sex, build them up through discipline, and then ride their spontaneous com-bustions into higher and higher states of consciousness and energy."

Heard envisioned Trabuco as a monastic community with men and women living together in celibate spiritual harmony. Most of the resi-dents were single, but Heard even insisted that married couples remain celibate during the time they spent at Trabuco. Heard's monastic rule would come back to haunt him when Felix Greene, the man who built the campus, had a falling out with Heard over the rule of celibacy. The troubles began with the arrival of Elena Lindeman, a strikingly beautiful actress and singer who took up residence at the college and began working as a teacher in a nearby one-room school for children living in this remote corner of Southern California. Lindeman, who was born in Mexico and had been a star in the Mexican cinema, fell in love with Felix. The couple soon ran off to get married, leaving Heard to deal with the more practical aspects of running the communal college.

"That was quite a blow to Gerald," William Forthman recalled. "Felix had been the managerial brain behind Trabuco. Gerald was not the best organizer of people. He surrounded himself with this miscellaneous collection of odd people, some of whom were quite remarkable, but several people he respected left Trabuco. Gerald was not a charismatic leader, which you need for a utopian community. You need someone with a good deal of personal magnetism, but also someone who wants to dominate, and Gerald didn't have that guru quality."

Isherwood saw Heard shortly after Greene dropped the news. "Felix Greene has announced that he's getting married, to a girl who lives up there, and Gerald is terribly upset about it," Isherwood wrote in his diary. "He [Heard] seemed depressed." Greene left and it soon became clear that Heard didn't have a clue how to run a college, let alone a monastery. Trabuco College fell into debt, and there were no more patron saints on the horizon.

·　　·　　·　　·　　·

Trabuco College may not have been a stunning success, but it did inspire reconciliation between Gerald Heard and Aldous Huxley. For decades, literary critics have credited—or blamed—Heard for inspiring Huxley to move beyond the satire and bemused cynicism of his early work and to focus on deeper philosophical and spiritual themes. There's some truth to that assessment, but the Heard-Huxley relationship was never that of teacher and student. They were close during most of the 1930s, during their final years in England and their early time in the United States. But the bond was always more of a literary and spiritual partnership.

Think of their work as a game of existential tennis. For nearly three decades, ideas and arguments about truth, beauty, and the meaning of life bounced back and forth between Huxley's novels and Heard's philo-sophical tomes. Heard appears, thinly disguised, as a learned eccentric in several of Huxley's novels. Other times, such as when they began to experiment with psychedelic drugs in the 1950s, Huxley took the lead.

Their shift from scholarly and literary pursuits to more mystical, phil-osophical endeavors horrified some of their old comrades in the literary establishment. Somerset Maugham, who moved to Hollywood in early 1940, mocked Heard behind his back, bemoaning the damage he'd done "to our great English literature" by luring Huxley and Isherwood off to California and into the vagaries of mystical speculation. Arthur Koestler lampooned the "Yogi-journalese of the Gerald Heard type" and scoffed at how Huxley had become the chief publicist for the wacky new religion emanating from the West Coast.

These attacks were, for the most part, cheap shots. As Huxley biogra-pher Dana Sawyer points out, if there was an ingrained tendency Huxley had to fight throughout his life, "it was not mystical dreaminess but cyn-icism." While there certainly was a mystical shift, it predates Huxley and Heard's 1937 journey across the Atlantic aboard the *Normandie,* their road trip across America, and their decision to settle in Southern California.

Huxley's spiritual quest is most poignantly reflected in *Eyeless in Gaza,* the novel he published in 1936, the year before he and Heard emigrated to the United States. Huxley's metaphysical angst is reflected in the char-acter of Anthony Beavis, the soul-searching sociologist in *Eyeless in Gaza.* Huxley signals his autobiographical intent early on in the book. As a boy, Anthony the character, like Aldous, struggles with the sudden death of his mother. It also turns out that Anthony has an uncle who coined the term *agnostic.* In real life, it was Huxley's grandfather, T. H. Huxley, who came up with the word. In the novel, the character, like the author in real life, comes to see self-knowledge as a necessary prerequisite for self-change and turns to his diary for a rigorous dissection of his own char-acter defects:

> Indifference is a form of sloth. For one can work hard, as I've always done, and yet wallow in sloth; be industrious about one's job, but scandalously lazy about all that isn't the job. Because, of course, the job is fun. Whereas the non-job—personal relations, in my case—is

disagreeable and laborious. More and more disagreeable as the habit
of avoiding personal relations ingrains itself with the passage of time.
Indifference is a form of sloth, and sloth in its turn is one of the symptoms of lovelessness. One isn't lazy about what one loves. The problem
is: how to love?

Anthony and a college classmate spend hours talking about "the fundamental metaphysical theory of mysticism," conversations that likely
mirror those Huxley had with Heard. Anthony asks, "You mean that you
can get at truth by some sort of direct union with it?"

"Yes. You get the most valuable and important sort of truth only in
that way."

"I'm content with only *knowing* the way of perfection."

"I think I should want to experience it too."

Anthony Beavis struggles in later entries in his diary—as does Aldous,
later in life—with the question of how to reconcile the mystical and the
political: How to combine belief that the world is to a great extent illusory with the belief that we must nevertheless try to improve the illusion?
How to be simultaneously dispassionate and not indifferent, serene like
an old man and active like a young one?

This is a question that Huxley and Heard would explore for the rest of
their lives. They began in earnest in the 1930s with their partnership in
the pacifist movement in England and the United States. Yet Huxley and
Heard each had a very different approach to the more personal spiritual
question of how far one should go in the search for mystical union—
resulting in a disagreement that led to what Maria Huxley called the
"lull" in their relationship.

As Heard and Felix Greene were building Trabuco, Aldous and Maria
Huxley were renovating a farmhouse they bought at Llano del Rio, on
the other side of Los Angeles, at the edge of the Mojave Desert. Huxley
needed a retreat from the Hollywood craziness, and he felt the dry cli-
mate might be just the cure for a variety of maladies that always seemed
to plague him. He was also fascinated by the history of Llano del Rio,
which was founded in 1917 as a socialist utopian commune but had long
since folded, and which was in ruins by the time the Huxleys arrived.

There was no electricity at the cabin, so the Huxleys installed their own gasoline-powered generator in a pit dug in the middle of the back-yard. The pit was covered by a trapdoor, on top of which Maria placed an otherwise unwanted terra-cotta bust of Gerald Heard. From that point on the pit was known as "Gerald's tomb."

Aldous and Maria would escape to Llano del Rio during much of the Second World War—the very horror that Huxley and Heard had worked so hard to forestall. And it was there that the Huxleys heard the news that the United States had entered the war. An old friend and her husband had come to visit them in December 1941. "We went out for a walk," the friend would later recall. "We came back across the field, the four of us. It was very sunny, and an old man came toward us and said, 'The Japanese have bombed Pearl Harbor.' And we all stood there and looked at each other and said, 'It's war.' Aldous just went blank. Maria said, 'Oh, God.'"

It was a long trek from Llano to Trabuco. At first, the distance only furthered Huxley and Heard's separation. But their bond was too strong to break. While Huxley was put off by Heard's asceticism and by some of the seekers who started looking to his old friend as some kind of guru, Aldous was also fascinated by Gerald's early vision of Trabuco as a kind of spiritual commune. He made the trek and they began to reconnect.

"It's nice to see that he and Gerald are good friends again," Maria wrote in a letter. "Gerald was for so long stimulating to Aldous that when there came a lull I was sad. Now it seems they are very pleased with each other and so I keep out of it all. I gather it is entirely intellectual and on 'principles.' But that is all right."

Later, in 1943, Maria accompanied Aldous on a visit to the place she liked to call "Gerald's monastery." To her surprise, she had a good time. Trabuco reminded her of some little convent in the Italian hill country, but with a Bohemian air. "The bells sing and we slip into the Oratory wearing blue jeans and red dresses," she wrote. A old friend from their Bloomsbury days, Iris Tree, a free-spirited poet who would go on to play herself in the 1960 Federico Fellini film *La Dolce Vita*, had been up at Trabuco for months, taking over the kitchen to prepare delicious vegetarian meals. "She writes hymns in the morning sun," Maria said, "and runs wildly with the goats in the afternoon."

Perhaps the most important work to come out of the Trabuco/Llano del Rio years was *The Perennial Philosophy,* Huxley's extended essay on how the religions of the world seek to explain and experience a common mystical truth. For his research, Huxley dove deep into Heard's Trabuco library, studying saints and sages of the timeless past—Lao Tzu, Saint John of the Cross, Meister Eckhart, the Buddha, and Saint Teresa. The fruit of his labor was this influential anthology and commentary on the writings of mystics East and West.

Huxley did not have a formal meditative discipline like the one Heard taught at his monastery. Huxley's method began with study and reflection, with the intellect, but soon moved into the heart. Those who watched Huxley work saw the importance of silently waiting, taking the time to think.

Like any writer, Huxley spent countless hours over his typewriter and his notes, but he would often lapse into a kind of desktop contemplation, sitting quietly, head in hand. "The goods of eternity," he explained, "cannot be had except by giving up at least a little of our time silently waiting for them." This advice follows a long tradition of spiritual contemplation, a discipline best explained by Meister Eckhart. "What a man takes in by contemplation," Eckhart says, "he pours out in love."

Huxley and his wife enjoyed their time at Trabuco, but they both thought the residents spent too much time *talking* about God. This was understandable, for if Gerald Heard was anything he was a talker. Huxley was a writer. He hated public speaking. Heard reveled in and shone from the podium and the pulpit. But it could all be a bit too much. One day Christopher Isherwood stopped by to visit Maria, to whom he was much closer than he was to Aldous.

"Off to Trabuco, Chris?"

"Not this week, Oh, no."

"Why?" Maria asked.

"I'm so fed up, sick and tired of hearing them yakking about God."

Maria replied without missing a beat. "*How* I understand you," she said.

Huxley begins *The Perennial Philosophy* with the same warning Heard issued to the novices at his monastery—that the seeker must change his or her way of being to truly understand and experience the "divine

Reality." To connect with "the immanent and transcendent Ground of all being," Huxley writes, one must first become "loving, pure in heart, and poor in spirit. . . . Why should this be? We do not know. It is just one of those facts that we have to accept."

Some fans of Huxley's satirical novels were shocked at such priestly conclusions. "If a choice must be made," one critic moaned, "the unregenerate Huxley of sixteen years ago seems to be infinitely preferable to the sour-faced moralist of today. The trouble with Huxley is and always has been intellectual whole-hoggery. Ideas will go into his head. He should read Aristotle on moderation."

Isherwood, on the other hand, considered *The Perennial Philosophy* to be one of Huxley's greatest books and defended his friend's embrace of the Vedanta philosophy. "It was widely represented as the selling-out of a once brilliant intellect," Isherwood would later recall. "As a matter of fact, it actually enlarged Huxley's already vast intellectual horizons by introducing him to mystical experience as a fact, a phenomenon of existence."

Huxley himself replied to the secular critics of *The Perennial Philosophy* in an essay published by the Vedanta Society. He did so in the name of "those of us who are not congenitally the members of an organized church, who have found that humanism and nature worship are not enough, who are not content to remain in the darkness of ignorance, the squalor of vice or the other squalor of respectability." His testimony shows that by the end of the Second World War, Aldous Huxley had clearly moved beyond his grandfather's infamous agnosticism. He now adhered to the philosophy of Vedanta. He believed in God, or at least in "the Godhead," described as "the unmanifested principle of all manifestation." Call it "Brahman" or "the Tao" or "the Clear Light of the Void," it was real. It was transcendent and immanent. The purpose of life was to know, love, and connect with it. There were spiritual laws that should be followed "if men are to achieve their final end." Huxley believed that "the more there is of self, the less there is of the Godhead."

His old secular comrades, the intellectuals and the hedonists and the humanists, were free to keep deluding themselves, to keep thinking *they* were at the center of the universe. "People like their egos," said Huxley, "and do not wish to mortify them, get a bigger kick out of bullying and self-adulation than out of humility and compassion, are determined not to see why they shouldn't 'do what they like' and 'have a good time.' They get their good time; but also and inevitably they get war and syphilis, tyranny and alcoholism, revolution, and in default of an adequate religious hypothesis the choice between some lunatic idolatry, such as nationalism, and a sense of complete futility and despair."

Huxley had finished *The Perennial Philosophy* in March 1945, less than two months before the end of the war in Europe. Harper and Brothers released the work in September, about two weeks after the Japanese surrender. The end of the Second World War brought a rush of recruits to Trabuco, pacifists and a few men who'd seen actual combat. But the monastery never really found its footing. Most of the returning war veterans were eager to get on with their lives—to go to a real college, get a job, and buy a house. The great postwar economic boom had begun. Materialism and consumerism were on the rise. Heard's ascetic program of meditation and simple living could not compete.

Heard was forced to shut the place down in the summer of 1947. There was a brief attempt by two of Heard's associates to open another kind of retreat center at the site, but that plan went nowhere. Heard was done. He signed over the entire campus, including three hundred acres of land, to Swami Prabhavananda and his old friends at the Vedanta Temple in Hollywood. He even let them keep his entire library of mystical texts. On September 7, 1949, Trabuco College was rededicated as Ramakrishna Monastery and formally taken over by the Vedanta Society of Southern California.

.   .   .   .   .

My journey to Trabuco begins at the Pacific Ocean, just north of Laguna Beach. It's been nearly seven decades since Gerald Heard opened Trabuco College. On my third morning at the monastery, something shifts inside me. Slowing down, getting out of that world and into this one, takes a few days. Shortly after six in the morning I leave my room to find a heavy mist hanging over Trabuco Canyon. The stillness of this world quiets mine. The only sounds are the soft drop of dew falling from trees and the quiet crunch of my scandals moving across the pebbles on the path that leads to the temple. A spider has spun a web across a brick archway. It collects droplets of morning dew that glisten like a long string of tiny Christmas lights. Inside the candlelight rotunda, which Heard called the Oratory, four monks sit in meditation before a framed photo of Sri Ramakrishna. This room had originally been built in the shape of a globe, with the floor dropping at the center in two descending concentric shelves. The Vedanta Society had the floor brought up one level in the early 1950s after a devotee entered the darkened shrine and went tumbling into the abyss.

We sit in silence for half an hour. When the clock strikes seven, the senior monk begins the morning prayer. *Chant the name of the Lord and His glory unceasingly. That the mirror of the heart may be wiped clean.* Thus begins the daily routine at Ramakrishna Monastery, with its prescribed periods of worship, meditation, ritual observance, work, study, and meals.

There's a mellow camaraderie among the eight monks living here now, including a twenty-eight-year-old novice who turns out to be a member of Alcoholics Anonymous with nine years of sobriety under his belt. That afternoon he hands me a first edition of the Big Book that he found in the library. Stamped "Trabuco College," it may have been hand delivered by Bill Wilson himself.

It's been half a century since Huxley and Heard walked these cloisters, but it's not hard finding signs of their lingering presence. The guesthouse where I'm staying was built after Heard signed the property over to the Vedanta Society, but the books left out for visitors include a faded 1945 hardbound edition of *The Perennial Philosophy* and a battered 1942 paperback booklet titled *Training for the Life of the Spirit,* by Gerald Heard. The booklet was sitting on the desk in my room when I arrived. I opened it, randomly, to page 30, where Heard warns against novices trying to glean instant wisdom from books on the spiritual life. "The spiritual life, as we have seen, is an evolutionary growth, the first stage of which is not called Purgation for nothing. At best it must be a stiff term of work, a grind in which there is seldom any very obvious reward."

Gerald Heard popped up on my second night here, when the public was invited to attend a weekly class on the Gospel of Sri Ramakrishna.

About forty guests turned out to sit by a fire in the library and hear a Dutch monk give an introductory talk on the doctrine of reincarnation. It was a sedate middle-aged crowd, plus some young Indian families who came here to remember their religious heritage. We sipped tea from Styrofoam cups and munched on snickerdoodle cookies. As I usually do at gatherings like this, I sat in the back corner of the room. Positioned near an open window, I looked out on a koi pond and a statue of Swami Vivekananda. It took me a few minutes to realize that I'd placed myself directly under a framed black-and-white photo of Gerald Heard taken a half century ago.

.   .   .   .   .

Trabuco College was a seminal stop on the spiritual journey of Huston Smith, author of *The World's Religions*. He was at the University of California, Berkeley, working on his PhD dissertation in 1945 when he stumbled upon the writing of Gerald Heard.

Smith, a doctoral student from the University of Chicago, came to Berkeley in 1944 to work on his dissertation. He had come out to California with his wife, Kendra, and their first daughter, Karen. He was already an ordained minister in the Methodist Church, and he spent his weekends down on the Monterey Peninsula, where he had a part-time job leading Sunday services at a small church, a congregation composed mainly of cannery workers. In exchange for his Sunday duties, the Methodist Church gave Smith's family a small house to use, plus sixty dollars a month for living expenses.

On weekdays, Smith passed most of his waking hours in the library or in his room, working on his dissertation. Every Friday at noon, he'd put away his books and take a series of buses from downtown Berkeley to Highway 101, where he would disembark and hitchhike down to Monterey to spend the weekend with his young family.

One weekday, back in Berkeley, Smith found himself thumbing through the card catalogue at Doe Library, looking for books with the word *pain* in the title. That's when he discovered Heard's book *Pain, Sex and Time: A New Outlook on Evolution and the Future of Man*. Smith checked the book out and took it back to his boarding house. He stayed up the whole night reading it, then went back to the library to get any book he could find by Gerald Heard. "Overnight," Smith said, "that book converted me from the scientific worldview to the vaster world of the mystics. I was taken by Heard's idea that we were on the cusp of an evolutionary advance—that the tide of evolution would allow mankind to merge with God's infinite consciousness."

Gerald Heard was still very much on Huston Smith's mind as Smith completed his 312-page dissertation ("The Metaphysical Foundations of Contextualistic Philosophy of Religion: An Inquiry into the Relation of Metaphysics to Religious Knowledge") and got his first teaching job at Denver University. Smith vowed to read every book Gerald Heard had ever written—no easy task—and then promised himself that he would meet the man. In 1947, Smith completed phase one of his project and wrote a letter to Heard in care of Heard's American publisher, Harper and Brothers in New York.

Heard replied with a handwritten note. "I'll be very happy to meet you," he wrote, "but you may have a little difficulty finding me." He explained that he was at a monastery in the Santa Ana Mountains, a place called Trabuco College. Even though he was broke, Smith decided there was no mountain high enough to keep him away from Gerald Heard. So he hitchhiked all the way from Denver to Los Angeles, then made his way out to Trabuco Canyon.

Huston Smith arrived shortly before supper. At the time, Trabuco was in its final months of existence. There was only a small group of men and women left at the college. They set an extra plate on the kitchen table and welcomed Smith into the fold. They ate their simple meal, listening to Heard give a little talk on the theology of the desert fathers. "After supper, Gerald led me out to a promontory," Smith recalled. "We sat on a rock and looked out over the canyon. I realized I had nothing to ask the man." Silent communion was enough.

Smith spent the night. The next morning, as he was getting ready to leave, Heard asked Huston if he was married. "With a wilting heart," Smith recalled, "I said, 'Yes. I'm married.' My heart was wilting because, at the time, I really wanted to become a monk, to give up everything and study meditation."

But that was not to be. Smith had his young family to consider, and he was about to begin a new teaching job at Washington University in Saint Louis. And before long, Smith began to have second thoughts about Heard's all-encompassing theory about the mystical destiny of mankind.

Smith told me this story one afternoon as we sat in the sun-filled living room of his home in Berkeley. He was ninety-one years old and had to laugh at his youthful enthusiasm for the writings of Gerald Heard. "It sounds silly now," he said. "You wonder why someone would stay up all night with a book like that, but I was young and gullible. I thought about it some more and realized that there was very shaky evidence to support Gerald's ideas. Sure, there were some people who have a talent for mystical experience, but there is no real evidence that that is happening across the board. There is no evidence pointing to an evolutionary wave leading us all toward mystical consciousness."

Before he left Trabuco Canyon, Heard told Huston that he might like to meet a man Gerald knew in Los Angeles. "He would like you," Heard said, scribbling the name and phone number on a scrap of paper. "He likes to meet people who share our interests." Huston looked at the piece of paper and could hardly believe his eyes. The man's name was Aldous Huxley, one of the most famous writers in the world.

The following morning, when he was back in Los Angeles, Huston pulled out the paper and made the call. Aldous answered. It turned out that the Huxleys were at their retreat in the Mojave Desert, but Aldous gave Huston directions on how to make the journey by bus.

After a long ride and bumpy ride, Huston finally saw Huxley's cabin off the highway out in the desert, exactly where Huxley said it would be. "I spotted it and asked the bus driver to stop." Huston recalled. "Aldous came out to welcome me."

Maria had just finished sweeping some sand out of the cabin and had started making their bed. Huston offered to help with the chores. He'd been somewhat dumbstruck, stunned by the realization that he was actually standing there with Aldous and Maria Huxley at their desert hideaway.

They sat down for tea. Huxley asked Huston where he was born, so Smith explained how he'd been brought up in rural China by Methodist missionaries. Huxley picked up the tin canister of Chinese tea from the table and asked Huston if "lapsang souchong" was only a brand name, or if it had some deeper meaning.

"I'm not sure," Huston said.

"It's probably just the Chinese translation for 'Lipton's,'" Huxley replied.

They finished their tea and took a walk together out in the desert. Aldous started talking about how he loved the emptiness of the landscape. Smith looked up at his new friend, amazed at his imposing height and magnificent profile, enthralled by the sonorous British accent and the almost magical way Huxley struck together a sentence. "You know, the Nothingness of which the Desert Fathers spoke is not nothingness," Huxley said. "The desert is, and it is in order that we may discover for ourselves, by direct experience, that God *is*."

They walked in silence. Huston, who was still in his twenties, considered the past incredible hour of his life and thought to himself, "Life can only go downhill from this point on."

Gerald Heard and Aldous Huxley encouraged Huston to explore the teachings of the Vedanta Society and put him in touch with a spiritual teacher in Saint Louis named Swami Satprakashananda. In his memoir, Smith writes that Gerald Heard "revolutionized my understanding" by passing along the teachings of the great mystics and showing him "that the world that we can see and touch is not all there is." By introducing him to Vedanta, Heard and Huxley "revealed to me depths in the religions that I had not suspected existed." And if it had not been for that swami in Saint Louis, Huston Smith says, he "would have had no career in the world's religions nor have written a book by that name."

And it all began with a short visit to Trabuco Canyon.

·   ·   ·   ·   ·

By the time I get to Trabuco, California is an altered state. Its population has jumped from seven million to thirty-seven million. Laguna Beach has grown up and prospered, but the place retains a faint countercultural aura. You can still hear echoes of an earlier time, not that long ago, when Laguna was a sleepy beach town and art colony favored by Southern California hippies.

Trabuco Canyon is about twelve miles from the coast. It's still a pleasant drive as you wind up Laguna Canyon Road. But the scene changes the closer you get to Interstate 5, the massive freeway that begins in San Diego and slices through the Central Valley on its march to Sacramento. Suddenly, you're surrounded by the soulless, automobile-centered culture of Orange County, with its endless parking lots and suburbs and gas stations and shopping malls and franchise restaurants.

It saddens me when I remember that this was where Aldous Huxley marveled at "orange groves—hundreds of miles of them, alternating with avocados, pears, persimmons, walnuts, peaches, cotton and fields of lettuce and artichokes." Today, suburban Orange County is neither farm nor city but a sea of asphalt and cement. Fortunately, I'm heading into the Santa Ana Mountains, away from all this. But just as I expect the road to narrow, it becomes a six-lane thoroughfare, almost a freeway in itself, and for no apparent reason.

It's a mystery for a mile or so, then the reason for this highway to nowhere reveals itself at the intersection of El Toro Road and Portola Parkway. It turns out that the road to Trabuco is also the road to Saddleback Church. This is the intersection where, once a week, the SUVs of an army of evangelicals pull into parking lots of biblical proportions.

Saddleback is the mother of evangelical megachurches, the Christian campus presided over by the Reverend Rick Warren, the best-selling author of *The Purpose-Driven Life* and the man President Obama chose, despite some controversy, as the prayer leader at his first inauguration. I realize I've forgotten that Saddleback Church is here, and I have to laugh when I come to the crossroads. If you don't turn left, into those parking lots, the road to Trabuco soon narrows.

That's right, I took the road less traveled.

About fifteen minutes later I pull into the small, unpaved parking area near Ramakrishna Monastery, just past the vegetable garden. I've come to interview a couple of monks who live here, including one who knew Heard during the Trabuco College years. Looking at my watch, I see that I'm nearly an hour early for my first interview. That's when I notice a trailhead at the end of the dirt lot and decide to take a walk through the woods, over to a nearby ridge, to check out the view.

About five minutes into my hike, I turn a corner and find myself facing a large Jewish shrine, a metal sculpture of the Star of David. What's *that* doing at a Hindu monastery? Then I remember the spiritual journey of Ramakrishna, who practiced and found truth in all the world religions that he came across in his life.

I sit down and look up at the Star of David. My mother and my lost Jewish heritage come to mind, followed by a memory of a man I met many years earlier in Jerusalem, Rabbi Adin Steinsaltz. There have been moments in my career as a skeptical religion reporter when I've felt a personal, dare I say "spiritual," connection with a story. Walking into the Orthodox rabbi's book-lined study was one of those moments. Actually, the feeling began even before I reached his office, when I was walking through the streets of the Jewish Quarter in the old city.

There have been many times in my life when I've felt Jewish, especially when hanging out with Jewish friends, connecting with that sardonic, world-weary wisdom that feels so right. This meeting with the rabbi was one of those times.

My encounter with Rabbi Steinsaltz happened in the spring of 1986. I was in the Middle East, reporting for a series of articles for the *San Francisco Examiner*. Tensions between the Israelis and the Palestinians were, once again, rising and would soon erupt into the first intifada, or uprising, in Gaza and the West Bank. One of my Jewish friends had recommended that I interview Steinsaltz, a noted Torah scholar and authority on the kabbalah, ancient Jewish mystical teachings that were finding a new audience among the spiritual seekers of my generation.

Something hit me when I walked into the rabbi's office. Perhaps it was only the random movement of cumulus clouds, but the sunlight seemed to pour into this room on cue. The bearded, bespectacled sage leaned back in his chair and another burst of light illuminated the arching white walls of his office.

Steinsaltz, then a frail five foot six, with sparkling eyes and elfin charm, was born in Israel in 1937 to Zionist settlers from eastern Europe. He read Marx before he ever opened the Torah. But at fifteen, he shocked his family and friends by enrolling in a yeshiva, a traditional school of Orthodox Judaism.

"In my generation," he told me, "that was something people wouldn't even think of as a remote possibility. You could do whatever you wanted—become a Communist or leave the country. But a return to religion was beyond madness. It was unthinkable." So what led him to that path? "I'm by nature a skeptic," he replied. "Skepticism is the ability to look at things for truth, not just accepting them. I'm not a believer, so I ceased believing in atheism."

Then the rabbi turned the tables. "Are you an atheist," he asked me, "or a believer?"

I hate it when the interview subjects ask me about my religion. More often than not they are evangelical Christians. I have a variety of answers, but I never lie. Sometimes I skirt the question. "For our purposes here, my religion is journalism." Sometimes I'll simply say "Yes" when an evangelical asks if I'm a Christian. Sometimes I'll say "Presbyterian." Jewish interviewees often warm up when I say something like: "I understand. My mother's Jewish." I decided to give Steinsaltz the complete answer to his question about whether I'm an atheist or a believer.

"Neither," I said. "My mother is Jewish, so I guess I'm Jewish. My father was Protestant, so I'm a baptized Christian. If you want to know which religious philosophy seems, to me, like the truth, I'd have to say its somewhere between Buddhism and Taoism."

"You know," the rabbi replied. "Judaism is usually depicted as a purely Western religion, but that's just not true. We are a mixture of East and West. Many of our basic notions are from the East."

Back in Trabuco Canyon, Steinsaltz is still on my mind as I stand up, turn my back on the Star of David and continue my walk through the woods. Soon, around another corner, I come across a stone statue of the Buddha. Here's a religious symbol from a culture so far from my own, yet at the same time it's the one that feels the least exotic, the most comfortable. This Buddha before me is a much larger version of one found on a little altar in my basement office, a few feet from where I sit to meditate and a few more feet from where I sit writing this book. If you force me to pick one religion, to choose a single spiritual label, I have to call myself a Buddhist.

My press credentials have given me the privilege of sitting down to interview such Buddhist luminaries as Tenzin Gyatso, the Fourteenth Dalai Lama, and Vietnamese Zen Master Thich Nhat Hanh. But only in more recent years, in my struggles with drug addiction, have I truly experienced the truth behind the Buddhist teaching that our suffering and selfishness flow from our attachment, craving, and endless desire.

I've been meditating—off and on, but more off than on—since I sat my first weekend retreat back when I was still in my twenties. A Korean Zen master named Seung Sahn led the retreat. He told me—and everyone else he came across—to keep a "Don't Know" mind. That sounded like advice I needed to hear, so I stuck around for a while. During one of the forty-five-minute periods of *zazen* with Seung Sahn, I experienced an amazing flash of something—a kind of centered, detached, almost hovering state of pure awareness. It lasted long enough that the shadows moved a few feet across the carpet of the meditation room. Then I started worrying that I might forget the feeling. I started to write a poem about it in my head and—poof!—it was gone.

That extraordinary state of mind I experienced during that first meditation retreat has never returned, but for some reason I have returned to the cushion countless times. Nothing much has ever happened, other than the constant chatter of the "monkey mind." Huxley called it "the whirligig." But I keep practicing, not nearly as much as I should. At one point, not that long ago, I realized that I must have faith in Buddhism. *Faith.* Imagine that. It was the first time I really thought of myself as a "man of faith."

That is not something I can say about my official religion, the one that awarded me a piece of paper documenting the fact that I am a baptized member of the Presbyterian Church USA. I don't have faith in that faith. I have respect and admiration for the carpenter from Nazareth, for the rebellious prophet whose life and teachings continue to inspire the multitudes. But I can't say I have faith in Christ. Yet on this afternoon in Trabuco Canyon, I do feel the presence of Jesus in my life.

As I continue my walk in the woods, a small still voice tells me Jesus will be just around the corner. And there he is, or at least his symbol, farther on down the trail, a simple cross standing tall against the Southern California sky.

It's always bothered me that the religion into which I was born and raised seems to have so little to do with the way I see the world and live my life. At the same time, there have been moments—meaningful encounters with Christian teachers whose message rang true. There was a Russian Orthodox priest in Saint Petersburg who gave me a gilded icon of Jesus, not nailed to the cross, but standing on the ground as a teacher of wisdom, holding the world in his hands. That icon sits on my altar, right next to Buddha.

And then there's the memory of my weekend retreat at the Immaculate Heart Hermitage, a Roman Catholic monastery perched on a bluff a thousand feet above the Big Sur coast. I was walking down the road with Brother David Steindl-Rast, a Benedictine monk who preaches a blend of Christianity, mysticism, and humanistic psychology. "When Jesus used scripture from the Hebrew Bible," he told me, "it was not like the teachers of his time who laboriously interpreted from the text—like the church does today. Jesus talked about experience, about daily experience. That was such an enormous change in the history of religion— especially in a culture like that in Israel, where the idea of God was so strongly theistic."

Brother David stopped talking, and we stood in silence. The sun dropped into the sea and a deep orange glow melted into a distant fog bank. "There is something happening in our time, and one of the most significant shifts is in the realm of religion," he said. "The emphasis is moving from the institution to personal experience. It is happening in people's lives on a very large scale, and it is absolutely irreversible."

My encounter with Brother David at Big Sur was more than twenty years ago. But right here, right now, I am in Trabuco Canyon and I have an appointment with another monk at another retreat center overlooking the California coast. It's supposed to start in ten minutes, so I interrupt my reverie and hurry up to Ramakrishna Monastery, once known as Trabuco College. I'm looking forward to meeting Swami Yogeshananda, who first came here in early 1945 and considered taking Heard on as his guru. He decided after two weeks there was something not quite right about Gerald Heard. So he headed north from Trabuco, where he wound up taking refuge—and becoming a monk—at the San Francisco temple of the Vedanta Society. For the next sixty years Yogeshananda served at Vedanta centers in the United States and India. He'd only recently returned to Trabuco Canyon to live out his retirement at Ramakrishna Monastery. It's not easy finding people who spent time with Heard and Huxley back at Trabuco in the 1940s. There was William Forthman, and Huston Smith, and here was another one of those rare sources.

Yogeshananda meets me outside the archway that leads into the monastery's cloisters. There's a bell tower rising from the high brick wall that encloses the sanctuary. It's been nearly seventy years since Gerald Heard and Felix Greene erected these buildings, but very little has changed. A few things are different. Yogeshananda points up the brick archway. "Back in the Trabuco days," he says, "there were words around the arch that read, 'This world is a bridge. Cross over it, but build no house. Enter into this place as onto a bridge.' As I remember it, those words were carved in stone, but now they're gone. I think they should put them back, but no one around here agrees with me."

We sit down on a bench under the rough-hewn beams supporting the cloisters, which embrace a little garden growing around a bronze statute of Vivekananda, turbaned and robed, sitting in the lotus position. Yogeshananda is now eighty-six years old. He's a short man with a ruddy face and thin white hair. He's wearing jeans and an open-neck shirt with pens and an eyeglass case poking out of his pocket.

I ask him what brought him to Trabuco back in the 1940s. "I was a conscientious objector in World War II and was assigned to a civilian public service program in Pennsylvania, working with the mentally deficient. I was twenty-two. We weren't popular. People would call us 'yellow bellies,' or they wouldn't talk to us at all. My brother and I had been raised on the liberal side of the Presbyterian Church, but we were getting into Quaker mysticism when the war started. My brother and sister-in-law were out here going to college in Pomona in 1943, and discovered that Gerald Heard had started this college. They began coming here for lectures and classes."

Yogeshananda, known then by his given name, Phillip Griggs, had read some of Heard's books during the war, and he headed straight to California upon his discharge in January 1945. "I was looking for a guru, and thought for a while that Heard might become my teacher," he tells me. "He was a fascinating speaker, tremendous. He had this elevated personality. He could talk over your head without making it seem like he was talking over your head. We talked a lot about spiritual problems, about the obstacles to living a spiritual life." Yogeshananda leads me into the kitchen, where Heard used to sit on a high stool and lecture at mealtime. "They had excellent vegetarian meals. The women did the cooking. They even served high tea. It was all pretty lavish for me. I was already living the life of an ascetic. I wanted to live a monastic life, so it seemed a little strange to me to have men and women living here together."

We walk into the library, where Yogeshananda has just finished going through the library and reorganizing the volumes. "This was Heard's library. We haven't changed it. All the Christian mystics are here. He'd talk at length about them. He knew all of these writers. Heard was basically a Christian mystic but could also talk about Buddhism or the Sufis or the Jewish mystics."

In his time, Heard was a known and respected authority on religious mysticism—enough so that he attracted other leading scholars to Trabuco. In just the two weeks that Yogeshananda was here in early 1945, the guest speakers included D. T. Suzuki, the noted authority on Zen Buddhism, and W. Y. Evans-Wentz, the American Theosophist who had traveled to the Himalayas and returned with the Tibetan Book of the Dead. That text, first published in 1927, would fascinate Huxley, who would later pass it on to Timothy Leary, who would turn it into a guidebook on how to take an acid trip, which would inspire John Lennon to write the one of the strangest Beatle songs—"Tomorrow Never Knows."

And it all started right here, in the library of Trabuco College.

But it was not enough to inspire a young World War II conscientious objector to make Gerald Heard his spiritual teacher. Yogeshananda and I sit down on a couch in the library. I ask the monk why he decided to leave Trabuco and look elsewhere for a guru. He tells me he was most impressed by another guest teacher who was there during his sojourn— a British nun from the Buddhist Theravada tradition named Sister Dhammadinna. She taught *vipassana* Buddhist practice, which would become popular decades later. In fact, she may have been the first *vipassana* practitioner to teach in the United States.

"Heard was a dabbler," Yogeshananda explains. "I wanted a guru who was perfected, and I didn't think he fit the bill. He talked about three stages of spiritual advancement, but it seemed like he was stuck in the middle. There was something about the way he dealt with individuals, and the way he handled himself. He was a bit of a preener. I didn't see the kind of selflessness there that you'd expect in a teacher."

"That's interesting," I say. "Is that why you think Trabuco failed?"

"Who knows? For one reason or another, people stopped coming. They were running out of money. The place started getting seedier when there was no one around to do the work." Yogeshananda paused and thought for a moment, then added, "I guess the world just wasn't ready for Gerald Heard."

Maria Huxley had her own explanation for why the college closed. In the end, she said, Heard proclaimed that it was "God's will to end Trabuco and Trabuco ended." "But there is no doubt," Maria said, "that Gerald really made a mess of the whole thing, chiefly by having favorites and then dropping them to take up another and so often making the dropped favorite despair of everything and leave Trabuco and God; forgetting that God and Gerald were not the same thing."

.   .   .   .   .

As an institution, Trabuco College was an obvious failure. But as an idea, it would survive. Seeds planted at Trabuco would germinate over the next two decades before taking root in the fertile soil of the 1960s. Michael Murphy, a cofounder of the Esalen Institute at Big Sur, would use the college as a model for a retreat center that would keep Heard's ideas alive into the new millennium. Huston Smith would be inspired by Heard, Huxley, and Vedanta and go on to write *The World's Religions*, perhaps the most successful and influential textbook ever written on comparative religion.

Then there was that other visitor to Trabuco Canyon, the man who wound his way up El Toro Road on that brilliant January day in 1944, the traveler at the beginning of this chapter.

Bill Wilson lived in New York, yet he still managed to make at least three visits to Trabuco College between 1944 and 1947. Miriam King, the

Stanford student who chose Trabuco over a Catholic convent, remembers one of those visits, a brief one by Wilson and his wife, Lois. King
met Wilson, and she was not impressed. He seemed like a man with an
agenda, a guy who wanted something out of his visit. He was certainly
warm toward Heard but seemed a bit standoffish to Miriam.

Another of the women residents took Lois off on a tour of the college.
Miriam stuck close to Heard and a small group that gathered to hear Bill
Wilson tell his story. Wilson told them about how he had been a stock-
broker back East and nearly drank himself to death. He told them about
the night at Towns Hospital in New York, when he was shaking with
the DTs and had a sudden mystical experience that changed his life. Bill
Wilson had crafted a stump speech about his spiritual conversion by the
mid-1940s, so we can imagine that it went something like this:

"Now I'd always believed in some kind of power greater than myself.
I was never an atheist. But I had a bone to pick with religion. I didn't
see much evidence of a personal, loving God who answers our prayers
and acts in human history. I'd been through the Great War. I'd been in
Europe, and it sure seemed to me like the power of God in human affairs
was pretty damn negligible. It seemed that, if anyone, the devil was the
Boss Universal. It wasn't until many years later that I started to change
my mind about God. I saw what he did for a friend of mine, a drunk
more hopeless than I. That friend of mine liked to talk about God. Maybe
not as much as Gerald here, but he wouldn't shut up about it. One day
he made an intriguing suggestion. He said to me, 'Why don't you choose
your own conception of God?'"

That, Wilson explained, was the power behind AA. Nobody was
going to tell a bunch of drunks how to worship God. Alcoholism was a
disease of the ego, Wilson explained, and the first step along the road to
recovery was to find a way to get over the selfishness, the arrogance, and
the egomania of the alcoholic state of mind. They seemed to have found
a way. AA was growing by leaps and bounds. The fellowship had been
struggling for ten years, but now, all of a sudden, the movement was taking off. And that, Wilson explained, was the problem he must face now.
How to deal with the success of AA?

Miriam King was right. This guy *did* have an agenda.

"It was very clear what Bill Wilson's purpose was for coming to Trabuco," King recalls. "He wanted to get advice from Gerald on what
direction AA should take in the future."

King was present at the meeting when Wilson popped the question.
"Where do we go from here?" Wilson asked.

Heard had an answer. "Don't build a big organization," he counseled.
"Keep it in discrete, small units that are independent of each other and
that are centered around the twelve steps." Wilson certainly followed
this advice. Some in AA wanted the fellowship to go in another direction, to set up a strong central organization that could keep control of all
the little chapters popping up across the country.

Gerald Heard was not the only one urging that AA keep the power in
the local chapters. Wilson had studied earlier movements organized to
encourage sobriety and was starting to see that the secret of success was
having the wisdom to let go.

AA initiates are told they must surrender to a power greater than
themselves if they ever want to free themselves of alcoholism. That's
what the first three steps of AA are all about—turning one's will and life
over to a power greater than oneself, however one wishes to understand
that power. Wilson and other AA leaders came to see that they had to
practice what they preached. They had to surrender their will and control over to G.O.D., also known as the Group Of Drunks. They had to
trust that Alcoholics Anonymous was best run from the bottom up, and
to base whatever decisions they made, at any level, on group conscience.

It's impossible to say exactly how much Gerald Heard influenced Bill
Wilson, but one thing is clear. Their first meeting at Trabuco was the
beginning of a personal friendship and collaboration that would continue over the next two decades.

Bill W. and Dr. Bob were both familiar with Heard's early writings on
spirituality and social organization. Eugene Exman, the religion editor at
Harper and Brothers, probably introduced them to Heard's ideas. Exman
was Heard's editor at Harper in the 1930s, at exactly the same time that
he was helping Wilson find a way to get AA's still-evolving "Big Book"
into print.

There are many similarities between Heard's ideas and the principles

outlined in *Alcoholics Anonymous* (the "Big Book"), which was first published in 1939, and *Twelve Steps and Twelve Traditions,* another central AA
text, released in 1952. Wilson was the principal author of both works. He
was drawing on many sources of inspiration, including *The Varieties of
Religious Experience,* the 1902 classic by American psychologist William
James, and the teachings of the Oxford Group, which promulgated a
similar step-by-step program for Christian conversion.

Heard's influence is most clearly seen in *Twelve Steps and Twelve Traditions,* especially its explanation of how a dedicated program of prayer
and meditation can lead the seeker and the alcoholic to a powerful spiritual awakening. "When a man or a woman has a spiritual awakening, the most important meaning of it is that he has now become able to
do, feel, and believe that which he could not do before on his unaided
strength and resources alone. He has been granted a gift which amounts
to a new state of consciousness and being."

In his book, Wilson describes God as *he* understood him, as "the ultimate Reality," a phrase Heard uses in his 1941 book *Training for the Life of
the Spirit.* Both books stress the importance of surrendering to a mystical
power "greater than ourselves," then using rigorous honesty and self-
examination to tame the ego and overcome self-centeredness. "We tried
to struggle to the top of the heap, or to hide underneath it," Wilson wrote.
"This self-centered behavior blocked a partnership relation with any one
of those about us. Of true brotherhood we had small comprehension."

Of course, writing about a mystical awakening is not the same as actually having one. But in the spring of 1953, a year after Wilson published
Twelve Steps and Twelve Traditions, Aldous Huxley would find a powerful
new tool for actually experiencing that "ultimate Reality that we glibly
call 'God.'" Huxley, sitting in the study of his home in the Hollywood
Hills, would be given a dose of mescaline by a Canadian psychiatrist
who had been treating alcoholics with another psychedelic drug, a much
more powerful agent called lysergic acid diethylamide-25. Humphry
Osmond's chemical approach to cosmic consciousness would soon have
a profound effect on the lives of Heard, Huxley, and Wilson, and on millions of other Americans, myself included.

Bill Wilson in the army during the First World War. COURTESY OF THE
STEPPING STONES FOUNDATION ARCHIVES, KATONAH, NEW YORK. NO
PERMISSION IS GRANTED FOR ANY OTHER USE OR REPRODUCTION.

Alan Joseph Lattin, born December 18, 1948, died January 23, 1953.
© DON LATTIN.

The Lattin family at home in Chesterland, Ohio, in the fall of 1959, in the calm before the storm of the tumultuous 1960s. Donnie and his father, Warren, front, with sister, Denise, and mother, Muriel, behind. © DON LATTIN.

Don Lattin in London in the early 1970s. © DON LATTIN.

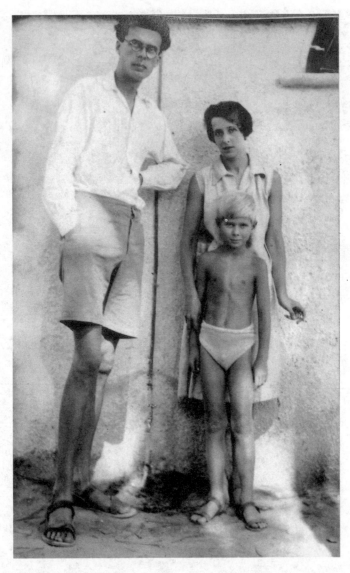

Aldous and Maria Huxley, with their son, Matthew, in the 1920s.
Photo by Lady Ottoline Morrell. © THE NATIONAL PORTRAIT
GALLERY, LONDON.

Aldous Huxley and Gerald Heard at Black Mountain
College in North Carolina in 1937, shortly after their
arrival in the United States. PHOTO PROVIDED BY THE
VEDANTA SOCIETY.

Bill Wilson during his drinking
days, with Lois in the sidecar.

Lois and Bill Wilson on their first trip to California, in the mid-1940s.

Gerald Heard and Christopher Wood near Laguna Beach, circa 1960. PHOTO BY JAY

Gerald Heard in England in 1930,
just after he met Aldous Huxley.

Bloomsbury days. Jack Sprout, Gerald Heard, E. M. Forster, and Lytton Strachey (from left), outside Ham Spray House in the 1920s. USED WITH THE PERMISSION OF KING'S COLLEGE, CAMBRIDGE, ENGLAND.

Drinking in Rome. Don Lattin (at right) with other religion writers covering a Vatican meeting in the mid-1980s. © DON LATTIN.

Swami Prabhavananda, Aldous Huxley, and Christopher Isherwood (from left) at the Vedanta Center in Hollywood in the late 1940s. COURTESY OF THE VEDANTA ARCHIVES. © VEDANTA SOCIETY OF SOUTHERN CALIFORNIA.

Don Lattin with the Dalai Lama at Stanford University in 1992.
© DON LATTIN.

Aldous Huxley at his retreat in the Mojave Desert during the Second World War.

SEVEN   Psychedelic

> I am certain that the LSD experience has helped
> me very much. I find myself with a heightened
> color perception and an appreciation of beauty
> almost destroyed by my years of depression. . . .
> The sensation that the partition between "here"
> and "there" has become very thin is constantly
> with me.
>
> Bill Wilson in a letter to Gerald Heard, 1957

Forget everything you think you know about psychedelic drugs. Try to
get Timothy Leary and "Turn on, tune in, drop out" out of your head.
Free your mind from Ken Kesey and the Merry Pranksters. Think back
to a time when no one outside of San Francisco had heard of the Haight-
Ashbury. Grace Slick is in high school, and the White Rabbit is still only
a character in *Alice in Wonderland*. The Beatles have not come together, let
alone released "Lucy in the Sky with Diamonds," and the Grateful Dead
have yet to begin their long strange trip.

It's the early 1950s. Aldous Huxley is doing what he does best—sitting
in his study in his Hollywood home, reading obscure academic papers
that point toward new ways for humanity to better understand itself.
He happens upon a paper recently published by two Canadian doctors,
Humphry Osmond and John Smythies, in the *Journal of Mental Science*.

It's titled "Schizophrenia: A New Approach" and explores the biochemical similarities between that mental illness and acute mescaline intoxication. Huxley has already begun a correspondence with Osmond, in the spring of 1953, in which he suggests that mind-altering drugs like mescaline might do more than merely mimic the psychotic state. They might also help us understand aesthetic experience and mystical enlightenment, thus "permitting the 'other world' to rise into consciousness."

What's foremost in Huxley's mind is the problem of education. "Under the current dispensation," Huxley writes, "the vast majority of individuals lose, in the course of education, all the openness to inspiration, all the capacity to be aware of other things than those enumerated in the Sears-Roebuck catalogue which constitutes the conventionally 'real' world." Perhaps mescaline and similar drugs could reopen the door to inspiration and enlightenment.

Huxley ends his letter to Osmond by mentioning that he hopes to meet him at an upcoming psychiatric convention in Los Angeles. He even offers to let Osmond stay in his house. "We can provide a bed and bath," Huxley writes. "You will be free to come and go as it suits you, and there will always be something to eat—though it may be a bit sketchy on the days when we don't have a cook."

In another letter, written a week later, Huxley wonders if Osmond might be able to bring some mescaline down from Canada. "I am eager to make the experiment," Huxley writes, "and would feel particularly happy to do so under the supervision of an experienced investigator like yourself."

Osmond agreed, and the stage was set for one of the most influential drug trips of the twentieth century, one Huxley would write about the following year in a short book titled *The Doors of Perception*.

Aldous swallowed four-tenths of a gram of mescaline dissolved in a half glass of water. He was hoping to experience the inner world that has been described by such visionaries as William Blake—the animated architecture of mystical lands, kaleidoscopic geometries, and magical landscapes populated by mythic beasts and heroic figures. But it didn't happen, a disappointment Huxley would later attribute to the fact that he was "a poor visualizer." He was forever trapped in a world of words and ideas. But there *was* wonder to behold. After about ninety minutes he found himself gazing at a vase containing three flowers—a hot pink rose, a magenta-and-cream-colored carnation, and the heroic blossom of a pale purple iris. He'd looked at the flowers earlier that morning over breakfast but was now "seeing what Adam had seen on the morning of his creation—the miracle, moment by moment of naked existence."

Aldous tried to describe the experience to his guide, but it was beyond words.

"Is it agreeable?" Humphry Osmond may have asked.

"Neither agreeable nor disagreeable," Aldous Huxley could have replied. "It just *is*."

This experience may have been beyond words, but Huxley was a man of words, so he had to try describing it in *The Doors of Perception*. Looking back, what he saw in those three flowers was "a transience that was yet eternal life, a perpetual perishing that was at the same time pure Being, a bundle of minute, unique particulars in which, by some unspeakable and yet self-evident paradox, was to be seen the divine source of all existence."

In other words, Aldous Huxley had, for the first time, seen God. He saw the mescaline experience as a blessing of "gratuitous grace." He wasn't saved or enlightened, but he'd gotten a glimpse of the Beatific Vision. His revelation reminded him of a line in William Blake's poem *The Marriage of Heaven and Hell:* "If the doors of perception were cleansed everything would appear to man as it is, infinite."

It was a shift in perception both subtle and profound. Huxley looked down on his gray flannel trousers and was amazed at the "is-ness" of trousers. The draperies in his study glimmered, inspiring a transformative appreciation of "the miraculous fact of sheer existence." He suddenly understood what the Hindu mystics were talking about when they spoke of Brahman, the undifferentiated ultimate Reality, static and dynamic, underlying the world. Huxley was silent for much of his first mescaline trip, but there was one impression that he kept repeating. "This is how one ought to see," he told Dr. Osmond. "This is how one ought to see."

At the moment of Aldous Huxley's first mescaline trip in the spring of 1953, I was in my own altered state of consciousness. I was in my mother's womb.

Nineteen years later, in the fall of 1972, I had my first close encounter with God, or at least with God as I've come to understand him. It was my freshman year at UC Berkeley. I'd just met a girl, and we had come together fast and strong. Our first weekend away together would be a road trip down to Big Sur to drop some righteous acid that had been circulating through the hallways of our high-rise dorm. I'd taken LSD in high school, but that first experience gave me only a taste of what was to come.

My first acid trip had been with a couple of teenage friends on the edge of the Palos Verdes Peninsula, just south of Los Angeles. At a certain point I wandered off on my own to sit on a rock over the tide pools, watching the waves wash over the rocks and, somehow, feeling them wash through me. These tide pools were a place I used to go when I wanted to be alone. I dimly recall some revelation about the origin of life itself, but whatever it was disappeared, as LSD insights often do. After a few hours I headed home, wandering through open fields not yet turned into subdivisions.

My mother was home watching an old black-and-white movie on television. I sat down to watch the movie with her but found myself staring at Mom, feeling a love and compassion that I had not felt for years. The angry, sullen, slouching teenager of the past few years, the child embittered by divorce, had vanished. Mom offered me a piece of chocolate cake. I began eating it with my fingers because I liked the way it felt as much as how it tasted. I rubbed some frosting in my ear and started to laugh. I could *hear* the taste of chocolate, and it sounded *so* good.

Who knows *what* my mother thought?

Many years later, I would learn that this confusion of the senses is called synesthesia. In researching this book, I found some extraordinary television footage from the 1950s in which Dr. Sidney Cohen, the man who would supervise Bill Wilson's first acid trip, interviews a research subject after she takes her first dose of LSD. Nearly overcome with bliss, the woman tries using synesthesia to describe her ineffable experience. She whispers to Cohen, "I wish I could talk in Technicolor."*

It turns out that synesthesia arises in some people without the use of psychedelic drugs. It depends who does the diagnosis, but the condition can be seen as a mental illness or a rare artistic gift. Either way, a bite of really good chocolate cake still takes me back to my psychedelic encounter with my mother—not unlike what happened to Marcel Proust in the famous scene in which he relives the experience of his mother feeding him little cakes dipped in tea. "No sooner had the warm liquid mixed with crumbs touched my palate than a shiver ran through me and I stopped, intent upon the extraordinary thing that was happening to me," he writes. "An exquisite pleasure had invaded my senses, something isolated, detached, with no suggestion of its origin. And at once the vicissitudes of life had become indifferent to me, its disasters innocuous, its brevity illusory—this new sensation having the effect, which love has, of filling me with a precious essence; or rather this essence was not in me it *was* me."

My most revelatory LSD trip—the one during my freshman year of college—unfolded a couple of hundred miles up the coast from where I had my first one. My girlfriend and I arrived at Big Sur in the early afternoon. We found a spot just off Highway 1 and left the car. We dropped the acid and wandered through a maze of scratchy manzanita and out onto the edge of the continent, settling down on a cliff that was topped by whimsical wind-carved sculptures of sandstone, natural formations that looked trippy even before we started coming on to the acid.

It was cool on the coast that afternoon, so I'd curled up into a fetal position. My girlfriend was tall and thin, about the same height as my six-foot frame, so she could wrap her arms and legs around my torso. She fully embraced me. My body got smaller and smaller until I was no longer in a fetal position; I *was* a fetus, and I was inside the womb of my lover and the womb of the earth. I was an unborn child. I was within her and without her.

*Highlights of this interview can be seen on the "Harvard Psychedelic Club" page at www.donlattin.com.

We communicated without using words. Then I saw in my mind's eye a tableau of Victorian sunbathers, painted in cranberry, which I described to her in detail as I floated peacefully in the warm embryonic fluid of the womb. She listened, and then told me that exactly the same image was printed on her brother's favorite T-shirt. I'd never met her brother. I was her brother. I was her lover.

We stopped talking, and the fetal experience began to change. I was no longer inside her. We melted together into a single entity, neither male nor female, no longer mother with child. Immanence met transcendence.

We were one with one another and one with everything. Time stopped. We saw nothing but white light. We were born again.

At a certain point, we opened our eyes and remembered where we were. The sun was setting into the Pacific beyond glorious, electric clouds of bright purple and dark gray. Waves washed over the rocks below like land and sea making love. We reveled in the wondrous symmetry of the world around us, seeing with new eyes the pattern that connects.

Then it started to rain. We made it back up to the car and started driving back up Highway 1 like we were in some dream. We melted together whenever we touched, passing the night in a motel room in Salinas, a night like no other.

Decades later, this mystical union with my beloved came to mind as I was reading an article in the *New York Times* headlined "The Brain on Love." It seems there is now a scientific explanation for the magic at Big Sur. It comes to us from a new field of study called interpersonal neurobiology: "Brain scans show synchrony between the brains of mother and child; but what they can't show is the internal bond that belongs to neither alone, a fusion in which the self feels so permeable it doesn't matter whose body is whose. Wordlessly, relying on the heart's semaphores, the mother says all an infant needs to hear, communicating through eyes, face and voice. Thanks to advances in neuroimaging, we now have evidence that a baby's first attachments imprint its brain. The patterns of a lifetime's behaviors, thoughts, self-regard and choice of sweetheart all begin in this crucible."

What most amazed me was what happened in the immediate aftermath of the revelation at Big Sur. My fusion with my mother/lover continued. Our bodies and ourselves remained permeable. We were no longer stoned, but we continued to melt together every time we touched, not only sexually or spiritually or symbolically, but also physically. Our skin no longer divided us. The magical melting-together feeling continued for days, then weeks. We were truly one, and I was convinced we would remain so for the rest of our lives. This was love. This was forever.

I've often wondered over the years how much I've mythologized the ecstasy of that freshman trip. In writing this book, I've gone to libraries and archives across the country, digging up correspondence between Gerald Heard, Bill Wilson, and Aldous Huxley. Then I remembered that box of letters my sister and I found several years earlier, when we sent our mother off to memory care. I'd looked through it long enough to discover some letters I wrote home during college, but something stopped me from opening them and reading them. I'd stuck the box of letters on a high shelf in my basement office and tried to forget they were there.

In one of the letters written during my freshman year, I wrote:

Dear Mom,

I just came to the realization that I owe everyone I know a letter, so I'm sitting down and chaining myself to a desk. Things are really looking good for me up here lately. I think I'm finally getting my lifestyle adapted to fit in up here. The most important development, however, is a girl I've been coming very close to over the past few weeks. . . . We've been able to break down most of the fronts we put up to each other and open up totally. We went down to Big Sur last weekend. We're at a level that neither of us has ever experienced, and the last few weeks have been some of the happiest in my life. I think the honesty is something I really need. . . .

                                        Love,
                                        Don

I have no memory of writing that letter, but I'm pleasantly surprised that I would write something like that to my mother. It sounds like me and it doesn't sound like me. My experience at Big Sur happened nearly forty years ago. I've tried to understand it and to write about it over the years, but seeing this letter confirms my memory of the experience. It wasn't just that I was describing the experience without mentioning that we dropped acid that weekend in Big Sur. It reminds me that, at the time, I didn't think the LSD was the main reason that my lover and I came together in such a miraculous way. It was fate. It was true love.

I fold up the letter and carefully place it back in its envelope. Then I pick up my battered 1970 paperback edition of *The Doors of Perception.* The pages are yellow and brittle. The cover has separated from the binding, and some of the pages have fallen out. My eyes rest on the paragraph in the book after Huxley takes his first mescaline, but before he tries to describe its effects. "We live together, we act on, and react to, one another; but always and in all circumstances we are by ourselves. The martyrs go hand in hand into the arena; they are crucified alone. Embraced, the lovers desperately try to fuse their insulated ecstasies into a single self-transcendence; in vain. By its very nature every embodied spirit is doomed to suffer and enjoy in solitude."

Aldous Huxley was right. Yes, there are *moments* when lovers may fuse their insulated energies into a single self-transcendence—moments like my encounter at Big Sur. For a time, or perhaps outside of time, we are not alone, and in the process of that coming together we get a glimpse of God. That's what happened at Big Sur on the eve of my nineteenth birthday. But it turned out that the love—or at least *that* love— would not last forever. It would not even last a season, for my freshman ecstasy would soon be followed by the most painful agonies of my life.

.   .   .   .   .

Bill Wilson had been sober for more than two decades when he had his first acid trip. Gerald Heard was his guide, joining Dr. Cohen for the session.

Heard had been invited to join Huxley for the latter's first mescaline session, with Humphry Osmond, in May 1953, but other obligations prevented Heard from participating. He had his psychedelic baptism six months later, in November 1953, the month I was born.

Huxley and Heard began by experimenting with mescaline but soon moved on to a new and much more powerful compound that could truly blast open the doors of perception. LSD changed Huxley and Heard, like it changes many of us who take it. Alan Watts was inspired to try psychedelics after seeing the effect it had on his fellow "British mystical expatriates." He noticed "a marked change of spiritual attitude" in Huxley and Heard. "To put it briefly, they ceased to be Manicheans," Watts recalled. "Their vision of the divine now included nature, and they had become more relaxed and human."

Bill Wilson had his first LSD session at the Los Angeles Veterans Administration hospital on August 29, 1956. At the time, everyone, from humanistic psychologists to chemical warfare enthusiasts, was looking for something to do with the mind-blowing drug that Albert Hofmann first synthesized at his Sandoz laboratory back in 1938. A group of researchers, including Dr. Osmond, thought LSD could be used to treat alcoholism. At first, Osmond and his colleagues thought the drug would help them to better understand alcohol-induced hallucinations. It might terrify drunks into changing their ways.

By the time Wilson had his first trip, Osmond had begun to see that it was insight, not terror, that was helping alcoholics mend their destructive ways. At first, it seemed counterintuitive. They were using one drug to overcome addiction to another. But they were doing what Wilson and AA had suggested in the second of their twelve steps. They were using mind-expanding drugs to find what the twelve steps describe as "a Power greater than ourselves" that "could restore us to sanity." They were using a drug that mimicked insanity to find sanity.

Wilson was nervous about taking LSD, so he turned to his most-trusted spiritual advisor. He asked Gerald Heard to be his guide, a role in which Heard accompanied many others in the early years of the psychedelic movement. This was four years before Timothy Leary had his first trip and anointed himself the Pied Piper of the psychedelic sixties.

Heard turned on *Time* publisher Henry Luce and his wife, Clare Boothe Luce; Jesuit theologian John Courtney Murray; and William Mullendore, the chairman of the board of Southern California Edison. He also inspired Dr. Oscar Janiger, a Los Angeles psychiatrist who turned on Gary Grant, James Coburn, and Jack Nicholson. "It was the philosopher Gerald Heard who introduced me to psychedelics," Janiger said. "He told me that the emergence of LSD in the twentieth century was simply God's way of giving us the gift of consciousness. He believed that LSD was a device for saving humanity from Armageddon."

Heard was also the man who turned on Myron Stolaroff, a Silicon Valley pioneer who went on to introduce to LSD many of the other engineers and business people who launched the personal computer revolution. Stolaroff met Heard at a series of Bay Area spiritual retreats in the 1950s known as the Sequoia Seminars. At first, Stolaroff couldn't understand why a famous mystic like Gerald Heard would need to take a drug to find God. But Heard was so enthusiastic about LSD that Stolaroff took his advice and made an appointment to see one of the most mysterious men in the early history of the psychedelic era, a secretive Canadian businessman named Al Hubbard. In April 1956, Stolaroff, an executive with the Ampex Corporation, which popularized the first tape recorders, was baptized into the LSD church at Hubbard's Vancouver apartment. Stolaroff returned to Silicon Valley to become one of the region's first LSD evangelists, resigning from the Ampex board in 1961 to found the International Foundation of Advanced Study, which sponsored research to see if LSD could be used to inspire creative thinking. According to some observers of the era, psychedelic drugs fueled the burst of engineering and business genius that inspired Silicon Valley.

And it all started with Gerald Heard, who would soon set his psychedelic sights on another adventurous businessman—Bill Wilson.

In the summer of 1956, Heard was working with Dr. Sidney Cohen at the VA hospital in Los Angeles. Wilson had been battling his depression and was unsure how he'd react to such a powerful psychotropic agent. Heard told him that everyone had a different reaction to the drug, but tried to put his mind at ease. Cohen, one of the leading researchers in the field, would supervise the session, and Heard would be there as Wilson's spiritual guide.

One can imagine what Heard told Wilson about LSD by examining Heard's written and recorded suggestions for psychedelic voyagers: "This should not be undertaken alone," Heard may have said. "You'll have two people at your side who are intimately acquainted with LSD. We will not intrude on your experience, but neither will we leave you figuratively or literally in the dark. You'll feel nothing for the first forty-five minutes or so. Then, as the first hour wears away, some subjects become convinced that they are feeling odd. Some, like the witches of Macbeth, feel a prickling in their thumbs, or perhaps a tightening of the skin. Don't worry. This will pass."

"Then what?" Wilson may have asked.

"Well," Heard may have replied, "I don't know any of our friends who have taken it who haven't said this one thing: 'Well, I never knew *anything* like that in the whole of my life.' First, there are the colors and the beauties and designs and the way things appear. But that's just the beginning. At some point you notice that there aren't these separations that we normally feel. We are not on some separate island—shouting across and trying to hear what each other is saying. Suddenly you *know*. You know empathy. It's flowing underneath us. We are parts of a common continent that meet underneath the water. And with that comes such delight—the sober certainty of waking bliss."

By the time Wilson came to Los Angeles for his LSD session, he had developed a close relationship with Heard. Letters they exchanged from the late 1940s to the early 1960s document that friendship. They helped each other through painful bouts of depression. "Profitable and pleasant thoughts of our brief hour with you keep returning," Wilson wrote in the summer of 1948, following his last visit to Trabuco Canyon.

By then, it was clear that Heard would have to shut down Trabuco College, and his own future was equally as uncertain. "This I would like you to know, for just now you may need to feel that things do matter," Wilson wrote. "What a gulf there sometimes is between knowing and feeling. . . . Remembering our talk I was a little anguished at how much I had taken away and how little I probably left. You spoke of Trabuco and the question of its future." Wilson went on to suggest that Heard consider turning the college into a center for the serious study of psychic phenomena, which was then and is now dismissed in most academic and religious circles as magical thinking or irrelevant superstition. Setting up a research center at Trabuco to document and prove that psychic activity is real, Wilson wrote, "would place a truly hot blow torch against the scientific and theological icebergs that seem to chill that field. Maybe that's an idea for Trabuco."

Heard, Huxley, and Wilson had a lifelong interest in psychic phenomena. Wilson's longtime personal secretary, Nell Wing, shared her boss's fascination with the paranormal. "In the early forties," she wrote in her memoir, "Bill and Lois often held meetings—or 'spook sessions,' as they termed them—in a small bedroom at Stepping Stones [the name for the Wilsons' home in Bedford Hills, New York] for A.A. friends, a couple of Rockefeller people,* and even some Bedford Hills neighbors frequently participated in these sessions and experienced unusual phenomena."

In their letters, Heard and Wilson discussed their common fascination with psychic activity. In a letter to Wilson in the fall of 1950, Heard discussed new research into "telepathic linkage," but also included words of support for Bill, who was passing through another period of melancholy. "I do hope your spirits have been backing up your will and insight and that the valley you had to go through has given place to higher ground and brighter outlook," Gerald wrote.

Heard and Wilson also shared an interest in flying saucers, as did millions of other Americans in the 1950s. Heard was an early proponent of taking these UFO reports seriously. His book *Is Another World Watching? The Riddle of the Flying Saucers*, was published in England in 1950, and came out in the United States the following year. One of its more extraordinary conclusions was that giant, super-intelligent bees might populate Mars. "It is difficult to resist the conclusion," Heard wrote, "that Mars is ruled by insects."†

By 1954, Heard and Wilson's fascination with flying saucers and psychic activity was taking a backseat to their new interest in psychedelic drugs. One short letter, written by Wilson on September 9, 1954, documents this shift. It also indicates that Wilson may have been invited to a mescaline session that year with Humphry Osmond and Aldous Huxley,

---

*John D. Rockefeller Jr. was an early AA patron, and some of his operatives worked closely with Wilson in the early years in New York.

†Gerald Heard had a keen interest in bees. His most successful mystery novel, written under the name H. F. Heard, is the tale of a mad, ingenious apiarist who programs his swarms to kill. That 1941 bestseller, *A Taste for Honey*, was later turned into a British horror movie, *The Deadly Bees*.

and that Wilson had initially told them he preferred to be an observer, not a participant.

> Dear Gerald,
> Thanks so very much for your letter of July. I'm glad you like the saucer account; it seems an unusually clean-cut sighting.
> Am looking forward with great anticipation to your visit in September when I hope that I shall be able to join you along with brothers Osmond and Aldous. Though, for the life of me, I can't see where I have much to contribute. But I shall be an ardent listener and try not to talk too much.
>
> As always,
> Bill

Osmond confirms that Wilson was initially reluctant to experiment with psychedelics—even after he presented the AA cofounder with evidence that it was helping hardcore alcoholics. One study showed that 15 percent of habitual drunks who were given LSD recovered, compared to only 5 percent of patients who were not given the drug. Yet Bill was not impressed.

In a talk he gave at the Esalen Institute at Big Sur in May 1976, Osmond recalled the story of trying to turn on Bill Wilson twenty years before. "Early on I told Bill W. that this was good news. But he was far from pleased with the idea of alcoholics being assailed by some strange chemical," Osmond recalled. "Later on Bill got extremely interested and took LSD with Sidney Cohen in Los Angeles. He likened his LSD experience to his earlier vision of seeing this chain of drunks around the world, all helping each other. This caused various scandals in A.A. They were very ambivalent about their great founder taking LSD, yet they wouldn't have existed if he hadn't been of an adventurous kind of mind."

Historians have been left to guess whether Bill Wilson and Aldous Huxley ever tripped together. My guess is they did, perhaps on mescaline in 1954 or on LSD in New York City later in the 1950s, or even in the early 1960s, when Huxley was spending a lot of time on the East Coast. Wilson and Huxley may have be present at some LSD sessions at the

Santa Monica estate of Margaret Gage in the late 1950s, where Heard lived after he turned Trabuco College over to the Vedanta Society.

The reason we have to guess about all this is the dearth of surviving letters between Aldous Huxley and Bill Wilson. Both men were prodigious letter writers. Bill Wilson's longtime secretary, Nell Wing, states in her memoir that Wilson and Huxley "carried on a lively correspondence for nearly two decades." Lois Wilson says in her autobiography that Heard brought Wilson and Huxley together during the Trabuco College years, after which Aldous became "a lifelong personal friend and admirer" of AA.

Wilson's letters to Huxley were probably lost in a devastating fire that destroyed Huxley's home in the Hollywood Hills in May 1961. But there is one noteworthy letter from Wilson to Huxley in 1962, in which Bill thanks Aldous for sending him a copy of a Krishnamurti book, *Declaration of Freedom*. Wilson tells of how the old newspaper accounts of Krishnamurti's struggles back in the 1920s to free himself from his messianic role in Theosophy "oddly stirred me." He also saw how the AA philosophy and Krishnamurti's later teachings have a similar approach to "that very same problem of liberation." Wilson writes:

A.A.'s "Twelve Steps" for recovery and its "Twelve Traditions" for the unity of group life carefully avoid coercion. "Twelve Steps" are made as "suggestions" and implicit in our Traditions is the idea that these principles, too, can be taken or left alone. We exercise no personal authority, no money can be demanded, nor are any beliefs required.

However it is true that in early A.A. life we are subject to an enormous coercion—that of being hourly aware that Barleycorn will destroy us if we don't conform in some degree to A.A.'s attitudes and practices.

So men conform at first because they must. Still balking somewhat, we then conform because conformity seems right. Finally we arrive at the place of free choice—no fear of coercion. So long as we hold this plateau we know something of the freedom of which Krishnamurti speaks. In our rather fitful way the most of us are thus moving toward freedom.

There are several references to Wilson-Huxley meetings in the Wilson-Heard correspondence. "If you see Aldous Huxley, take him my renewed thanks for those engaging hours we spent together," Wilson writes in an October 13, 1950, letter to Heard. Most of this letter consists of Bill W. recounting the purported psychic abilities of his sister, Dorothy Strong. Wilson writes that his sister had begun channeling messages from Camille Flammarion, a deceased astronomer and spiritualist. These communiqués from the grave, Wilson writes, even contain references to Gerald Heard. Wilson tells Heard that his sister had "a bad crackup" and "extreme emotional difficulties" three years earlier, but that she had emerged from those troubles and was "developing marked psychic talents."

Heard responded to the letter within days of receiving it. Heard begins his reply to Wilson by suggesting that he and Aldous Huxley get together with Tom Powers, a close Wilson associate, for another séance. This foursome, Heard writes to Wilson, might uncover "still another chapter of your pioneering and explore—both for the insane and the so-called sane—the border country of psychical research of which you know so much."

In a letter written to Heard on May 1, 1956, the same year as his first LSD trip, Wilson refers to another meeting with the Huxleys at the New York home of David and Lucille Kahn, a wealthy couple who participated in some of the early LSD sessions with Wilson in New York. The Kahns were followers of the famous psychic Edgar Cayce. The letter shows how the longtime interest in psychic activity shared by Wilson, Huxley, and Heard led to their newfound enthusiasm for psychedelic drugs. "At the Kahn's I recently spent several pleasant hours with Aldous and his charming lady," Wilson writes. "Since then, Lois and I have most carefully read his recent 'Heaven and Hell.' It was one of the most integrating experiences we have known in a long time. We feel positive that he is on precisely the right track. It was astonishing to see how our own psychic experiences, and those of many friends, fitted in to the frame of reference that he has drawn. We could almost substantiate every chapter, page and verse. When you see him, will you please tell him this?"

Heaven and Hell was Huxley's second book on the psychedelic drug experience, a sequel to *The Doors of Perception*.

Fortunately, some of Gerald Heard's firsthand accounts of Wilson's psychedelic sessions have survived. Heard took notes during Wilson's first LSD experience at the VA hospital in 1956. He reports that Bill felt "an enormous enlargement" during the session, started laughing and said "people shouldn't take themselves so damn seriously."

Here's how Betty Eisner, a UCLA psychologist who worked with Cohen, describes Bill Wilson's thinking as he came into the session, and his reaction to the drug:

> Alcoholics Anonymous was actually considering using LSD. Alcoholics get to a point in the program where they need a spiritual experience, but not all of them are able to have one. Tom Powers was Bill Wilson's right-hand man in this. Tom had been through hell with alcoholism, so he brought Bill Wilson out to meet with us. Sid and I thought it might be a good idea to try a low dose together, but when I met Bill, I thought, "Uh-oh, this is going to be *his* therapy session." And that's one of the things it turned out to be. We each took twenty-five gamma, except for Bill. Sid offered him several pills, and Bill said, "Don't ever do that to a drunk," and took two. But the rest of us just took one.

At Bill's urging, Lois Wilson participated in that first session. She claimed to feel nothing spectacular, but did confess that she had "a very pleasant time." Bill Wilson's secretary, Nell Wing, who had dropped acid in one of the early Los Angeles sessions with Sidney Cohen, said Lois took a very small dose, which may explain the lack of fireworks in her trip.

There are seven letters between Bill Wilson and Sidney Cohen in the files of the Stepping Stones Foundation Archive in New York. They were written between 1956 and 1961. In one written in 1956, Wilson thanks Cohen for the time the psychiatrist spent him. Wilson then comments on his "Door of Perception" experience, writing: "The outstanding residue seem to be these: all of the assurances of my original experience were renewed, and more. The sense of the livingness of all things and a sense of their beauty has been considerably heightened and restored. . . . I can report this in spite of the fact that on my arrival home I had a severe reaction of anxiety, weakness, lack of focus and the like. But this time, the depression was pretty much absent."

In another letter Wilson reports that he keeps hearing gossip about his LSD use in AA circles, stressing to Cohen "the desirability of omitting my name when discussing LSD with A.A.'s." Cohen wrote back to assure Wilson that his series of LSD trials included no other active AA members. Not long after Wilson's LSD sessions in Los Angeles, Huston Smith invited Heard to give a talk at Washington University in Saint Louis, where Smith was a professor of religious studies. Wilson happened to be speaking that same week at an AA convention in Kansas City, and he desperately wanted to see Heard. So Huston drove Heard all the way to Kansas City and spent two hours with them in Wilson's hotel room.

They spent much of their time together talking about psychedelics, a conversation that helped inspire Huston Smith to begin a psychedelic partnership a few years later at Harvard with Timothy Leary. Smith's most vivid memory of the two hours he spent in the hotel room was Wilson describing his trip as "a dead ringer" for the epiphany he'd had back at Towns Hospital in the 1930s. On that night in late 1934, Wilson has recalled, "every joy I had known was pale by comparison. The light, the ecstasy. I was conscious of nothing else at the time."

There's a good reason why Wilson's 1956 LSD trip at the Veterans Administration hospital in Los Angeles would remind him of his 1934 vision at Towns Hospital in New York. In both cases, Wilson had been given hallucinogenic drugs. Doctors at Towns Hospital employed "the Belladonna Cure" to treat alcoholics. Patients were given an hourly dose of a potion that included belladonna. Also known as deadly nightshade, belladonna is a perennial herb with dark purple flowers and black berries. It can produce delirium. Patients at the hospital were given this potion *every hour for fifty hours*. Wilson's spiritual experience there, which he would also refer to as his "hot flash," could very well have resulted from this treatment, as well as from the delusions and hallucinations that often accompany alcoholic toxic psychosis.

Does the fact that drugs may have fueled Wilson's 1934 revelation diminish its legitimacy or importance? In my mind, not at all. What's most important is that it changed the way Bill Wilson lived his life. He stayed away from alcohol, a drug that nearly killed him and that caused so much anguish in the lives of his loved ones. And Wilson went on to help countless other alcoholics do the same.

Our understanding of what really happened to Bill Wilson that night at Towns Hospital is best understood by turning to the same book he opened the morning after his revelation. By his own account, the first thing Wilson did was read *The Varieties of Religious Experience*, the book Ebby Thatcher brought to him at Towns Hospital. He says he read it "cover to cover." About midway between the front and back covers is a chapter titled "Conversion." In it, William James argues that the worth of a religious conversion should *not* "be decided by its origin." It doesn't matter whether the revelation comes instantaneously or builds slowly over time—whether God or drugs or prayer or meditation induces it. "If the *fruits for life* of the state of conversion are good," James writes, "we ought to idealize and venerate it, even though it be a piece of natural psychology; if not, we ought to make short work with it, no matter what supernatural being may have infused it."

Bill Wilson idealized and probably inflated the story of his conversion. The tale seems to have gotten better with successive retelling, as stories do. Careful readers of this book will recall that the myth of AA's founding revelation is remarkably similar to the story that Wilson grew up hearing, the tale of Grandpa Willy and his sudden conversion from demon rum, when he met God on the mountaintop in Vermont and rushed down to proclaim it before the Sunday morning flock at the East Dorset Congregational Church.

It matters little that Wilson may have borrowed a bit of his grandfather's revelation. This is exactly how the stories of our lives are transformed into the religious movements of our times. Wilson's experience inspired one of the greatest spiritual revivals of the twentieth century. What matters is whether his revelation made him a better person and allowed him to help others. It didn't turn him into a saint—not even close—but it certainly helped him and countless others live better lives.

·   ·   ·   ·   ·

Looking back on my revelation at Big Sur, when my lover and I became one and we were bathed in the white light of divine bliss, I must ask this same question: "Did it make me a better person? Did it change the way I lived my life?"

It has taken me forty years—five of them lived clean and sober—to even approach the question. There were dozens of psychedelic drug trips over thirty-five of those years, many of them revelatory and a few of them hellish. There were countless nights when alcohol and other drugs truly *did* enhance my experience of life and my communion with others. But there were also years trapped in the pain and hopelessness of addictive despair.

Aldous Huxley warned us of the agony that sometimes follows the ecstasy. "Visionary experience is not always blissful," he cautioned in 1956. "It is sometimes terrible. There is hell as well as heaven."

Hell, for me, came on the heels of heaven. Several weeks after my blissful experience at Big Sur, my lover and I took another acid trip, this one with another couple from our dorm at UC Berkeley, where we were all first-year students. My roommate's family belonged to a private retreat deep in the woods of Northern California, about three hours north of Berkeley. We drove up there for another session with the amazing acid that was in circulation that semester. But this would turn out to be a journey to a place very different from where I went on my first experience. My roommate had neglected to tell me that this private retreat was actually his father's hunting lodge.

The nature of an LSD trip depends heavily upon the set and setting of the experience. You need to be in a safe, comfortable place with people you trust. That's the main reason I always took my LSD out in nature, far from the noisy crowd and the artificial, advertising-laden environment of city and suburb.

The setting for this trip was isolated, but it was not safe. As we were hiking in the wooded hills, coming on to the LSD, we could hear gunshots off in the distance. The gun-toting families back at the hunting lodge had not been happy to see four teenage acidheads show up for the weekend. We did not feel welcome. But we were young and foolish and not about to change our plans and sit around the lodge playing cards all weekend.

On this trip, my body shrank again, but this time I responded with fear and paranoia and psychosis. We were sitting out in the woods, still coming on to the acid and smoking a joint to supercharge the effect when

I began the "bad trip" from central casting. My three companions did not try to comfort me. They seemed to be laughing at me. I melted into the earth, but this time I did not feel a oneness with everything. I felt like I was disappearing, maybe even dying, and would never return.

By the time we made it back to the cabin the intense effects of the LSD had finally stopped, but the paranoia lingered. We had to eat in a dining room with the hunters and their families. Everyone in the room, including my friends, was staring at me, mocking me, or at least that's what I experienced.

There had been blissful communion in the light of Big Sur, but here in the dark northern woods the same drug brought isolation, fear, and brokenness. There were separate dorm rooms at the lodge for unmarried men and women, so I did not spend another wondrous night with my girlfriend. I spent a terrifying, sleepless night hearing voices offering insult and recrimination.

But what terrified me most was that the fear and paranoia and hallucinations did not leave once the drug wore off. On the drive back to Berkeley, I had to stop and turn the wheel of my car over to my roommate. I was driving too slowly for the traffic on the freeway. Every time a large truck would pass my little 1965 Mustang, it would seem as if the monstrous vehicles were towering over me, hundreds of stories tall, about to crush the car like a bug on the road. Of course, I didn't say this to my companions. I think I simply said I was tired or too spaced out to drive.

Back in Berkeley, my lover and I would soon part ways and I would be left alone, more alone than I had ever been in my life.

I'd always thought all the talk in the news media about LSD flashbacks was only propaganda, part of Nixon's war on drugs. Then I experienced them myself. I had mild hallucinations for days and then weeks after I stopped taking any drugs, including alcohol and marijuana. I had other mental problems too. I lost the ability to read. One word would set my mind off on such a tangent that I was literally unable to understand a single sentence—not a good state for a freshman at the University of California. I continued hearing voices at night and got very little sleep. I stopped eating. I was scared to death. I thought I'd permanently damaged my brain. I was insane, yet sane enough to know exactly what I had done. I kept all this to myself out of fear that I would be thrown into the nearest nuthouse.

Looking back on it, I realized that some of my delusions were almost amusing. For a while I fell into a kind of positive paranoia. I became convinced that people were secretly trying to *help* me. During my freshman year I was part of a short-lived experimental program at Cal called Arts, Technology and Society. It was a residential program, meaning we all lived together in the same dormitory. One of our art projects involved putting colored lights in the windows of our high-rise dorm and turning the building into a giant light show. This was called "alternative education" back in the early 1970s. Unable to read, I threw myself into this endeavor with a kind of insane glee. I'd decided that my teachers, most of them hippie or leftie graduate students, had designed the entire project for my benefit.

The most terrifying series of hallucinations came when I was home for the Thanksgiving holiday. My mother had already sold our house and moved into a condo. We were sitting in her living room watching the news when the face of Tom Brokaw, then a local newscaster in Los Angeles, turned into that of a hideous monster.* At first I thought his metamorphosis was some kind of television spoof, but then I realized that I was having another flashback. I quickly got up and headed for the guest bedroom, where I hoped to lie down and wait for the terror to pass.

My mother was dating the man she would later marry, Gideon "Russ" Russell, the man with the same name as my childhood imaginary friend, Russell. This is the man my mother would marry to avoid remembering the horrific loss of her first son, Alan, the son I replaced—the son whose imaginary friend was named "Donnie." There were twin beds in the room where I sought refuge. But what awaited me there was a hallucination more troubling than the monstrous Tom Brokaw. Russ had gone into the back bedroom to take a nap, or I assume he had, but that wasn't the problem. Russ was in both beds. There were two of him, and I didn't know which one was real.

*Brokaw would later write his own memoir of the 1960s, titled *Boom*.

Freudians could have a field day with this, but the lesson I take away from my twisted vision was not that I wanted to sleep with my mother and kill her lover. Thankfully, those Thanksgiving weekend horrors marked the beginning of the end of my temporary psychotic break—which would have been the official diagnosis. I somehow managed to get back to Berkeley, reassemble myself, and make it through the first semester of college. Decades later, a therapist told me that the smartest thing I'd done during my troubled freshman year was *not* to seek professional help. I would have been institutionalized and labeled, and probably would have wound up worse off than I did by getting through the crisis myself.

When I look back on all of this now, both the "good trip" and the "bad trip," I see that entire affair as the best and the worst thing that ever happened to me. I came out saner than I went in. I'd been to the other side and made it back alive. Later in my college career, when I read the works of Carl Jung and Joseph Campbell, I came to see all this as my own process of individuation. It's what I needed to do to leave home and find my own way.

Drugs gave me new life. Then drugs nearly destroyed my life. The same thing happened to Bill Wilson.

.   .   .   .   .

Bill Wilson returned to New York following his psychedelic baptism in California in the summer of 1956. His thinking as he went into the session was that an LSD experience might help him overcome two of his remaining demons—his depression and his addiction to tobacco. Gerald Heard's hourly notes from the August 29 session reveal that the trip did little to keep Bill away from cigarettes, a lifelong addiction that would kill him in the end. At 1 PM Wilson reported "a feeling of peace." At 2:31 P.M. he was even happier and proclaimed, "Tobacco is not necessary to me anymore." At 3:22 P.M. he asked for a cigarette.

His depression lifted for a while, only to return when he got back to New York. "On my return home, I fell into one of my fits of exhaustion, which bordered on serious," Wilson wrote in a September 26, 1956, letter to Heard. Yet, Wilson added, "I do not think that in any way my state is related to my experience in looking through 'The Doors of Perception.' In spite of my temporary condition, I do feel a residue of assurance and a feeling of enhanced beauty that seems likely to stay by me."

A few months later, Wilson was even more upbeat about the long-term benefits from the LSD session. "More and more it appears to me that the experience has done a sustained good," he wrote to Heard on December 4, 1956. "My reactions to things totally, and in particular, have very definitely improved for no other reason that I can see. Tom [Powers] says he has been thinking about the possibility of visiting you soon again with a friend with the idea of trying this out some more." Powers may have made that trip and returned to New York with a generous supply of the drug, for he and Wilson were certainly committed to "trying this out some more."

Wilson became so intrigued by the spiritual potential of LSD that he formed an experimental group in New York that included Father Ed Dowling, a Catholic priest, and Eugene Exman, the religion editor at Harper and Brothers. The "friend" of Powers that Wilson mentioned in his letter may have been a psychiatrist from Roosevelt Hospital in New York, who served as the supervising physician at Bill Wilson's psychedelic salon.

Meanwhile, on the West Coast, Gerald Heard was hosting his own LSD-fueled gatherings in the Santa Monica home of Margaret Gage. It was 1957. William Forthman, the teenager who'd met Heard at Trabuco College during World War II, was now a graduate student at UCLA. Both he and Heard were living at the Gage estate when the psychedelic sessions began. Forthman had already been living in a cottage on the property when Heard arrived. He surrendered the cottage to Gerald and took a room for himself in the main house.

"When it came to LSD, Gerald was a bit of a Pied Piper," Forthman recalled. "Gerald got Dr. Cohen to give LSD to lots of famous people, not just to Bill Wilson and the Luces. John Huston [the film director] and Steve Allen [the television show host] took LSD at Margaret's house."

They would gather at the Gage home in the morning. Dr. Cohen would arrive with little glass vials of LSD, which he could break open and dissolve in a glass of water. They would start to feel the effects in thirty to forty minutes. LSD "gave you a sense that whatever happened was very portentous," Forthman remembered. "It was a great focuser of attention. People would listen to music. Aldous used to say it wipes out all the normal distractions."

Bill Wilson thought LSD could help cynical alcoholics undergo the "spiritual awakening" that stands at the center of twelve-step work. It seems unlikely—as some have claimed—that Wilson once planned to have LSD distributed at AA meetings. Yet Wilson's enthusiasm for both psychedelics and spiritualism were among the reasons he decided to officially remove himself from the AA governing body—a move that was designed to free him to pursue outside interests without making it seem like they were endorsed by AA.

Nevertheless, "Bill W." remained the best-known member of Alcoholics Anonymous throughout the 1950s and 1960s. "Dr. Bob" died in 1950, leaving Wilson as the surviving founding father of the fellowship. Wilson continued to play a major role, appearing at AA conventions and writing for the organization's publications for the rest of his life.

According to the anonymous author of Wilson's official biography, the cofounder of Alcoholic Anonymous felt LSD "helped him eliminate many barriers erected by the self, or ego, that stand in the way of one's direct experiences of the cosmos and of God. He thought he might have found something that could make a big difference to the lives of many who still suffered." This explanation in *Pass It On*, published in 1984 by Alcoholics Anonymous World Services in New York, also addresses the AA reaction to Wilson's LSD experiments. "As word of Bill's activities reached the Fellowship, there were inevitable repercussions. Most A.A.'s were violently opposed to his experimenting with a mind-altering substance. LSD was then totally unfamiliar, poorly researched, and entirely experimental—and Bill was taking it."

Wilson defended his LSD use and psychic experimentations in a long letter written in June 1958—a statement that shows how his enthusiasm for the drug caused him to ignore its dangers. Wilson wrote that Osmond and his colleagues had given LSD to hundreds of subjects, and that there was "no record of any harm, no tendency to addiction. They have also found there is no physical risk whatever. The material is about as harmless as aspirin."

Wilson also began experimenting with adrenochrome, another drug Osmond was investigating as a possible treatment for schizophrenia. It is sometimes classed as a hallucinogen, although those effects may be diminished when a modified version, leukoadrenochrome, is administered. This time it was Bill Wilson who would turn Aldous Huxley on to a new drug. In a letter to Osmond written on September 16, 1960, Huxley writes, "Yesterday I lunched with Bill Wilson who spoke enthusiastically of his own experiences with leuko-adrenochrome and of the successful use of it on his ex-alcoholic neurotics. This really sounds like a breakthrough and I hope you are going ahead with clinical testing. Do you have any of the stuff to spare? If so, I'd be most grateful for a sample."

Wilson may have been following Osmond's lead and experimenting with a chemical cocktail that combined LSD and leukoadrenochrome.

Father Dowling, the Jesuit priest who had known Wilson since the early 1940s, and who participated in at least one of the early LSD sessions in New York, was initially as enthusiastic as Wilson, but would later warn Bill to be more careful with the drug. Dowling played a major role in promoting AA—which was seen by some as a Protestant sect— as a fellowship that Roman Catholics could join in good conscience. He also inspired Wilson to take another look at Christianity, especially at its long mystical tradition. In the 1940s, Wilson met regularly with Dowling and Monsignor Fulton Sheen, the popular Catholic radio host. For a time, Wilson considered Dowling to be his "spiritual advisor" and even considered converting to Catholicism. "I *feel* more like a Catholic," he once wrote to Sheen, "but I *think* more like a Protestant." In the end, Wilson did not convert, partly because he felt it could hurt AA, and partly because of his lifelong distrust of organized religion.

Some of the letters Wilson and Dowling exchanged between 1958 and 1960, the year Dowling died, concern Wilson's ongoing psychedelic drug experiments. "On the psychic front," Wilson wrote on December 29, 1958, "the LSD business goes on apace. . . . I don't believe that it has any miraculous property of transforming spiritually and emotionally sick people into healthy ones overnight. It can set up a shining goal on the positive side. . . . After all, it is only a temporary ego-reducer. . . . But the vision and insights given by LSD could create a large incentive—at least in a considerable number of people."

Nearly a year later, on October 26, 1959, Wilson wrote about the controversy the drug sessions had stirred up in AA, noting, "It must be confessed that these recent heresies of mine do have their comic aspects." He told Dowling that "the LSD business created some commotion. . . . The story is that 'Bill takes one pill to see God and another to quiet his nerves.'"

Dowling replied by urging Wilson to proceed with caution, and even suggested that the devil might be working through LSD. Quoting Saint Ignatius, the Jesuit priest wrote, "It is the mark of the evil spirit to assume the appearance of the angel of light."

．　　．　　．　　．　　．

While I don't think Satan was mixed up in my troubles with LSD, I do believe that some drugs can lead us into darkness and temptation. But they can also point us toward the light. They can, as Huxley said, show us a glimpse of heaven and then send us straight to hell.

For me, the trouble was not knowing when to stop. Not a big surprise, since that's what being an addict is all about. I've always liked (but not followed) the advice of Alan Watts, who was once asked if people should keep taking LSD after getting a glimpse of God on the drug. "When one has received the message," Watts said, "one hangs up the phone."

I stayed on the line too long. Even after my psychotic break, even after promising myself I would never drop acid again, I was heading off a few months later on another trip that could have posed a serious threat to my undergraduate education, not to mention my sanity. It was during spring break in my freshman year that I found myself in a car with two guys from my dorm winding our way up Mount Tamalpais. It was three in the morning. We'd been sitting around wondering what to do with ourselves when someone (probably me) suggested we drive over to Marin, drop acid, and watch the sunrise from the top of Mount Tam.

There was some blotter acid floating around the dorm at the time, so we snipped off three hits and tossed them into a little metal Sucrets box, along with three Quaaludes and a few joints. We were smoking one of the joints in the car when two officers from the Tiburon Police Department pulled us over for a busted taillight. They smelled the smoke, found the stash, and the next thing we knew we were being processed at the jail at the Marin County Civic Center—not just any jail, but a futuristic facility designed by the renowned architect Frank Lloyd Wright.

I guess the good news is that we had not yet dropped the acid. I spent two nights in that jail before I could get one of my teachers at Cal to bail me out. I didn't want to call my father, mainly because he'd warned me that I would become a drug addict if I went to school in Berkeley. I didn't want to give him the satisfaction of being right. In the end, the Marin County district attorney never charged us, probably because we were white, upper-middle-class college students and not seen as an imminent threat to civilized society. Whatever the reason, I dodged that bullet, but of course did not learn whatever lesson I was supposed to learn.

Still, I suppose the question I posed some pages back remains unanswered: Did my revelatory experience at Big Sur make me a better person? Did it and my other experiences on psychedelic drugs change the way I lived my life? They certainly showed me that there is more going on in the universe than the narrow, ego-driven, self-centered world that was once the only world I knew. Psychedelic drugs left me both fascinated with, and fearful of, mystical states and helped inspire my long career as a religion writer. They instilled a new sense of wonder at the natural world and the interconnectedness of everything in it. Drugs such as MDA and Ecstasy showed me another way of relating to my friends and lovers, with more empathy and compassion. The trick, of course, is remembering to live that way the morning after.

Recovery from decades of heavy drug use and abuse is a lifelong process. For me, it's important to remember the agony *and* the ecstasy. You sober up and move with new insight on to the rest of your life. In his book *Not-God: A History of Alcoholics Anonymous,* Ernest Kurtz points out that AA was always about more than simply finding a way to stop drinking and drugging.* It was about our conversion from total self-centeredness to a "constructive, creative and *fully human interaction* with others."

*Kurtz's dedication to that book reads, "To G. H. *with gratitude,*" which according to one account was his way of tipping his hat to Gerald Heard. (Italics in the original.)

That's where I am in my recovery, having gotten over the early cravings and beyond any real desire to regress to my drinking and drugging days. Recovery is a day-by-day wrestling match with my inner cynic, a constant effort to curb my tongue and keep an eye on my own self-centeredness.

My first attempt at recovering from a drug problem—the one during my freshman year of college—was not really about addiction. I was not addicted to LSD. My first recovery was about recovering my sanity. At that point in my life, what I needed was *more* self-centeredness. My self had been blown so far off center that I didn't know which way was up. I was not ready for the ego-dissolving power of a high-dose psychedelic journey, not prepared for either the ecstasies or the agonies. I had no experienced guide to show me the way.

My cosmic union at Big Sur was wondrous, but I had no context in which to understand what was happening. I was convinced that I had experienced true love. So *that* was what it meant to be one with your lover. I had no doubt that we would be together for the rest of our lives. Then we broke up shortly after that second, "bad" trip.

I didn't see my old college girlfriend for more than three decades. Then, suddenly, she stumbled across my name and tracked me down via the Internet. At the time, I was new to sobriety and had recently started a book about the psychedelic sixties.* I was thinking about her and our Big Sur communion the very day I got her email. We later got together, and I asked her about her version of what happened to us. Her memory of that time reminded me that this craziness had all been going on in my head. I had never really expressed it to her or anyone else. She was only vaguely aware of my bad trip. She remembered being put off by my "dark energy," and that she had then moved on to another lover and the rest of her life.

My agonizing trip and its psychotic aftermath were steeped in the deep disappointment and self-doubt that followed our breakup. I remember thinking, "What a fool! How could I believe all that crap about us

*The Harvard Psychedelic Club: How Timothy Leary, Ram Dass, Huston Smith, and Andrew Weil Killed the Fifties and Ushered in a New Age for America.

being one forever?" Looking back on it now, I see that I restored my sanity by building a great wall around my heart and soul. My ego had been blown away, and the only way I could recover from that trauma was to fortify my defenses to withstand any future attack on my sense of self. My "spiritual journey" over the past few decades has been about finding a safe way to—brick by brick—tear down that wall of self-centeredness.

Unfortunately, my freshman orientation packet at UC Berkeley had not included a copy of Gerald Heard's 1963 essay on LSD, which was titled "Can This Drug Enlarge Man's Mind?" Heard warned that LSD should be taken only with "the greatest care," and then only in the presence of "competent researchers." By the early 1960s he had become more skeptical about whether psychedelic drugs could supercharge the evolutionary march toward what he called "super-consciousness." LSD might provide an *experience* of the great mysteries, but it offered no instant answers. "It is true that mystics and saints have reported, time and again, 'out-of-this-world,' indescribable experiences that did change their lives and bring a 'better order' in their living. But these experiences came as the result of many years of severe mental and physical discipline carried out within a doctrinal frame of reference, which often brought them to the brink of insanity." For most people, Heard wrote, the psychedelic experience "remains a beautiful anomaly, a gradually fading wonder—fading because it has no relevance to 'the life of quiet desperation' which Thoreau saw most of us living and which we cannot help but live."

EIGHT

Sixties

My own belief is that, though they may start by
being something of an embarrassment, these
new mind changers will tend in the long run
to deepen the spiritual life of the communities
in which they are available. . . . From being an
activity mainly concerned with symbols, religion
will be transformed into an activity concerned
mainly with experience and intuition.

Aldous Huxley, *Saturday Evening Post*, 1958

Something happened between Gerald Heard's warning to psychedelic
voyagers to proceed with caution and my mind-blowing acid trips of
1972. The sixties happened. This would not go down as a decade remembered for its cautious, reasoned approach to spiritual growth and social
change. By the end of "the sixties," which came sometime in the mid-
1970s, we'd start looking back on this era as the Dionysian decade.

Much of this can be ascribed to economics and demographics. Waves
of baby boomers born in the prosperous two decades following World
War II came crashing onto the shores of mainstream culture. They came
of age and gave birth to the sixties' counterculture. By my reckoning, the
era began in earnest with the 1963 assassination of President Kennedy
and ended with the Nixon resignation in 1974.

That decade saw the maturation of the civil rights movement, the sexual revolution, the successful organizing of young people to stop the war in Vietnam, the rise of rock and roll, the birth of the feminist movement, and the flowering of the psychedelic drug subculture. Jim Morrison, the stoned prophet of reckless abandon, summed it up in nine words: "We want the world and we want it . . . NOW!"

It may seem a long way from the intellectual musing of Aldous Huxley to the libertine lyrics of Jim Morrison, but in the time line of the 1960s they are separated by only a few seasons. Huxley died at his home in Los Angeles on November 22, 1963, on the day President Kennedy was gunned down in Dallas. In the summer of 1965, a UCLA film school graduate named Jim Morrison met Ray Manzarek, a composer and keyboard player, on Venice Beach in Los Angeles. Manzarek had just met a drummer at his meditation class. They formed a band and decided to name it after one of their favorite books, *The Doors of Perception*.

Aldous Huxley, Gerald Heard, and Bill Wilson set the stage for the spiritual revolution of the 1960s and 1970s. They distilled the spirits of organized religion into a powerful new blend that would help change the way Americans practice their faith and live their lives. These changes are so pervasive that many fail to notice them. At first glance, we might see rising religious fundamentalism among Muslims, Christians, Jews, and other true believers. There seems to be less peace and love, and more holy war, more religious intolerance. It's hard to ignore the noisy and violent pockets of religious extremism at home and abroad, but surveys of the American religious landscape paint a different picture.

They show *rising* religious tolerance.

According to the 2008 Pew survey, 70 percent of Americans affiliated with a religion or denomination said they agreed with the statement "many religions can lead to eternal life." Even a surprising 57 percent of those calling themselves "evangelical Christians" stated they believed there was more than one way to heaven.

In another Pew survey, in 2009, two out of three Americans expressed belief in or reported having experience with at least one of the following spiritual concepts or phenomena: reincarnation, astrology, "spiritual energy," yoga as spiritual practice, the "evil eye," making spiritual contact with the dead, or consultation with a psychic.

The American Religious Identification Survey of 2008 found that those who claimed "no religion" were the only demographic group that grew in every state within the last eighteen years. Between 1990 and 2008, the number of those who claimed no religious affiliation nearly doubled, from 8 percent to 15 percent. Yet the majority of these Americans still pray, meditate, or believe in God. They are, in other words, "spiritual but not religious." They are more likely to practice mix-and-match spirituality, to take a little from East and West, to go to church on Sunday and the yoga studio on Monday. They are more interested in religious experience and less concerned with religious dogma.

There are other statistics to back this up. Pollsters with the Gallup organization asked, "Do you think of spirituality more in a personal and individual sense or more in terms of organized religion and church doctrine?" Almost three-quarters said "personal and individual." Gallup found that one-third of the American population now describe themselves as "spiritual but not religious."

Nine out of ten Americans believe in God. But what kind of God? More and more of us envision an abstract, impersonal force or intelligence as opposed to an anthropomorphic deity. Another poll found that more than eight out of ten Americans saw God as "everywhere and in everything," opposed to "someone somewhere."

Princeton sociologist Robert Wuthnow has identified a shift from a "dwelling spirituality," in which a "spiritual habitat [such as a church] defines one's relationship to God," to a "seeking spirituality," where "we seek God in many different venues." His research also finds that the number of people who believe the Bible is the literal word of God has "dropped remarkably since the 1960s."

One of the most dramatic shifts in the spirituality of the baby boom generation has been a declining loyalty to the religion in which the individual was raised. In 1958, only one in twenty-five Americans said he or she had left the religion or religious denomination of his or her childhood. By 1984, one out of three of us had switched religions or religious denominations.

The new American spirituality that came of age in the 1960s and 1970s is experiential, antiauthoritarian, eclectic, utilitarian, and therapeutic.

It's not about believing in God as much as experiencing the power of the divine. It shows a deep distrust of religious hierarchies. It draws from the world's religions. It's about stress reduction, not salvation. It's practical, not pious. It's as much about feeling good as about being good.

There were many forces behind these changes, but one of them is most certainly the fact that, in the three decades following Huxley's prophesy about "these new mind changers," more than twenty-three million Americans tried LSD. Psychedelic drug use would explode in the 1960s and 1970s as the consciousness-expanding torch was passed from Huxley and Heard to a more volatile trio—Timothy Leary, Richard Alpert, and Ken Kesey.

.   .   .   .   .

Aldous Huxley and Bill Wilson were already in their sixties when the 1960s began. Gerald Heard had just reached the eighth decade of his life. Wilson and Heard would make it through the 1960s, but time was not on their side. Medical problems took their toll. Heard had a series of strokes, and Wilson was slowly dying from a nicotine habit he could never shake. But that wasn't the only reason for their seeming irrelevance. The times were changing too fast for Heard and Wilson to keep up with the whirlwind—even if they had stayed healthy.

Two Harvard researchers, Timothy Leary and Richard Alpert, would soon steal the show. They, along with Ken Kesey, the West Coast leader of the Merry Pranksters, would become the joyous ringmasters of the mindblowing circus that was the psychedelic sixties. The Beatles dropped acid, went to India, and started writing songs about being "within you and without you." Alpert made a pilgrimage to India, returned as Ram Dass, and emerged as the spiritual teacher best positioned to help psychedelic drug devotees find kinder, gentler means of mind expansion.

But it was Heard and Huxley who set up the circus tent. But Huxley would be the only one of these sixties icons to make it onto the cover of *Sgt. Pepper's Lonely Hearts Club Band*, the Beatles' 1967 psychedelic masterpiece. Huxley stands in the crowd right behind the Fab Four.

Huxley and Leary crossed paths in Cambridge, Massachusetts, in

the fall of 1960, a few months after Leary had his first magic mush-
room trip on his summer vacation down in sunny Mexico. Leary and
Alpert soon began a research and partying protocol called the Harvard
Psilocybin Project. Huxley happened to be at the nearby Massachusetts
Institute of Technology giving a series of lectures and hanging out with
his host, Huston Smith. Humphry Osmond also happened to be in town,
so he and Huxley and Leary met for dinner at a Boston restaurant. Their
encounter occurred the night John F. Kennedy was elected president of
the United States.

Huxley and Leary discussed the direction of psychedelic drug research in a series of letters they exchanged from 1961 to 1963. After seeing an exhibition of paintings by Max Ernst at the Museum of Modern
Art in New York, Huxley suggested that Leary recruit Ernst as a research
subject. "It might be interesting," Huxley wrote in the summer of 1961,
"to get in touch with him, find out what his normal state is, then give
him mushrooms or LSD and get him to compare his normal experiences
with his drug-induced ones."

After he was burned out of his house in the Hollywood Hills, Huxley
wrote to Leary saying that he'd lost more than all of his letters, diaries,
and papers. "Among the uncommon objects which vanished was the
bottle of psilocybin tablets you gave me—full but for a single dose. If you
have any more to spare, I would be grateful for a new supply."

In early 1962, Huxley replied to a letter from Leary in which the
Harvard researcher asked him if the Indian philosophy of Tantra could
help him understand the psychedelic experience. "LSD and the mushrooms should be used," Huxley wrote, "in the context of the basic Tan-
trik idea of the yoga of total awareness, leading to enlightenment within
the world of everyday experiences—which of course becomes the world
of miracle and beauty and divine mystery when the experience is what
it always ought to be."

Leary also corresponded with Heard, inviting him in the spring of
1961 to stay in his home in Newton, Massachusetts. Heard declined and
choose to stay in a nearby hotel, but by the following summer the two
were close enough that Heard was signing his letters to Leary: "Love,
Gerald."

Wilson, too, corresponded with Leary. In a letter sent in the summer of 1961, Wilson wrote that Huxley has "referred enthusiastically to your work." Wilson goes on to write that, "though LSD and some kindred alkaloids have had an amazingly bad press, there seems no doubt of their immense and growing value."

.   .   .   .   .   .

Bill Wilson didn't know it, but the bad press had only just begun. Leary and Alpert's psychedelic research project spun out of control and became a crusade. They were kicked out of Harvard in the spring of 1963 and thrust into the national spotlight as the spiritual leaders of the burgeoning drug culture. Leary christened himself "High Priest" and would go to such lengths in his campaign to turn on America that Richard Nixon would call the former Harvard researcher "the most dangerous man in America."

Huxley thought LSD should be carefully given to a select group of intellectuals, artists, and opinion leaders who would gradually influence the direction of the culture. In a letter to Humphry Osmond, Huxley explained why he chose *not* to talk about psychedelics in television interviews. "We still know very little about psychedelics, and, until we know a good deal more, I think the matter should be discussed, and the investigations described, in the relative privacy of learned journals, the decent obscurity of moderately highbrow books and articles. What one says on the air is bound to be misunderstood."

Leary and Alpert had no such reservations. They wanted to turn on everyone, all at once. Huxley saw the direction Leary was taking the psychedelic movement, and did not like what he saw. In another letter to Osmond, Huxley described Leary as a ticking time bomb. He saw that Leary had become a "nonsense-talking . . . mischievous Irish boy" whose obsession with "flouting convention" was bound to upset the Harvard authorities and set back the psychedelic movement. "I'm very fond of Timothy," Huxley wrote, "but why, oh why, does he have to be such an ass!"

Leary's crusade would eventually get him tossed in prison and inspire a backlash against serious scientific research into the beneficial uses of psychedelic drugs. That backlash would continue into the new millennium, which finally saw a blossoming of new, government-approved research projects, including one on the use of Ecstasy (MDMA) to treat returning Iraqi and Afghan war veterans suffering from post–traumatic stress disorder.

While Huxley favored a more cautious approach to spreading the psychedelic gospel, he quickly saw the positive impact that mind-expanding drugs could have in the West. His "mind changers" prophesy, highlighted at the start of this chapter, came two years before Leary had his first trip. "Biochemical discoveries," Huxley said, "will make it possible for large numbers of men and women to achieve a radical self-transcendence and a deeper understanding of the nature of things."

Huxley was right. Psychedelic drugs would inspire millions of young Americans in the coming generation to begin calling themselves "spiritual but not religious." But the impact of Heard and Huxley on the counterculture of the 1960s was about much more than drugs. The two would help lay the foundation for the human potential movement, which Michael Murphy and Richard Price would build upon at their Esalen Institute at Big Sur. Esalen provided the template for other "growth centers" that would spring up across the country and around the world in the last half of the twentieth century.

The human potential movement has its roots in the humanist ideas of nineteenth-century thinkers such as T.H. Huxley and in the early American psychology of William James, and it continued through the work of humanistic psychologists such as Abraham Maslow, Fritz Perls, Carl Rogers, and Rollo May. But the ideas that would take form in the human potential movement can be seen in some of the earliest writings of Aldous Huxley and Gerald Heard. Their fascination with psychic activity and paranormal phenomena in the 1930s and 1940s would later find expression in the so-called New Age movement of the 1970s and 1980s. That movement's emphasis on spiritualism and "channeled" teachings can be traced back to the Theosophical Society of Helena Blavatsky and Annie Besant, but Heard and Huxley helped keep those ideas alive in the middle decades of the twentieth century.

Huxley laid out the ideas that would become the human potential movement in a series of lectures he gave in 1959 at the University of California, Santa Barbara. He talked about how we must first satisfy our basic physical needs for food, shelter, and security. Then we need to face such psychological needs as our yearnings to love and be loved and feel a sense of belonging. We must then follow the way of Socrates and seek to know our true selves. Here many of us will face the greatest obstacle to self-knowledge, our neuroses. Huxley defines *neurosis* as "a fixation upon a single aspect of life, a looking at the world through one particular set of distorting lenses, and hence as the inability to see a wider angle of life and to perceive realistically what is going on around us."

What a great definition of addiction.

"We need to be sufficiently aware of the newness and uniqueness of every event here and how to be able to react appropriately and spontaneously to it," he said. "This business of being aware of everything within and without is a standard procedure in Buddhist, Tantric and Zen psychology. . . . Now, after so many years, it is coming to the surface and will prove to be of very great value." Huxley then moved on in his lecture to what he called "problems in love. . . . Love and knowledge go very closely together," he said. "Love without knowledge is largely impotent, and knowledge without love is frequently inhuman. . . . Our problem is to find some way in which we can make it more possible for more human beings to love in an aware and knowledgeably directed way."

Price, the Esalen cofounder, heard Huxley give this same lecture the following year at the University of California, San Francisco. At the time, Price was studying with Alan Watts at the American Academy of Asian Studies in San Francisco (now called the California Institute of Integral Studies). Murphy and Price wrote a letter to Huxley. They were heading down to Mexico and wanted to meet with him to talk about their ideas for their Big Sur property. Huxley told them he would be out of town when they were passing through Southern California, but he made two suggestions. Since they were going to Mexico, they should visit a place south of the border called Rancho la Puerta, a resort that offered health food, yoga classes, and self-improvement lectures. And on the way down, they might want to stop and meet a guy named Gerald Heard, an old friend of his who once ran an interesting little retreat center in the Santa Ana Mountains, a place called Trabuco College.

Murphy and Price met Heard at his cottage behind Margaret Gage's house, and they left spellbound. Heard told them about the "gymnasia for the mind" that he oversaw in the 1940s. It failed, but perhaps the time was right to try it again.

Murphy and Price would try again when they created Esalen. This time, the time was right. Huxley spent two days at the Big Sur resort in 1962, the same year Murphy and Price put on their first seminar series, which would feature Gerald Heard and a session devoted to a discussion of "drug-induced mysticism."

Aldous Huxley supplied the Sandoz LSD for Michael Murphy's first LSD trip in Mexico in 1962, a journey on which Huxley's second wife, Laura, served as Murphy's guide. Later, on the Esalen grounds in 1964, Murphy had a second LSD session, led by none other than Richard Alpert and Timothy Leary. Murphy stopped taking the drug in 1966. "Each trip got worse, more painful," Murphy told Leary scholar Robert Forte. "The whole message was, 'this is not good for you.'"

When I last spoke to Murphy, in the summer of 2011, a half century had passed since his first meeting with Gerald Heard in Santa Monica. Esalen was still going strong. "Gerald was a seminal influence for many people—for Aldous, and certainly for Dick and me," Murphy told me. "He was classically Irish. He embodied that Irish Druid spirit. He was a teller of tales. Some of his ideas were fanciful, but he was a true visionary."

.   .   .   .   .

It's the early 1980s and I've just begun my duties as the full-time religion reporter at the *San Francisco Examiner*. I'd snuck into the Esalen baths a few times back in the 1970s, but this is my first official visit. I've persuaded my editor that there's a good story to be found at the Esalen Institute at Big Sur, a leisurely three- to four-hour drive down Highway 1 from the city.

It's a brilliant afternoon on the coast, and I'm lying nude on an outdoor massage table getting the royal treatment from one of Esalen's sea-soned bodyworkers, who is also nude. She works my body in a most sensual way. There's nothing sexual about it, but *oh my God does it feel fine.* All I hear are the waves crashing against the cliffs below and the happy moan of another Esalen seminarian slowly sinking into the silky radiance of the natural hot springs. I open my eyes.

Behind the sun-bronzed body of my masseuse, I see butterflies dancing playfully in the cool ocean breeze. She tells me that these Monarch butterflies have stopped here on their two-thousand-mile migration to Mexico. They come to Big Sur to mate. The males spiral through the air in pursuit of females, coupling with their mates as they carry them aloft in acrobatic flight. My masseuse smiles. I close my eyes and feel the sun on my skin, just warm enough to balance the cool ocean breeze. The cynical reporter in me melts away. My heart fills with joy, and I'm struck by a profound realization.

"Jesus," I suddenly remember. "I'm actually getting paid for this!"

There's something about this spectacular stretch of coastline that opens my heart and frees my spirit. Sure, there are the obvious associations—my teenage pilgrimage up Highway 1 in the summer of 1970, and my psychedelic communion with my lover two years later. These are moments I long to relive, but there's more to it than that. Big Sur instills meaning in the story of my life. My first eighteen years were spent with my family, bouncing across the country from New Jersey to Ohio to Colorado to Southern California, running from the pain of the past. One of my ways of tuning out my parents' bitter arguments was—along with getting high—leaving our house and heading down to the cliffs and tide pools of the Palos Verdes Peninsula. Here there was nowhere to run, nowhere to go but off the cliff or into myself. Big Sur is another such place.

In his voluminous history of the Golden State, Kevin Starr traces the outlaw spirit that radiates from this isolated edge of the North American continent back to its obscure Indian tribes and early homesteaders. People have always come here looking for a place to hide. In the twentieth century, artists and poets, including Robinson Jeffers, came to Carmel and Big Sur in the aftermath of the great San Francisco earthquake and fire of 1906, followed by writers like Henry Miller and others fleeing the air-conditioned nightmare. In their wake came the Beats and the hippies and the other disillusioned seekers of truth. Big Sur is a land of extremes, of dark canyons and brilliant beaches, raging wildfires and freezing fog. It's a place that looks solid but is sliding into the sea. Its spirit was instilled in a culture that became "especially vibrant at mid-twentieth century." People came here looking for another way, and they turned this rugged stretch of the California coast into a place that "stood for art, rebellion, contemplative value, and transcendence."

In the 1960s and 1970s, the Esalen Institute attracted an eclectic collection of psychologists, spiritual teachers, movement therapists, and other purveyors of wit, wisdom, and joy. They offered what Esalen scholar Jeffrey Kripal calls "the religion of no religion."* To Kripal, "the history of Esalen can be read as an American moment in a much broader Tantric transmission from Asia to the West." For many spiritual seekers in my generation, "Tantra" brings to mind the exotic and the erotic, a magical means to enlightenment, through the practice of "sacred sex." But what Kripal is talking about is the importation of an esoteric blend of Hinduism, Buddhism, and Taoism. It's the idea that the universe we experience is "nothing other than the concrete manifestation of the divine energy of the godhead."

Kripal may be onto something. Michael Murphy certainly thinks so. But it's not my intention here to make Esalen fit into any grand theory. Esalen, it seems to me, is a place for people trying to find themselves, for those looking for direction in a time of transition, and I'm here for all of those reasons. I'm not really here to write a newspaper story. That's only an excuse. I have this bad habit of dividing time into decades—like "the sixties" or "my forties." It's one of my many ways of *not* being here now. On this trip, in the fall of 1983, I am leaving my twenties behind, but I'm also putting down the pipe dream that I am going to find love or the meaning of life by taking psychedelic drugs.

One of the teachers in residence this week is a Chinese-American t'ai

---

*This phrase comes from *The Religion of No Religion* (1953) by Stanford professor Frederic Spiegelberg. Murphy and Price were both Stanford undergraduates in the early 1950s and were deeply influenced by Spiegelberg.

chi teacher named Chungliang Al Huang. He has been teaching here since the mid-1960s, when he began leading workshops with Alan Watts on Chinese philosophy, calligraphy, and martial arts. Watts was another of my favorite authors in the 1970s. His books—unlike Huxley's and Heard's—were a joy to read. His message was deep, but he never seemed to take himself too seriously.

Here was a spiritual teacher I could follow. Watts's public pronouncements and private explorations of free love got him kicked out of the Anglican Church, where as a young man he had become an ordained priest. He was also a serious drinker. You could often hear the ice tinkling in his glass as Watts gave his talks in the 1970s over the airwaves at KPFA, the left-leaning public radio station in Berkeley.

Back in the early 1960s, Watts, along with Huxley and Heard, helped Esalen find its way. The institute's first mailing lists drew names from Watt's network at the American Academy of Asian Studies and from a directory of people who'd seen Gerald Heard at a series of lectures in San Francisco in the late 1950s.

Watts died from complications related to his alcoholism on November 16, 1973, the day after my twentieth birthday. He was fifty-eight, my age as I write these words. Watts's last piece of writing published in his lifetime was a preface to Huang's 1973 book, *Embrace Tiger, Return to Mountain—the Essence of T'ai Chi*. Watts's final project—published posthumously—was a collaboration with Chungliang titled *Tao: The Watercourse Way*.

Following the death of Alan Watts, Chungliang would find another mentor and Esalen coteacher in Joseph Campbell, the popular mythologist. Campbell was another of my favorite writers and thinkers, so much so that my editors at HarperCollins gave him a nod by titling my second book *Following Our Bliss*. In the introduction to that book, I quote one of my favorite Campbell lines. "People say that what we're all seeking is the meaning of life. I don't think that's what we're really seeking. I think that what we're seeking is an *experience* of *being* alive."

That's what I was seeking. It's what I had been after with drugs and alcohol. I felt more alive when I was high. But I'd finally come to the realization that I would have to find another way to follow my bliss.

Like many psychedelic drug devotees, I tried to rediscover that feeling through meditation, but sitting for hours on a meditation cushion was not my way. T'ai chi, the flowing meditation of movement, seemed better suited for my restless soul.

That state of being seemed where my mind, body, and spirit would go whenever I'd take my favorite drug, MDA. I began taking t'ai chi classes and studying the teachings of Lao-tzu and Chuang-tzu. T'ai chi was embodied meditation, a way to integrate body, mind, and spirit. It was a way for me to recall the feeling of psychedelics. T'ai chi certainly wasn't as intense, but a natural high does have its advantages.

It won't kill you.

Taoist teaching is paradoxical, but perhaps the crooked path points directly to the truth. T'ai chi is a way to experience the Tao. "T'ai chi exemplifies the most subtle principle of Taoism, known as wu-wei," Watts writes in his introduction to the book. "Literally, this may be translated as 'not doing,' but its proper meaning is to act without forcing—to move in accordance with the flow of nature's course which is signified by the word Tao, and is best understood from watching the dynamics of water. . . . As Lao Tzu said, although water is soft and weak it invariably overcomes the rigid and hard."

Or as Chungliang would say, "Don't push the river."

My first t'ai chi teachers were *serious* teachers. They taught a traditional form where the student mimics the teacher's form in every detail. When I saw Chungliang teach at Esalen in 1983, I saw another way to approach the practice. There was form to his teaching, but it was also free-form. It seemed a bit flaky, even silly at times, but it felt right. It was about feeling the spirit of the Tao, not imitating Chungliang. It was a dance—something to enjoy. It wasn't only a practice. It was a way of life.

Chungliang had an infectious, childlike spirit. I was hooked. So hooked, in fact, that I dropped my newsman skepticism, joined his merry band of Taoists, and followed him—twice in two years in the mid-1980s—all the way to China, to a remote region of Fujian province, to Wuyi Mountain.

We were among the first Westerners allowed to enter the district after China began reopening to the West in the 1970s. We would rise before sunrise and ascend stone stairways carved into the sides of cliffs in perfect symmetry with nature. One day, we wandered down a trail that seemed to end in a dark cave. Only when we got down on our knees and crawled through a small opening did we discover a hidden meadow of blossoming peach trees and an old monastery inhabited by two Taoist monks, one old and one young. It was so well hidden that it had survived the destruction of China's Cultural Revolution. Another day, we found a temple that was hidden during the rainy season behind a curtain of falling water.

I'd always loved Chinese landscape painting, those ephemeral depictions of Taoist temples floating on clouds or perched on outcroppings of rock, formations that seemed to rise from the earth like giant fingers pointing heavenward. I thought those painted scrolls were some mad monk's vision of the celestial kingdom, but when I came to Wuyi Mountain I saw that those old Chinese artists were simply painting the landscape as it is.

Chungliang's idea of bringing a band of artists, dancers, and assorted truth-seekers to this wonderland was not a new one. Such gatherings date back to the Six Dynasties, when Wang His-chih, China's greatest calligrapher, gathered forty-two of his friends in the Lan Ting, or "Orchid Pavilion," for a Purification Festival. It was the ninth year of Eternal Harmony, or by our reckoning, A.D. 353. Wang described the gathering in his famous Orchid Pavilion Preface: "Talented people, young and old, came. Here, lofty mountains and handsome peaks, thick forests and tall bamboos. Next, clear streams, rushing torrents. Like silver belts, they reflected both sides. With these, floating goblets on meandering waters. We sat down in groups. Although we did not have strings and pipes, we drank and chanted, enough to fully pour out our feelings."

Perhaps Chungliang Al Huang, in an earlier incarnation, lifted one of those meandering goblets, toasted the future, and vowed to return to the Orchid Pavilion. For, 1,632 years later, in the Year of the Ox, Chungliang's dream of resurrecting the Orchid Pavilion came true—right down to the floating wine goblets.

Thirty-eight talented people, young and old, gathered at the base of Great King Peak. We sat down in groups. We rose with the sun. We climbed 853 stone steps above Nine-Twist Stream and brought the spirit of Far-Flung Wisdom back to Heavenly Wandering Temple.

We spent one wondrous night there playing flutes, drinking Chinese brandy, and teaching our Chinese hosts how to sing the blues. We were a collection of thirty-four Americans, three Canadians, and a West German—a psychic from Manhattan, banker from San Francisco, school counselor from Iowa, flutist–dowser–retired sociology professor from Ohio, dance therapist from British Columbia, doctor from Duluth, psychologist from Beverly Hills, electrician from Toronto, Sufi priestess from Santa Cruz, California, and myself, a newspaper reporter looking for another way to get high. We brought New Age Americana, with its marvelous spontaneity and freeze-dried wisdom, to the People's Republic, planting a seed that, given the right conditions, might eventually blossom in this tradition-bound society or, if not there, at least within us.

China's reopening to the world would come screeching to a halt five years later in the horror in Tiananmen Square. But the seed of that spirit would stay with me, buried for a decade in the despair of addiction but ready to blossom when conditions were right.

Looking back, my time at Wuyi Mountain seems like a mystic dream, but it was real. We wandered through lush bamboo forests, looking up at mountain peaks with names like Jade Lady and Tiger Roaring. We sat by mountain streams that meandered between those peaks or, as the Chinese poets say, "mountain and water in perpetual embrace." We climbed up to ornate pagodas perched atop towering cliffs that were inscribed with centuries-old calligraphy, painted bright red. These giant poems always have multiple meanings. One of them was written as a warning to the king but also as practical advice for careless hikers. It would take another decade for me to see that it had warned me about the danger of looking for God by getting high on drugs. It read:

Perched high,
Contemplate danger.

Aldous Huxley's psychedelic baptism came as Maria, the love of his life, was dying of cancer. She'd had a mastectomy in 1952, a year before Aldous had his first mescaline trip, when it was already clear to Maria that the end was coming. She told a friend, "I mustn't die before Aldous. How would he manage without me?" By early 1955, Aldous could no longer remain in denial. "The news here is discouraging," he wrote in a letter to Humphry Osmond. "Maria is not getting better."

Maria died on February 12 with Aldous at her side. Just before Maria took her last breath, in peace and without struggle, Aldous leaned over and spoke softly in her ear. "I am with you," he said. "I will always be with you. I will be with you in that light, which is the central reality of our being. You are surrounded by my love, and by a greater love. Let go, my love. Leave your body here like a bundle of old clothes. Let yourself be carried away, like a child is carried, into the heart of the rosy light of love. No memories, no regrets, no looking back. Only the light. This pure being, this love."

Aldous and Maria's son, Matthew, and a close family friend were at Maria's bedside. After her passing, they recited a passage from the Tibetan Book of the Dead. Aldous read with tears streaming down his face, but in a quiet, unbroken voice. Gerald Heard would later recall that Maria had "been wonderfully and gently brave through it all." She was buried two days later at Rose Dale Memorial Park in Los Angeles, with a small group of close friends, including Heard and Christopher Isherwood, in attendance.

Huxley would revisit Maria's death in a scene in his final novel, *Island*, where he presents his utopian dream, the counterpoint to the dystopian nightmare of *Brave New World*. Lakshmi, one of the main characters in *Island*, is on her deathbed, surrounded by family, friends, and unconditional love. "Lightly, my darling, lightly," she's told. "Even when it comes to dying. Nothing ponderous, or portentous, or emphatic. No rhetoric, no tremolos, no self-conscious persona putting on its celebrated imitation of Christ or Goethe or Little Nell. And, of course, no theology, no metaphysics. Just the fact of dying and the fact of the Clear Light. So throw away all your baggage and go forward."

After Maria died, Huxley threw himself back into his work, finishing a series of articles for *Esquire* magazine and his second long essay on the psychedelic journey, titled *Heaven and Hell*. He scheduled another mescaline session—this time with a therapist in Los Angeles known for her ability to bring up repressed childhood memories.

Aldous explained his goal in a letter to Humphry Osmond. "I decided that it might be interesting to find out why so much of my childhood is hidden from me, so that I cannot remember large areas of early life." But no memories were recovered, he told Osmond. "Instead, there was something of incomparably greater importance; for what came through the closed door was the realization—not the knowledge, for this wasn't verbal or abstract—but the direct, total awareness, from the inside, so to say, of Love as the primary and fundamental cosmic fact. The words, of course, have a kind of indecency and must necessarily ring false, seem like twaddle. But the fact remains."

That same month, in October 1955, Huxley had his first experience with LSD. He took it in the presence of Laura Archera, a family friend who'd been spending more and more time with Aldous in the months following Maria's death. It was a moderate dose, and Huxley reported no fantastic visions. Huxley and Archera listened to Bach's First Brandenburg Concerto. Laura did not take the drug herself, but when she got up to change the record she strongly felt Maria's presence in the room. It almost seemed like she *was* Maria. Laura didn't say a word about it to Aldous, who nevertheless turned to her and said, "Don't ever be anyone but yourself."

Laura Huxley said Aldous took about a dozen psychedelic drug trips in the final decade of his life, including at least one group trip with Heard and several psychiatrists at the Margaret Gage estate. "It was never casual," she said. "It was absolutely one of the most important things we did. It was never saying, 'Let's have whiskey and soda,' or 'Let's have LSD.' We would plan a psychedelic session very carefully."

One month after his first LSD trip, Huxley returned to give a lecture at the Vedanta Society in Hollywood. It had been nearly two decades since he and Heard had first settled in Southern California and begun their association with Swami Prabhavananda. The swami did not approve of Huxley's praise of mescaline-induced mysticism in *The Doors of*

Perception. In his talk, Huxley mentioned neither the book nor his recent experience with LSD, but the subject kept coming up during a question-and-answer period. One of Prabhavananda's American devotees challenged Huxley on his advocacy of "chemical yoga," asking if he really thought one could have a true "union with God" by taking drugs.

"If we look at the history of religion, we see that drugs have been used from time immemorial," Huxley said. "Without question, we are on the verge of developing any number of chemicals, such as lysergic acid, that can produce extraordinary changes in consciousness—some desirable and some not, but I don't see why some of them might not be considered most excellent."

Another member of the audience asked whether drug-induced mysticism wasn't "abnormal." Huxley answered by noting that there are many ways to induce states of spiritual transcendence. There are traditional methods like fasting or meditation, he said. Then he cited new research showing that subjects put in sensory deprivation chambers soon begin having "full-blown mystical experiences." "Isn't this what the Tibetan Buddhists do in caves in the Himalayans, or what Christian hermits seek by living in a restrictive environment?" Huxley asked. "They are having tremendous visionary experiences. Is that normal or abnormal?"

Around this same time, Huxley discussed the use of liquor as a mind-changing substance in an essay he wrote for his friend Bill Wilson, who published it in the November 1957 edition of the *A.A. Grapevine*, the organization's monthly newsletter. "Alcohol is one of the oldest and certainly the most widely used of all consciousness-changing drugs," Huxley writes. "Unfortunately, it is a rather inefficient and, at the same time, a rather dangerous drug." He cites the Hebrew prophet Isaiah, who denounces priests and prophets who have "erred through strong drink." "Traditionally, Dionysus was the god of prophecy and inspiration," Huxley notes. "But, alas, the revelations of alcohol are not altogether reliable."

Huxley ends his essay in the AA newsletter by praising Wilson's fellowship for inspiring "self-transcendence through social means," noting his and Wilson's shared belief that "the spirituality of small-groups is a very high form of religion."

That same year, in 1957, Huxley appeared as a guest on the NBC television network program *Look Here*. He faced a series of hostile questions from host Martin Agronsky, who interviewed Huxley in a TV studio overlooking New York City's Central Park. "You are always predicting these totalitarian developments," Agronsky said. "Doesn't this indicate a contempt on your part for your fellow human beings?"

"I don't feel any contempt," Huxley replied, "but I do feel there are tendencies in the modern world that are pushing people in that direction."

Agronsky remained on the attack. "Alfred Kazin said your books show a dislike for people and a fear of sex."

Huxley was nonplussed. He sat in his chair twiddling his fingers and watching the smoke rise from Agronsky's cigarette. "Maybe other people know one better than oneself," Huxley replied, smiling.

Agronsky went on to cite critics who questioned Huxley's literary abilities, but the author refused to get defensive. "I don't think I'm a born novelist," he replied. "I'm an essayist who writes novels, and sometimes they come off well and sometimes they don't."

In March 1956, Huxley's family and friends were shocked by news reports that Aldous and Laura had married. The two had hoped to have a secret wedding, but the story of their nuptials was told in newspapers the following day. "NOVELIST HUXLEY WEDS VIOLINIST," the *Los Angeles Times* reported. Aldous and Laura had driven across the California-Arizona border to quietly tie the knot at an establishment that called itself the Drive-in Wedding Chapel. "As you have probably read in the paper," Aldous wrote to his son, "Laura Archera and I got married today, at Yuma in a naïve hope of privacy that has turned into publicity all the same. You remember her, I am sure—a young woman who used to be a concert violinist. . . . She is twenty years younger than I am, but doesn't seem to mind."

Aldous would spend the last eight years of his life with Laura. Cancer would take his life, as it had taken his beloved Maria. Christopher Isherwood remembered both Aldous and Maria as "great connoisseurs of doctors" who would "consult absolutely anyone, at least once, in a spirit of disinterested experimentation." "Aldous was an exceptionally sensitive human instrument, and his heath was correspondingly variable,"

Isherwood recalled. "He suffered from all kinds of ailments; but they seemed to interest him quite as much as they distressed him."

But by October 1963, it was clear that Aldous would soon be passing. Isherwood visited Huxley at the Cedars of Lebanon Hospital in Los Angeles in early November. "Aldous looked like a withered old man, grey-faced, with dull blank eyes," Isherwood recalled. "He spoke in a low, hoarse voice which was hard to understand. I had to sit directly facing him because it hurt him to turn his head." Huxley told Isherwood that his writing days were over, adding, "I feel more and more out of touch with people."

Huxley was taken home on November 15, 1963. He lived another week. He'd told Laura that he wanted to leave this world in a psychedelic state, and Laura was ready. Sometime around noon, on November 22, Aldous asked Laura for a pad of paper. He scribbled the following words, barely legible. "Try LSD 100 mm intramuscular." In the next room, a nurse and a doctor who'd come by the house to assist stared blankly at a black-and-white television set, which was showing the first footage of the assassination of President Kennedy. The doctor refused to inject Aldous with LSD, so Laura did it herself.

"You are going towards Maria's love," Laura told her husband, "with my love."

Bill Wilson was among a small group of close friends and family to receive a long letter from Laura Huxley describing the way Aldous left this world. Wilson's secretary, Nell Wing, said he was "possibly the only person outside his family to receive it."

Gerald Heard, it turns out, was at Esalen the day Huxley died. Mike Murphy and Dick Price led a cliff-side vigil with Gerald and Jay Michael Barrie, who would spend much of the 1960s caring for Heard in his final years of life. There was a small earthquake on the coast that day.

After Huxley's death, Heard looked back on his thirty-two-year friendship with Aldous and his "long and intimate struggle with the obscure issues lumped together under the name of 'religion.'" "The tempered metal of Huxley's mind was made of that amalgam of curiosity with skepticism," Heard wrote. "The web of his thinking was shot with doubt as to systems, with their closed 'laws' and sacred canons."

·   ·   ·   ·   ·

Gerald Heard began the 1960s by releasing a trilogy of record albums about death—the death of the body, or perhaps the death of the ego. His January 1961 album, *Explorations, Volume 2: Survival, Growth and Re-birth,* can be heard, like the Tibetan Book of the Dead, as a guide for living and for dying, or as the soundtrack for one of those sometimes blissful, sometimes terrifying, LSD trips when one's body disappears.

"Suddenly, you are finding yourself free from all burden of the body and all the dreaming dimness of the mind," Heard intones. "Listen with vital care. Now you know that the soul does not die with the body. . . . This is no dream. You have woken from the dream. . . . Here where time itself falls back and the timeless begins to reveal itself. Here where that which is unreal and a dream dissolves like a cloud and the real is laid bare. . . . Stepping out from this dim world into the yonder light as then this great change comes upon you. There is now being lifted from you the confining armour and defenses of the body."

"Remember," Heard continues, "who you truly are and listen to me, to this voice which gives words to what you know and gives understanding to what you must experience. . . . All doing is illusion unless it can be known as being. All acts are vain if they cannot be seen as the door to understanding. . . . As inevitably as the comet plunges into the sun, your essential nature now must seek its union with the infinite sun of all being."

As usual, Heard's album was a few years ahead of its time. In 1964, Timothy Leary, Richard Alpert, and Ralph Metzner would release their own guide for an acid trip, *The Psychedelic Experience: A Manual Based on the Tibetan Book of the Dead.*

Two of the most influential Americans Heard initiated were Henry and Clare Boothe Luce, which helps explain why the publications of Luce's Time-Life empire ran some of the most positive stories about the early years of psychedelic research. There was a glowing, richly illustrated *Life* story in the summer of 1957 by R. Gordon Wasson, a New York banker and amateur mycologist who liked to travel the world with his Russian-born wife in search of magic mushrooms. Later, in the 1960s,

Time ran a rave review of Leary-inspired LSD research under the headline "Mysticism in the Lab."

Heard's friendship with Henry and Clare dated back to the 1940s. Even before her 1935 marriage to Henry Luce, Clare Boothe was a rising writer and editor in American media. She was ambitious—some would say ruthless. "She used sex, street smarts, acid humor and money to plot a career more improbable than anything in her own fiction and drama," her biographer writes. "She confessed to a 'rage for fame.'"

Clare worked her way up the chain of command to become one of the top editors at *Vanity Fair*, and then married one of the nation's wealthiest and most powerful publishers. But the death of her only child—a daughter from her brief first marriage to a wealthy alcoholic—in 1944 forced Clare to reexamine her life. She fell into a depression and turned to religion and psychotherapy in her search for another way of living.

That search led her to Gerald Heard. They began a friendship and correspondence that continued into the 1960s. Heard was her spiritual advisor, a role that became clear to me after I spent a day looking through their letters, which can be found in one of the special collections at the Library of Congress in Washington, D.C. It was hard staying focused on Gerald Heard, for Clare Boothe Luce wrote to and received letters from a who's who of American cultural and political leaders. She was elected to Congress in 1942 to represent Fairfield County, Connecticut, and she later served as the U.S. ambassador to Italy. She corresponded with Sir Winston Churchill, Walt Disney, William Randolph Hearst, Alfred Hitchcock, Herbert Hoover, Chiang Kai-shek, John F. Kennedy, Joseph Kennedy, Cole Porter, Father Thomas Merton, and Gertrude Stein.

One of the more intriguing lines in the Heard correspondence is from a July 26, 1949, letter from Clare to Gerald written not long after the collapse of Trabuco College. "I wish that I could write with utmost frankness about why your great spirit does not carry the force it could. You wouldn't agree, of course, but it would make me feel fine to have said it. . . . Now why did I slip into that?!"

Over the years, Henry and Clare became increasingly close to Gerald Heard and Jay Michael Barrie. Heard and Barrie spent holidays together and vacationed with the Luces. On December 15, 1959, Heard introduced

Clare and Henry to the wonders of LSD. "The LSD experience," Heard wrote to Clare, "is a death-deliverance experience and those that share it can have a rapport which is a profound communion. . . . This [LSD] is the free gift of God which He may mediate through them and they themselves may receive from Him as His supreme reward."

In the spring of 1962, Barrie wrote to Clare, "Since we left you we have both had a most wonderful (feeble word!) experience. On Easter Sunday we voyaged (literally!) to outer space! Gerald, Sid [Sidney Cohen], two other people and I took a 'journey'—and what a journey! Out of thirty times which I have taken the journey this is only the second time that I felt I had to at least attempt to get [write] some of it down."

In the final years of Gerald's life, the Luces provided some financial assistance to Heard and Barrie, including money for two European vacations. Beginning in 1966, a series of strokes left Heard bedridden. Clare set up a short-lived foundation in Heard's name to fund studies in Christian mysticism.

Heard was a mystic, but he was also a scientist, philosopher, mystery writer, historian, and more. Writing under the pen name D. B. Vest, he contributed to the early gay liberation movement with a series of articles on the evolutionary and spiritual significance of homosexuality. Huxley called him one of those rare individuals (Aldous was one himself) who found "his mental home on the vacant spaces between the pigeonholes." "The pigeonholes must be there because we can't avoid the academic specialization," Huxley said, "but what we do need are a few people who run about on the woodwork between the pigeonholes and peek into all of them and see what can be done. They are not closed to disciplines, but they don't happen to fit into any of the categories that are considered valid by the present educational system."

John V. Cody, a longtime scholar of Heard's work, said Heard had "influenced the thought of our time, directly or indirectly, to an extent that will not be appreciated for another fifty years. . . . Heard was, in a nutshell, a scientific shaman . . . a prophet of postmodern consciousness. . . . A fascinating hermetic figure, he aimed at bringing to birth a postmodern, psychologically aware mythos that would empower humans in new ways of being."

According to Jay Michael Barrie, "Gerald Heard felt his role was similar to that of a cuckoo bird, which lays its eggs in the nests of other species of birds. Heard, preferring anonymity to the limelight, would sow his ideas and allow others to develop and receive credit for them."

Jean Houston, a psychologist and early leader in the human potential movement, knew Heard during the final decade of his life. In the early 1960s, when she was a twenty-three-old graduate student, Houston was asked to review a manuscript by the seventy-three-year-old Heard. The long treatise was wildly speculative—too dramatic, too daring, and too original. Much of it was outrageous, but the manuscript had "a core of truth that would not go away." It haunted her. The book would be published in 1964 as *The Five Ages of Man*.

Houston knew the book would be ignored by critics and read by few, but she also knew that Heard would have a seminal influence on the spirituality of the 1960s and beyond. "When I knew him," she recalled, "Gerald Heard was a beautiful old gentleman of boundless curiosity, elegant playfulness, and a passion for discovery. We would walk down New York City's Madison Avenue together, and his long, poetic hands would carve out the air in front of him, his bushy eyebrows would dance arcs of questions, and he would laugh as a child might laugh when some inquiry met with a response that brought our worlds of interests together."

Gerald Heard died at his Santa Monica home on August 14, 1971. He was eighty-one. The next day, Christopher Isherwood wrote in his diary that he longed to "tell the brute stodgy thick-skinned world that it has lost one of its few great mythmakers and revealers of life's wonder."

. . . . .

My father died in the fall of 1995 in his own bed in Santa Rosa, California, with his fourth wife, Valeska, at his side. I wasn't there. I was drunk.

It was a typical night of carousing. We started out at the M&M Tavern at the corner of Fifth and Howard, just down the block from the *Chronicle*. By now, I'd become one of the old drunks. I was drinking with a young reporter and his wife. We wound up moving on to another bar in North Beach, and then another in the Tenderloin. We were probably looking for

drugs. I don't remember where we went after that. I do remember getting ticked off at my young friend about something and good-naturedly
stubbing out my cigarette on the back of his hand. His flesh sizzled, but
he didn't flinch. He laughed. He was as drunk as I was. I only remember
this because he had a wound on his hand for weeks, and the story was
retold many times.

His wife was a beauty and liked to flirt. At a certain point in the evening the three of us were discussing the size of women's breasts. I said
something about how her breasts were small but very nice. "Small!" she
replied. "You call these small?" She lifted up her pullover and proudly
displayed them. That's the last thing I remember. I woke up on their
couch with their cat attacking my feet. I looked at my watch and saw
that I was already late for work. I found some aspirin in their medicine
cabinet and downed four of them. The couple had a little flat on Nob Hill
that was only about a fifteen-minute walk, downhill, to the newspaper.

There were nine messages on my voicemail. *Shit,* I thought. I must
have missed some big story. I'd slipped out of the office the previous
afternoon to ride over to Oakland to score some coke and had never
returned or checked my messages. It was before cell phones, or at least
before I carried one around all the time. The messages were from my
stepmother, my sister, and my ex-wife. It was the first time my ex-wife
had called me since our divorce.

My dad was dying. I didn't get there in time. I started beating myself
up as I drove across town, over the Golden Gate Bridge and up Highway
101 to Santa Rosa. Somewhere in Marin County I came to the conclusion
that Dad would have wanted me to be out drinking the night he died. He
would have loved hearing the story about the girl in the bar.

My father was a sailor, so it's not surprising that my fondest memories of him involve water. Some of my first memories are of standing tall
on his shoulders in the shallow waters of some lake in Ohio. I felt ten
feet tall and probably was, since he was six foot six. In Colorado, we'd sit
alongside little rivers in the Rocky Mountains fishing for rainbow trout.
He'd catch fish and I wouldn't. "Let me tell you a secret, kiddo," he said.
"You've got to think like a fish." Off the beach in Southern California,
he'd float in the sea on his back with his hands crisscrossed behind his

head like a pillow. He'd fall asleep floating in the ocean until a wave would crash over him, pushing him underwater, but then he'd pop up to the surface in the same position like nothing had happened.

Around the time he died I'd been trying to get back into my meditation practice. I was reading books by the Vietnamese Zen master Thich Nhat Hanh, whom I'd interviewed at a monastery in the Santa Cruz Mountains. My father was not a religious man, so I struggled to come up with something to say about him and his life and his death at a memorial I organized for his friends and our family. I wound up telling the story about him and the waves and read a passage by Thich Nhat Hanh.

> Some waves on the ocean are high and some are low. Waves appear to be born and die. But if we look more deeply, we see that the waves, although coming and going, are also water, which is always there. Notions like high and low, birth and death, can be applied to waves, but water is free of such distinctions.
>
> Once you are capable of touching the water, you will not mind the coming and going of the waves. You are no longer concerned about the birth and the death of the wave. You are no longer afraid.

· · · · · ·

Bill Wilson was not a child of the sixties, but he did have his moments.

Alcoholics Anonymous began as a self-help fellowship for white businessmen and other professionals who were drinking themselves to death. Pick up a copy of the Big Book today and it reads like it was written by a committee of salesmen. That's because it was. "A business which takes no regular inventory usually goes broke," it advises. "We did exactly the same thing in our lives."

There is much wisdom in the Big Book, but its tone initially turned me off. So did my early encounters with "AA Nazis." There's a fundamentalist element in AA—members who view the Big Book as Holy Scripture that can never be changed, even the sexist sections. Many women must gag when they get to chapter 8. It's titled "To Wives," and it urges patience with and understanding for the alcoholic husband who chases women. "Try not to condemn your alcoholic husband no matter what he says or does," the book advises. "When he angers you, remember that he is very ill."

It warns that the wives of early AA members often had to put up with philandering husbands. "Sometimes there were other women. How heart-breaking was their discovery; how cruel to be told they understood our men as we did not!" The chapter goes on to warn that the wife of an alcoholic "must not expect too much. His ways of thinking and doing are the habits of years. Patience, tolerance, understanding and love are the watchwords." To many women, the chapter must read like helpful hints on how to stay happy while playing the role of long-suffering wife, which was the way of Lois Wilson.

By the 1960s and 1970s, the Big Book seemed hopelessly out of date. Many young people of my generation were struggling with their addiction to drugs other than alcohol. Yet to this day many AA meetings still discourage members from talking about their addiction to heroin, speed, pot, cocaine, or prescription drugs. Bill Wilson appeared to be of mixed mind about whether AA should expand its fellowship to include all kinds of addicts. In a 1968 missive that has come to be known as "Bill W.'s Letter about Hippies in A.A.," he encouraged "thoughtful A.A.s" to welcome drug addicts to open meetings, which are open to the general public, but not to closed meetings, where "the only requirement for membership is the desire to stop drinking."

"We know that we cannot do everything for everybody with an addiction problem," he said.

While Wilson doubted that AA could help hardcore heroin and cocaine addicts, he thought it might be useful for "hippies who have LSD or marijuana troubles. . . . Many of these kids appear to be alcoholics also, and they are flocking into A.A., often with excellent results."

Bill began to change his mind about the hippies after he ran into four of them in 1968 at a convention of young AA members. "I saw one young gal prancing down the hall, hair flying, in a miniskirt, wearing love beads and the works," he recalled. "I thought, 'Holy smoke, what now!' She told me she was the oldest member of the young people's group in her area—age twenty-two! They had kids as young as sixteen." Curious about this new development in his fellowship, the seventy-three-year-old AA founder took the hippie girl and her friends out to lunch. "They were absolutely wonderful," Wilson said. "All of them said they had had some kind of drug problem, but had kicked that, too."

Wilson ends his "Letter about Hippies" by urging the AA old-timers to welcome these young seekers into the fold. "We shall have to put up with some unconventional nonsense—with patience and with good humor, let's hope." These seekers with "LSD or marijuana troubles" could form their own meetings within AA. Those with problems with heroin and similar drugs, Wilson said, were free to set up their own fellowship along AA lines. If they did so, he said, "we need deny them only the A.A. name."

That's what happened. Many people who struggle with alcohol and other drugs find a place in AA, especially at meetings where alcoholics are free to talk about their struggles with other addictive substances. Then there are other twelve-step fellowships, the largest of which is Narcotics Anonymous. It grew out of an AA meeting in Los Angeles in 1953. By 2007, Narcotics Anonymous had developed into a worldwide fellowship of more than 25,000 local groups. That same year, AA reported that its 1.8 million members were meeting in more than 106,000 local groups scattered around the world.

Over the last three decades, other twelve-step fellowships have been formed for people addicted to everything from marijuana to cocaine, from sex to shopping. There's even a twelve-step group for Christians trying to break free from religious fundamentalism. Then there are the many "codependency" groups for people addicted to living with other addicts. Lois Wilson founded Al-Anon, the largest of those fellowships, in 1951.

Bill Wilson's inability to remain faithful to Lois led to the founding of another group that split off from AA in the early 1960s. Tom Powers, a former ad man who worked closely with Bill W., met Wilson in the early 1940s. In 1961, Powers began his own organization called All Addicts Anonymous. He saw the need for a self-help organization that would help people dealing with all kinds of addictive behavior, from alcoholism to compulsive sexual activity.

Powers had quit drinking, but it took him another five years to control his impulse to have sexual affairs. Then Powers spent the next five years trying to convince Wilson that he had to face the fact that he was a sex addict. Powers told Wilson that he thought his struggle with depression was caused, at least in part, by the guilt he felt over his unfaithfulness to Lois. "Bill would always agree with me. 'I know,' he'd say, 'you're right.' Then just when I would think we were finally getting somewhere, he would say, 'But I can't give it up.'" Powers continues: "When I would press him as to why the hell not, he would start rationalizing. What would really kill me is when he'd say, 'Well, you know, Lois has always been more like a mother to me.' Which somehow was supposed to make it all right for him to cheat on her."

"Besides what he was doing to the women he was chasing and to Lois," Powers said, "his behavior was a huge source of controversy in A.A. He would be very blatant about it, and there were times when it seemed like the reaction to a particularly flagrant episode would end up destroying everything he had worked for. But then people would scurry around and smooth things over, or cover it all up."

The section in the Big Book on sexual infidelity has Bill Wilson written all over it. "One set of voices cry that sex is a lust of our lower nature, a base necessity of procreation. Then we have the voices who cry for sex and more sex; who bewail the institution of marriage; who think that most of the troubles of the race are traceable to sex causes. They think we do not have enough of it, or that it isn't the right kind. They see its significance everywhere. One school would allow man no flavor for his fare and the other would have us all on a straight pepper diet. We want to stay out of this controversy."

Wilson was a full-flavored sexual connoisseur. He goes on to address the delicate question—especially for him—of whether a husband who sobers up must confess his sexual affairs to his wife. Making such amends is one of the central practices in AA. "We must be willing to make amends where we have done harm," Wilson writes, "provided that we do not bring about still more harm in doing so." Let's call that line "the Bill Wilson escape clause."

In the mid-1950s, around the time of his LSD experimentation, Wilson began a fifteen-year-long affair with a woman named Helen Wynn. They met at an AA meeting when Helen was new to sobriety. He was in his early sixties. She was an attractive woman in her early forties. According to Francis Hartigan, who worked as Lois Wilson's secretary, this affair "was different than any he had before." "Bill Wilson and Helen Wynn had an intimate, and at least in the early years, a passionate relationship," Hartigan writes in his biography of Bill Wilson. "At age sixty, Bill Wilson may have found a soul mate."

Wilson got Helen a job at the AA headquarters in New York, where they would rendezvous during his frequent overnight visits to the city. Wynn participated in some of Wilson's LSD sessions in New York, which may explain why this affair was different from the others.

Did Lois know? "By the time Bill and Helen met, Lois had been long practiced in ignoring her husband's peccadilloes. From all the evidence, Bill never stopped loving Lois. . . . During the years Helen and Bill were together, Lois seems always to have had first call on Bill's time and to have participated in his life as much as she cared to."

In 1963, Hartigan says, AA executed a new agreement, which upon his death gave Helen 10 percent of his book royalties. Lois, who was twenty-two years older than Wynn, got 90 percent. Lois Wilson died in 1988 at age ninety-seven.

Wilson's extramarital affairs, his LSD experiments, and his fascination with spiritualism and psychic phenomenon were a long-lasting source of embarrassment for other AA leaders. So was his tireless promotion of vitamin B_3 therapy for the treatment of alcoholism and depression, which became an issue at the 1967 AA convention. Wilson was told to stop using his AA stationary and AA's mailing address in New York City for his vitamin crusade, which was seen as a violation of AA guidelines that the organization's name never be used to promote "outside enterprises."

Bill Wilson had officially withdrawn from AA leadership at the fellowship's "Coming of Age" convention in Saint Louis in the summer of 1955, but he never really faded into the background. He continued to write letters, publish essays in the AA newsletter, and lobby for changes in the organization's governing structure for more than a decade. He had long advocated that AA change its original bylaws, which stated that a majority of its governing trustees be outside, nonalcoholic members. That rule was finally changed at AA's 1966 governing convention. Wilson continued to give keynote addresses at AA's annual conventions in the late 1950s and throughout the 1960s.

His final appearance was in 1970, before the thirty-fifth anniversary convention in Miami, while Wilson was being treated at the Miami Heart Institute. Bill W. was brought into the hall in a wheelchair with an oxygen tank. But he insisted on standing up at the podium, which he gripped with both hands to slowly raise up his six-foot-three frame. He was welcomed one last time with a prolonged standing ovation. Wilson spoke for only four minutes and had to be held up by two people standing at his side.

In the end, the other addiction that Bill Wilson could never shake, his dependency on tobacco, was clearly killing him. He was dying from emphysema and chronic bronchitis, which would lead to pneumonia. As late as 1969, those who came to visit him at his home in Bedford Hills reported that Wilson would take hits from an oxygen tank, then from a cigarette. He came down with pneumonia in the fall of 1970.

Two male nurses cared for him at his home. On Christmas Day, one of the nurses noted in his log that Wilson "asked for three shots of whiskey" and became belligerent when told there was no liquor in the house. He continued to make this demand over the final couple of weeks of his life—a testament to the enduring power of alcohol. He was flown to Miami by private plane for more treatment at the heart institute, which was where he died on the night of January 24, 1971.

Bill Wilson was—like most of us—a flawed human being. But on the night he died, more than three hundred thousand men and women around the world were staying sober by trying to live their lives in accordance with the principles outlined by Alcoholics Anonymous. Many of them would get up the next morning, go to a meeting, and recite the following words: "Do not be discouraged. No one among us has been able to maintain anything like perfect adherence to these principles. We are not saints. The point is, that we are willing to grow along spiritual lines. The principles we have set down are guidelines to progress. We claim spiritual progress rather than spiritual perfection."

NINE

Sober

Either we were shy, and dared not draw near
others, or we were apt to be noisy good fellows
craving attention and companionship. . . .
There was always that mysterious barrier we
could neither surmount nor understand. It was as
if we were actors on a stage, suddenly realizing
that we did not know a single line of our parts.
That's one reason we loved alcohol. It did let us
act extemporaneously.

Bill Wilson, *Twelve Steps and Twelve Traditions*, 1952

On a Sunday morning in January 2011, on the day before the fortieth anniversary of Bill Wilson's death, I find myself sitting at the head of a long table. "Good morning," I say. "Welcome to the Serenity Now meeting of Alcoholics Anonymous. My name's Don, and I'm an addict, an alcoholic, and your cosecretary."

"Hi, Don," the assembled voices reply.

"Alcoholics Anonymous," I say, "is a fellowship of men and women . . ."

We're meeting in the boardroom on the fifth floor of the old Providence Hospital on "Pill Hill" in Oakland. Forty recovering alcoholics and drug addicts sit in blue plastic chairs arranged around the table and along the four walls. The congregation is a mix of alumni and current patients with various amounts of sobriety under their belts—from a few days to a few decades. The newcomers tend to sit in the back, by the door, and there's usually at least one guy sitting there with his arms crossed and a smirk on his face. He's thinking, "What a load of crap. What the fuck am I doing here?"

I used to be that guy.

Checking myself into rehab was one of the most difficult moves I ever made. But it certainly wasn't the first time I'd tried to kick my addiction to alcohol and cocaine. Sometime in the 1980s I began a tradition in which I'd refrain from alcohol and cocaine for the month of January. I made it through the first couple of years, then it was three weeks, then two weeks, then I'd say something like: "That's a week. I've made my point." I'd promise myself that I would wait until February 1 to go see my coke-dealing friend, but I'd near his neighborhood on the freeway and my car would steer itself off the highway and onto his street. My addiction was in the driver's seat. When my January sobriety diminished to a few days, sometime in the 1990s, I ended that doomed attempt.

This time, the time I checked myself into rehab, was different. I was truly surrendering, or at least I thought I was. I went to great lengths to keep the world from knowing that I was entering a twenty-eight-day treatment center. No one—other than my wife and one close friend—knew what I was doing. I made up a story about another illness for my bosses and coworkers at the *San Francisco Chronicle*. I told my teenage stepdaughters that I was away covering a story. I lied to my friends. I was ashamed and embarrassed that I was so weak that I had to subject myself to rehab. I'd spent my entire life constructing my identity as a hard-boiled, hard-drinking newspaper reporter.

AA was not for me. I was the irreverent religion writer, the guy you called "Father Lattin" because it was so damn funny putting those two words together. I was not ready to turn my will and my life over to God, as the third step suggests, nor was I willing to swallow the seventh step and humbly ask him to remove my shortcomings.

If I had a problem, it was cocaine, not alcohol. I came to Providence Hospital to get medical information. I was concerned about the state of my liver, my nose, and my memory, but the people at this hospital seemed more concerned about the state of my soul. I wanted to find out if I was addicted to coke because I was depressed, or if I was depressed because I was addicted to coke. If I could only stop the coke, then I could control my drinking. I'd finally come to see that my ingenious regime of licit and illicit drugs was not sustainable.

The rehab center assigns a counselor to work with you. It turned out that my counselor had seen my name on the intake list and recognized me as the *Chronicle* religion writer. He'd been enjoying my stories for years. That was flattering but also disconcerting. Newspaper reporters don't like to admit it, but we love it when someone remembers our byline or a story we wrote. I was more worried that my cover was blown. Word would soon leak out that the religious editor at the *Chronicle* was a drug addict. I was worried that people I'd exposed over the years—like pedophile priests or abusive cult leaders—would use that information to get back at me for ruining *their* careers.

My efforts to sober up coincided with my involvement in a very public dispute with San Francisco Archbishop William Levada, who didn't like some of my stories about his track record with pedophile priests. Levada would soon become the Vatican's top doctrinal watchdog, after Cardinal Joseph Ratzinger's election to replace Pope John Paul II. I didn't know it at the time, but the stakes were high for Levada. He was playing hardball. He denounced my reporting in the local Catholic newspaper.

The *Chronicle* had a new ethics policy of *not* covering up the story when its own editors and writers got into trouble. One of the reasons I went to rehab was that I had imagined my enemies might begin spying on me. My mind would start spinning, and I'd see agents of the Catholic Church tipping off the cops to keep an eye on me. Soon the headlines would read, "Chronicle Religion Writer Arrested in Drug Bust."*

My counselor assured me that the hospital had strict guidelines to protect the confidentiality of its patients. Then, later in the day, I was told that a TV news crew was filming a story about a standup comic who'd returned to entertain the patients. "Don't worry," we were told. "The camera will be shooting only your back." That didn't do me any good, because I knew the reporter who was doing the piece. He'd see me in the audience or sitting in the dining room and word would get out, and soon

---

*Acute cocaine intoxication may lead to paranoia and grandiose thinking.

every reporter in town would know that Don Lattin was in drug rehab. So I was hidden away in a large closet, which is where I spent the first afternoon of my twenty-eight-day treatment.

So why, you may ask, am I now so out of the closet about being a recovering alcoholic and drug addict? Why am I writing a book about it? And aren't people in Alcoholics Anonymous supposed to be *anonymous*?

.   .   .   .   .

People in Alcoholics Anonymous have various ideas about what "anonymous" means, and they always have. At some early AA meetings, people introduced themselves using their full names. Other chapters had members wear masks or hide behind curtains. One of the reasons that AA originally stressed anonymity was out of concern that its early leaders would fall off the wagon and discredit the entire fellowship, and some of them did.

Those days are gone. AA is now an established grassroots organization with some two million members. At the same time, public attitudes have changed since 1934. Substance abuse does not carry the same stigma it once did, especially for people who are sincerely trying to overcome it. Addiction has come to be seen by many as a disease, perhaps even a disease that can be passed on genetically. We are not sinners. We are not weak willed. Or at least that's not all we are.

Nearly all AA members, myself included, believe that everyone in our fellowship has the right to his or her own anonymity. I have not outed any AA member in this book other than myself. Nevertheless, by putting my name on this book I probably *am* violating what AA calls "tradition eleven." It states, "We need always maintain personal anonymity at the level of press, radio and films." This is meant as "a constant and practical reminder that personal ambition has no place in A.A." I have at least one AA friend who will be so ticked off that I put my name on this book that he'll probably refuse to read it, let alone buy it.

Is this book an expression of my personal ambition? Yes, but that's not all it is. Writing this book upholds other AA principles, such as the instructions to practice "rigorous honesty" and put "sobriety first." AA states, "The only requirement for membership is the desire to stop drinking," so I have fulfilled my membership duties. They can't kick me out. One of my favorite AA sayings is: "Take what you need and lose the rest."

My early obsession with anonymity in rehab and AA backfired. I completed my treatment program at Providence Hospital. I got a sponsor. I went to meetings. I worked the steps. And it was all done in secret. Two weeks after finishing treatment, I went back to drinking and using. It would take me more than another year before I was able to string together a couple weeks of sobriety. As they say in AA, I had to go out and "do a little more research."

Today, as I write this final chapter, it has been more than five years since I downed a drink or snorted a line of coke. That is a miracle, which is not a word I'm known to throw around. What changed? How was I finally able to stay sober?

What changed was my attitude about anonymity. I started telling the story of my struggle with alcohol and other drugs. First I told my sponsor. Then I told it at AA meetings. Then I told my extended family and friends. Then I told my coworkers. Now I'm telling the world, or at least anyone who picks up this book. And I'm doing so because I've come to see that telling the truth can set me free. If I am going to construct a new sense of myself, a new identity, a new life, I must proclaim the end of my past life. I'm not being noble. Personal pride in my sobriety keeps me sober. I'll use everything at my command to not take that first drink or snort that first line, including my own egomania and self-centeredness.

· · · · ·

AA is a place where you can tell your story, listen to other stories, and, as part of a group, learn another way of life. Some of the tales you hear stick with you. There are the outrageous drunk-a-logs. One morning we hear from a former U.S. soldier who had been stationed in Japan—until he went on a bender and woke up in a hut in the Philippines, not *just* with a strange woman but also with her four young children sleeping on the ground all around them.

Some accounts break your heart, like that of a woman confessing she was so ashamed to admit she was an alcoholic dying from the disease that she prayed God would give her cancer so she could "die with dignity." Her story inspires another man sitting at the table, a successful businessman, to speak up. "My hands were shaking so bad toward the end that I went to a series of doctors trying to find someone to diagnose me with Parkinson's disease," he recalls. "Anything was better than admitting I was just a drunk—especially if that meant I had to stop drinking."

There are all kinds of AA meetings, including gatherings for men, women, gay people, disabled people, agnostics, whatever. Those who stick around long enough discover that there are also countless off-the-schedule groups, private meetings of people who have met at Alcoholics Anonymous or Narcotics Anonymous and have spun off to form their own private gatherings.

One of those, known as the KooKoo Faktory, helped me make it through my first couple of years spent relapsing and recovering. A guy named Steve, a former actor and heroin addict with an interest in Buddhist meditation, started it. Steve and about a dozen other junkies from a Narcotics Anonymous meeting that meets on Saturdays in San Francisco starting getting together Monday evenings to meditate. We gathered at Steve's place, a funky crash pad and performance space in an old warehouse on a dingy alley in the Mission District.

It was an edgy blend of local characters—aging punk rock musicians, writers, computer programmers, a carpenter, and a retired Shakespeare scholar. We would meditate for twenty minutes. Someone would read a page or two from a book about Buddhism, and then we would talk about the passage or about what was going on that week in our own lives.*

I found the KooKoo Faktory a year or so before I finally checked myself into rehab. I was living on my own in a small bungalow in Berkeley. My first marriage had ended. I no longer had to be concerned about my wife worrying about me staying up all night somewhere drinking vodka and snorting coke, so I found myself drinking more and using more. In my mind, I already knew all I needed to know about AA. In the late 1980s

---

*Steve died and the KooKoo Faktory closed.

and early 1990s, I'd written several long newspaper articles and magazine pieces about AA and the larger recovery movement. That was my way of testing the waters without diving in for a full-immersion baptism.

There's a page-1 story I wrote for the *Chronicle* of December 17, 1990, headlined "Going to Church the 12-Step Way." It focused on the many Bay Area churches where the number of people meeting in recovery groups in the basement far exceeded that of the Sunday morning congregation. "It freaks out our members," said a Lutheran pastor in Marin County. "They're asking, 'What are we doing wrong?'" At the time, there were more than five hundred AA meetings within the city limits of San Francisco alone.

Around this same time I wrote a long magazine profile of John Bradshaw, an author, television personality, and recovery evangelist who was wildly popular in the late 1980s and early 1990s. My article was published in the summer of 1991. Looking back on that story two decades later, in the summer of 2011, reminds me that I began my "recovery" many years before I checked into drug rehab.

I first discovered Bradshaw when he appeared, uninvited, on my television screen. He was one of those self-help gurus that public television stations shamelessly promote during pledge drives because these gurus' devotees tend to donate money—just like the followers of TV preachers do on other channels. Most of these self-promoters make me want to throw my shoe at my TV set. That was my first thought when I saw Bradshaw, but then I started listening to what he was saying about the psychology and spirituality of addiction. I flew up to interview him in Eugene, Oregon, where he was making a public appearance. Here's how I began my story:

> John Bradshaw paces the stage, clenches his fist and with the soul-shaking power of a preacher on fire, tells his story. Inside the soaring Hult Center for the Performing Arts in Eugene, Oregon, it is mostly silent, except for an occasional sob, sniffle or sigh rising from some 2,000 souls gathered here. People are listening, really listening. You can tell they are from the tears, the sympathetic nods, the quiet "yes" flowing from hearts.
> Speaking through his Texas drawl, Bradshaw tells of his alcoholic

father who abandoned him, his mother who turned him into a substitute husband. He talks about his struggles in Catholic seminary, his battles with alcohol and sex addiction. For a moment, he stops pacing and leans against the wooden pulpit on stage.

"When I put that Roman collar on, they called me 'Father.' Hell, I didn't even know who I was," he tells the audience. "I remember times in seminary when I would sneak out and get pornography. I would look at pornography and have actual conversations with the pictures. Now that's lonely. But when you're numbed out emotionally, the only way to feel is through your addiction. It's the only way you become connected with yourself."

Looking back on that story, I now see that I was telling my story through the story of John Bradshaw. That's the same thing I've tried to do in this book, to tell my story through the lives of Aldous Huxley, Gerald Heard, and Bill Wilson. What began as a group biography turned into the book you've almost finished—a blend of memoir and biography.

I never got a chance to interview Huxley, Heard, or Wilson, but I do vaguely recall the long conversation I had with John Bradshaw in his room at the Hilton Hotel in Eugene. I started searching through the many boxes of papers in my basement office and found a stuffed folder with "Bradshaw" written on the tab. It turns out I still have a transcript from that interview, so I looked back to see if I'd talked about my addiction during our conversation. There's nothing about it in the story I wrote. I read through the long transcript, and at the very end, we had this little exchange:

"You know, I fit the profile," I said. "My father is a successful functioning alcoholic, and not abusive to me. I'm in a profession where there's a lot of alcoholism, and I have to watch it. You know, I wish there were some sort of group you could go to where you didn't have to stop drinking. You could just help one another keep an eye on it."

Bradshaw laughed. "You might just do that, with some chosen people. And say, 'Look, let's just kind of monitor each other.'* A lot of times, I

*Reading this old transcript of my conversation with Bradshaw reminded me that I actually took him up on that suggestion. I convinced a few of my drinking and drugging

didn't know how out of line I was getting with my drinking. I remember thinking that I was pontificating, but that I was really making sense. Then the next day my friends would say, 'You were off the wall last night.'"

I asked Bradshaw if he thought alcoholism was genetic. "I don't think everybody whose father is an alcoholic becomes an alcoholic. But I know that my dad was a genetic alcoholic. I'm a genetic alcoholic, and I'm pretty sure my son is."

"My father's mother died of alcoholism, and then there's my dad," I said. "But I just can't swallow AA. There seems to be a kind of fundamentalism, a new Puritanism, to all this recovery stuff that really bugs me. It's all very black and white."

"I agree," Bradshaw said. "People get in there and they become very rigid. It's 'my way or the highway.' But that's starting to change. Young people are coming in and breaking that down."

That turned out to be what I would find twenty years later. My first sponsor was a bit of an AA Nazi. But that's what I liked about him. I needed someone who could see through my bullshit, who wouldn't let me rationalize my way into a relapse. That didn't work. I relapsed anyway. After a few more months of drinking, using, *and* going to meetings, I started looking around for another sponsor. One of my colleagues at the *Chronicle* suggested I have coffee with a guy who'd helped him sober up. By now, I had been through my month of rehab and another six months of relapsing.

My twenty-eight days on the Providence Hospital rehab ward (eight as an inpatient and twenty as an outpatient) taught me a lot about the disease of alcoholism—too much, it turned out, to keep using. While I

---

buddies that we should try to get together and just talk one night a week without drinking vodka and snorting cocaine—to see if we could have the same intense conversations, and make the same connection, without the drugs. It was our version of a men's group. We met a half dozen times, but found we couldn't keep the meeting together. The only rule was you couldn't drink or use for an entire day before our meeting. Several of us had trouble following that guideline. Looking back on this noble experiment, I now see that I was trying to reinvent the wheel. There are meetings like this going on all the time. They call it Alcoholics Anonymous. Today, I get together with another group of men every other week to talk about our sobriety. We meet at one of our homes every other Thursday night for an hour and a half. It's not an official AA meeting, but we are all members of that larger fellowship.

kept drinking and using off and on for more than a year, it was never the same. What little enjoyment I'd gotten from getting high was gone.

They say alcoholism is a progressive disease, and mine was definitely progressing. I'd started hiding bottles of vodka in my basement. I'd started buying larger quantities of coke to supply my habit. I'd started selling it to friends, then to friends of friends. I was on the verge of becoming a drug dealer, and I was putting myself in some dangerous places, liking hanging out in East Oakland late at night, waiting for my connection with a large wad of cash in my pocket.

My new sponsor stuck with me through this period of "further research." I'd disappear for a month and then resurface and call him, ready to try again. I kept coming back. I kept going to the KooKoo Faktory and to follow-up recovery groups that met at the hospital. I went to AA meetings and almost always found something worth hearing. I also went to meetings of Cocaine Anonymous, which helped me see my patterns of abuse with that enslaving substance.

At a certain point, my efforts started working and I stopped using. I got a month of sobriety, then another month, then a year, then another year. One day at a time. The cravings continued for a year or so, but I warded them off by following one of the lessons I learned at rehab. For me, it starts like this: something happens, like some minor annoyance at the newspaper, and the little addict in my head says, "Fuck it. Let's get high." I learned to recognize the relapse even before the little addict spoke up, when he was just clearing his throat, or when the idea first arose in *his* mind. That's when I'd call my sponsor, or call another addict, or go to a meeting.

Addicts and alcoholics can't wait until they down the first drink or snort the first line of coke. By then it's too late. This is exactly what they tell you over and over again in recovery, but it only works if you actually choose to remember this and pick up the phone or go to a meeting. My sponsor would say something obvious when I'd call him, something that I already knew but had to hear someone else say, like: "Is the situation really going to get better if you go out and get drunk?" Or he'd say, "Here's all you have to do. Don't drink or use until tomorrow, and call me before you do." It really is that simple, and it isn't.

Talking about feelings was not something I'd ever learned to do. Real men don't feel or reach out for help. I had to unlearn that and learn to feel my anger, fear, frustration, and loneliness, not sedate them or intensify them with drugs and alcohol. Feelings pass. That's what they do. I had to stop doing what I do. I had to stop pushing the river.

.   .   .   .   .

At a certain point in my recovery it dawned on me that the road I was on was taking me to another place. It turned out that my recovery was not really about whether or not I drank vodka or snorted cocaine. It was about finding another way of living. Alcoholism and drug addiction were symptoms of a deeper malaise. Giving up alcohol and cocaine was the first step in treating a malady the church used to call acedia, a state of spiritual apathy and stupor. Addiction may be a disease, but it's not really like other diseases. It is dis-ease, a kind of soul sickness, or at least it was for me. I got high to recover the ease, to overcome the dis-ease.

The twelve steps are a spiritual program designed to help drunks and addicts recover from this dis-ease. I admitted to myself and then to others that I couldn't go it alone. I needed to find a power greater than myself, which can be God, Buddha, or simply the realization that I am not God. I took a hard look at my own shortcomings and tried to make amends to those I'd hurt in the past. Now I try to do that every day, and sometimes I even succeed. I try to admit it when I'm wrong. I try to remember that I don't have all the answers.

Now I try to think about the consequences of what I am about to say. I may not be able to stop "the stinkin' thinkin'," as they call it in AA, but at least I can keep my mouth shut. I try to talk less and listen more, and sometimes I actually do. I try to say three things several times a day in my interactions with other people, things I never used to say: "I don't know" and "You might be right" and "Do you have any suggestions?" You might want to try that—even if you're not an addict or alcoholic.

In the 1930s, Bill Wilson wrote a paragraph that applied to more than only him and his fellow drunks. "Selfishness—self-centeredness! That, we think, is the root of our troubles. Driven by a hundred forms of fear, self-delusion, self-seeking, and self-pity, we step on the toes of our fellows and they retaliate. Sometimes they hurt us, seemingly without provocation, but we invariably find that at some time in the past we have made decisions based on self which later place us in a position to be hurt."

Gerald Heard was not an alcoholic, but he understood this program of recovery. In 1958, Bill Wilson asked Heard to write a "think piece" for the May issue of the *A.A. Grapevine,* the organization's newsletter filled with corny jokes and folksy wisdom from Bill W. and other members of the fellowship. It was the first time a nonmember had written for the publication. Heard titled his article "The Search for Ecstasy." Here's how it began:

> Nobody, in or out of A.A., can doubt that this—A.A.'s most remarkable attack upon a major complaint, alcoholism—has resulted in something much bigger, even, than its success against this most damaging social and individual disability.
>
> Look first at the rise of what some of us call the "ad hoc churches." These are the many anonymous groupings which, modeled on A.A. and using its main principles, have helped people to endure ordeals other than alcoholism and at the same time to help their fellow sufferers. These other ordeals range from narcotic addiction through epilepsy, cancer, and heart surgery to the trials of bereavement and divorce.
>
> Why has this happened and how may we in society as a whole avail ourselves of this widening applicability of the A.A. basic principles?
>
> I think that it's generally taken for granted by experts on the subject that alcoholism is a particular symptom of a very widespread distress, a kind of psycho-physical illness.

Heard goes on to attribute this dis-ease to the ever-increasing stress that many of us face in our lives. The problem, he writes, is that "none of us is living in a sufficiently tonic way." We are searching for comfort and security. We seek a firm foundation. But this will only lead to more stress. We don't need a rock on which to stand. We need a river to ride.

"Deep down we are a current," Heard wrote. "Our little surface crust wants to 'stay put.' Our deep self wishes to move on, to grow. Though alcohol is a narcotic, alcoholism (like all addictions) is not at base a search for utter sedation. It is a desire for that *ecstasis*, that 'standing out' from the land-locked lagoons of conformity, out onto the uncharted high seas where the only map is the star-set heavens."

Heard believed three things must happen for the twelve-step program to work. The addict must have "a personal experience of purposive power." It must be "brought to him by one who had also been aghast at the emptiness of our way of living." Finally, "the salvaged person must find a group, a model society, whose members have gone through the same ordeal."

"Only thus," Heard concludes, "can all events come to be regarded as opportunities for an embryonic growth, here and now, which prepares us for a maturity yet to come."

My embryonic growth as an adult began on that cliff at Big Sur in the fall of 1972, when I was reborn with the assistance of a drug that a Swiss chemist accidentally invented the year Aldous Huxley and Gerald Heard came to California. That wondrous experience was not a good trip followed by a bad trip but the beginning of a process of recovery that *is* my life. It was and it is all grist for the mill.

Psychedelic drugs showed me the way. Buddhism and Taoism helped me bring those insights into the rest of my life. I learned that I was looking not so much for the meaning of life but for the experience of being alive. I stopped pushing the river; or as they say in AA and elsewhere, I learned to "take it easy." I had to "let go and let God."

That's pretty much the same sentiment expressed in the Serenity Prayer, which was written by theologian Reinhold Niebuhr and popularized by the twelve-step movement. "God," it begins, "grant me the serenity to accept the things I cannot change, the courage to change the things I can, and the wisdom to know the difference."

I've come to see that drugs may produce religious experiences but do not necessarily produce religious lives. Drugs may give us altered states but not altered traits. "What promised to be a short cut will prove to be a short circuit," Huston Smith warned in 1964. "Religion cannot be equated with religious experiences, neither can it long survive their absence."

·   ·   ·   ·   ·

Many people who come to AA have trouble with "the God stuff." Some are like Gerald Heard. They had an abusive religious upbringing and want nothing to do with God—or at least with the punishing, vindictive God of their childhood. Others are like Aldous Huxley. They were raised to believe in modern science, not holy scripture. They may call themselves atheists or agnostics, but either way they're turned off by an AA meeting that ends—as many of them do—with the Lord's Prayer.

Bill Wilson and some of the other early AA leaders brought their own skepticism about organized religion into the program of recovery they created. There's an entire chapter titled "We Agnostics" in *Alcoholics Anonymous*, the movement's guiding text. "Some of us have been violently anti-religious," it states. "To others, the word 'God' brought up a particular idea of Him with which someone had tried to impress them during childhood. Perhaps we rejected this particular conception because it seemed inadequate. With that rejection we imagined we had abandoned the God idea entirely."

AA solved this problem by suggesting that its members find a God of their own understanding. "Much to our relief, we discovered we did not need to consider another's conception of God," the Big Book states. "As soon as we admitted the possible existence of a Creative Intelligence, a Spirit of the Universe underlying the totality of things, we began to be possessed by a new sense of power and direction, provided we took other simple steps. . . . To us, the Realm of Spirit is broad, roomy, all inclusive."

Alcoholics, addicts, and others who seriously begin to work the twelve steps are forced to think about what they mean by "God." To me, this is one of the most useful and intriguing aspects of AA. Many of us grew up with the idea of God as "our Father." Many people never develop a more sophisticated understanding of God. He remains up there on some cloud in heaven, stroking his long white beard, judging, punishing, or loving us, depending on how we behave or what we believe. He's the Santa Claus god.

For many in my generation, this god died sometime in the middle of the 1960s. In fact, we may even know the exact date. That's because *Time* magazine, in its notorious cover story on April 8, 1966, dared to ask, "Is God Dead?"

Perhaps my father read that issue of *Time*, for it came out around the time that he asked me if I wanted to keep going to church, then expressed relief when I told him I did not. God the Father left our not-so-happy home, followed a couple of years later by my real-life father, the towering lord of the Lattin household.

God was dead, but not for long.

Psychedelic drugs would soon inspire many in my generation to think about God on another level. We didn't want to worship God. We wanted to *experience* God, and the quickest and easiest way to do that—or so we thought—was by swallowing a tab of Orange Sunshine.

Decades later, my recovery from drug addiction forced me to once again reexamine the way I envision the divine. And I finally began to see that there's more to religion than religious experience, no matter what generates it.

.   .   .   .   .

My recovery from addictive behavior and my new understanding of God doesn't account for much if it doesn't change the rest of my life—such as the way I make a living or how I relate to friends and family. My efforts to stop drinking and drugging came as I was ending a twenty-five-year-long newspaper career and beginning my second marriage. I took a buyout from the *Chronicle* and quit the newspaper at the same time that I was buying into my new role as reluctant stepfather of two resistant stepdaughters. My recovery turned out to be a package deal.

My second wife, Laura, was one of my old college girlfriends. We met at the *Daily Californian*, the student newspaper at the University of California, the same month that newspaper heiress Patricia Hearst was kidnapped from her Berkeley apartment by members of the Symbionese Liberation Army, which turned into one of the more sensational cult stories of the mid-1970s. It was a crazy time, the end of the era we would later call "the sixties." Laura and I split up when I went off to England for my junior year abroad. Twenty years later, we both found ourselves at the corner of Fifth and Mission Streets, working for a San Francisco newspaper. Laura and I had remained friends during the intervening decades. Our first marriages each lasted about one decade, with mine ending a few years before hers.

There are a couple of ways of looking at our reunion. Perhaps the old flame never died, or maybe we simply have trouble meeting new people.

Divorce is never easy, especially when children are caught in the middle; it seems that in matters of the heart we often find ourselves reliving the drama of our family of origin. That was certainly my experience. You can call it karma or destiny or the unfinished business of life, but the patterns in my family saga are hard to deny. After my parents' divorce in the 1960s, my father wound up marrying my mother's former best friend. This was the woman who had introduced my mother and father to each other in New York in the 1940s. I was the teenage child caught in the middle of that family feud.

Laura's older daughter was fifteen years old when I married her mother, the same age I was when my parents finally split up. Her sister was eleven. I entered into my new role with no prior parenting experience. It was trial by fire, and we all got our wings singed.

A friend of mine at the *Chronicle* had gone through a similar trial when he remarried and moved in with two stepdaughters who were the same age as mine. "Good luck," he warned. "They barely said a word to me for four years. They tried not to acknowledge my existence."

It wasn't quite that bad for me, but I was not exactly welcomed into my new family with open arms. So be it. I was getting the same silent treatment I'd handed out to my parents after their divorce. The girls responded to my unwelcome presence by simply acting as if I did not exist. I wasn't really there. I quickly became a coconspirator in this game, escaping to my "man cave" in the basement to nurse my melancholy or fuel my resentment with a line of coke or another drink.

Laura and I survived that trial, and so did the girls. I stopped drinking and drugging and our relationship improved. I made more of an effort to talk to the girls and, at a certain point, started getting more than one-word answers. They went off to college and into the rest of their lives. We all grew up a little. Meanwhile, I got a puppy and relearned one of the great lessons of life. If you want unconditional love, get a golden retriever.

Looking back on it, I've come to see that Laura's kids handled divorce better than I did during my teenage years. I responded to my parent's divorce by beginning a pattern of drinking and drugging to numb emotional pain, a pattern that, thankfully, the girls chose *not* to repeat. Assuming the role of pseudoparent the year I turned fifty forced me to grow up.

One of the more embarrassing reminders that it was finally time to clean up my act came after a night I spent with my nephew tooling around San Francisco. We'd gone out to dinner and I'd consumed, as usual, copious quantities of vodka and wine, in addition to making frequent trips to the men's room to secretly snort cocaine. My nephew, Jamie, had had a brief drinking and drugging binge as a teenager, but he'd stopped using in his twenties, when he and his wife gave birth to a son and daughter and they became born-again Christians. We got back to my house in Berkeley late enough that Jamie spent the night on my couch before heading home to Sacramento. Laura and I were engaged, but I had yet to completely move out of my place and in with her and the girls.

I woke up with the usual hangover and vague recollection of saying inappropriate things the previous night. My nephew had already headed home by the time I awoke, but he'd left a note on my kitchen table, along with a small vial of coke that he found on the passenger seat of his car. It must have fallen out of my pocket on the way back from San Francisco. "Dear Uncle Don," the note read. "You left this in my car. You might want to think about giving this stuff up now that you're about to become a parent."

·   ·   ·   ·   ·

Similar hints were being dropped at work. One day I was called into the city editor's office and told I was setting a bad example for the younger reporters. I was talking back to my editors and doing so in a voice that the entire newsroom could hear. This often occurred after lunch and an ample serving of loudmouth soup. The boss made it clear during our meeting that he was giving me an official warning. It would go in my personnel file.

My drinking wasn't mentioned, but it was the pink elephant in the room.

Of course, this little reprimand didn't set me straight. It only pissed me off more, gave me something else to bitch about over another three-martini lunch. I seem to recall going out and kicking over a newspaper rack. In my mind, I wasn't corrupting young reporters. I was maintaining one of the sacred traditions of American journalism. Newsrooms were supposed to be raucous places full of disheveled, gin-soaked characters that rose to the occasion when the big story broke. We were not meant to be pious, pliant employees. We were difficult to deal with, but we had what the editors needed when the shit hit the fan. We'd been there, done that, and we could do it again, do it fast, and get it right.

We reveled in our arrogance.

Resentments are a form of poison, and I was killing myself with mine. My old colleagues at the *Chronicle* remind me that my resentments about the direction of the newspaper and the competency of some of its managers fueled more than a few explosive outbursts in the city room. I tended to use words like "fucking idiots" and "beyond clueless." I was often drunk, but not always. I see now that I was the idiot. I was poisoning myself—not only with alcohol and cocaine, but also with resentment.

One day I came back to the office after a long lunch. I was tight and on a tight deadline. I needed a scriptural reference to start off my story but couldn't find my copy of the Good Book. Other reporters were always taking books off my desk and not returning them. After frantically searching through the mountain of files, books, and other debris, I stood up and yelled out across the city room, "Who stole my *fucking* Bible!"

There was a new hire working that day. Puzzled by my blast of blasphemy, he turned to the reporter next to him and asked, "Who *is* that guy?"

"Oh, that's Father Lattin. He's the religion editor."

It was me, and it wasn't me. When I started working the Godbeat, I found that an irreverent approach to religion was the easiest way to be taken seriously in the newsroom. Any hint that I actually believed this stuff would only arouse suspicion from my comrades in cynicism.

Christopher Isherwood, the British mystical expatriate who became the most dedicated disciple in the Vedanta Society, had a similar problem when he found God. Isherwood was an openly gay man who'd already made a name for himself chronicling the risqué scene that unfolded in Berlin between the two world wars—stories that would inspire the 1951 Broadway production *I Am a Camera* and the 1966 Oscar-winning film *Cabaret*. He laid out two strategies for defusing secular suspicion among old colleagues. "If a member of the so-called intellectual class joins any religious group or openly subscribes to its teachings, he will have to prepare himself for a good deal of criticism from his unconverted and more skeptical friends," Isherwood observed. "Either he will preach to his old friends and bore them; thus confirming their worst suspicions. Or he will make desperate efforts to reassure them, by his manner and conversation, that he is still 'one of the gang.' He will be the first to blaspheme, the first to touch upon the delicate subject. And his friends, far from being relieved, will be sincerely shocked."

This was the strategy I employed in the newsroom by creating the role of the irreverent religion writer. It worked for many years, but I finally got tired of playing the part.

At the same time, the newspaper was slashing its staff and downsizing its way out of existence, unable to find advertising or a business model that worked in the brave new world of the World Wide Web. I don't think I could have sobered up if I'd stayed at the newspaper. I survived my last half dozen years only by taking leaves of absences to work on books. It got harder and harder to go back to the paper and watch its steady decline. The Hearst Corporation offered a series of buyouts and finally made me (and half the staff) an offer we couldn't refuse. I was ready to leave. I'd found myself saying with increasing frequency, "I did that fucking story ten years ago." I'd stayed at the party too long.

In the end, I quit the newspaper business for the same reason I quit drinking and drugging. It wasn't fun anymore. I wasn't getting that old high. But there was another reason I had to leave the newspaper. I had to stop covering religion to let religion cover me. I had to stop writing about religion to get right with religion.

It wasn't simply because religion reporters tend to cover religious conflict rather than religious reconciliation, or that we are more interested in scandal than spirituality. When we write about religion, or anything else for that matter, we approach the subject with a manipulative agenda. We're exploiting religion to get a good story.

We do not really understand religion. We stand outside religion. We are not experiencing religion. We can be graceful writers without being open to grace. We cannot be "objective" about religion and at the same time infused with its higher power. We can't turn our will and our life over to the care of God as we grind out yet another newspaper story about him. Or at least I couldn't. Hitting bottom and checking myself into rehab was the first step in my recovery from being a religion reporter.

.   .   .   .   .

There's an old saying in the guru business about how, when the student is ready, the teacher appears. My teachers are a bunch of drunks and drug addicts.

About a dozen of us get together every Saturday morning to talk, drink coffee, meditate, and read scripture together. We meet at a Catholic retreat house in Oakland—a short walk from the hospital where I first sought treatment. It's not an AA meeting, but most of us met at the rehab center.

If I try to deconstruct this group, I can't help but come up with equal parts Aldous Huxley, Gerald Heard, and Bill Wilson. We follow a medieval mystical tradition known as *lectio divina*, where we recite a passage of scripture four times, employing different types of listening to cultivate deeper understanding. Working with a teacher well versed in this tradition, and who is also in recovery, we practice a related spiritual discipline called "centering prayer," a mix of Christian contemplation and Buddhist meditation.

Father Thomas Merton, the Catholic monk who did so much to find common ground for Eastern mysticism and Western spiritual traditions, first popularized this approach. The Reverend Thomas Keating, a Cistercian monk, and other teachers further developed it. Merton and Keating were not focusing on addicts or alcoholics—but the practice works for us.

It helps that the room in which we meet reflects my Jewish-Christian heritage and my Taoist-Buddhist leanings. There's a white stone statue of the Buddha on the altar, an Orthodox Christian icon glowing in the candlelight, and a depiction of the *I Ching* hexagram hanging on the wall. One of the first sessions I attended featured a reading from the Hebrew Bible. "Be glad then, you children of Zion. Your sons and daughters shall prophesy. Your old men shall dream dreams. Your young men shall see visions" (Joel 2:23–32).

One of this contemplative tradition's founding texts is *The Cloud of Unknowing*, the same anonymous fourteenth-century text that Gerald Heard used as the basis for his Trabuco College seminar on Christian mysticism back in the 1940s. "And so I urge you, go after experience rather than knowledge," the text reads. "On account of pride, knowledge may often deceive you. Knowledge tends to breed conceit, but love builds. Knowledge is full of labor, but love, full of rest."

Father Keating is not in recovery himself, but he understands the program. "One of the great strengths of the Twelve Step Program of Alcoholics Anonymous is that it emphasizes how serious one's illness is. Participants in A.A. know that their lives are unmanageable and will never become manageable unless they work the Twelve Steps," he writes. "The advantage of being an addict is that you know you will never get well without help. Unfortunately, the average practicing Christian, because of a certain modicum of respectability, does not seem to know this. . . . The practical question for all of us is, 'How addicted *are* we?'"

Keating goes on to explain that addicts of all kinds (and that includes most of us) must repent, a word he defines as "that fundamental call in the gospel to begin the healing process." By "repent," Keating means "change the direction in which you are looking for happiness. The various orientations for happiness that we brought with us from early childhood are not working. They are slowly killing us."

For me, there was no more happiness in another drink or another line of coke. There was no contentment in cynicism and resentment. Stopping the drink and drugging was only the first step. Finding a way to bring God *as I understand him* into my life has been an entirely different struggle. Our Saturday morning meetings give me a ray of hope. But who knows? This is still a work in progress. The memoir is almost finished, but life goes on. My critical mind still questions "the God stuff" and may ultimately sabotage this latest chapter in my ever-reluctant spiritual search.

My judging, calculating mind draws me away from experience, back into intellectual analysis. It encourages me to separate, not integrate. My critical mind leads me to a new book titled *God Is Not One*, which reminds me of how I used to think about religion. "The idea of religious unity is wishful thinking," writes Stephen Prothero. "This naïve theological groupthink—call it Godthink—has made the world more dangerous by blinding us to the clashes of religions that threaten us worldwide. It is time we climbed out of the rabbit hole and back to reality."

My head agrees with Prothero, but my heart and soul long to follow Huxley, Wilson, and Heard. Stay focused, I tell myself, on *The Cloud of Unknowing*. "Knowledge tends to breed conceit, but love builds. Knowledge is full of labor, but love, full of rest." I don't really understand what happens when we gather, but there have been moments when I've truly felt the presence of God in our midst. I'm not sure what that means, but it has something to do with the sum of our work being greater than the parts. Maybe God is the glue, the secret ingredient.

Our meditation opens us up to a higher power or ultimate Reality, to the Ground of Being or the Clear Light of the Void, whatever words you want to use to describe the ineffable. After we sit in silence for twenty-five minutes, our teacher tries to put our practice into words, saying:

> When we come to this practice, we bring with us everything we made
> to create ourselves—our habits, defenses, fantasies. We bring our
> inner sense of separation. We see how we live so far from ourselves.
> Yet also, within us, the spirit works. Clearing, little by little, we
> become one with our self. This is the practice. Receive exactly what
> is here. Receive the sound received in your ears. Receive without

comment. It's just here. Receive your capacity to hear just what is
there. Receive your mind. Receive your body. Receive this moment.
   If you look and do not observe love, that is because you are love.
And just as an eye cannot see itself, you cannot see love.

Our *lectio divina* reading encourages us to focus on a word or phrase in
the scripture that resonates with us. We ask ourselves, "What does this
tell me about God?" But our gathering is not a discussion group. We're
reaching for something deeper, a distillation of the personal and the universal, a distillation of the spirit.
   At one of our gatherings, the *lectio divina* begins with a reading from
the Psalms about how "those who walk hand in hand with goodness"
and "delight in the Spirit of Love" are "like trees planted by streams of
water, that yield fruit in due season." At first, that phrase calls out to me.
Then, another line from the morning's reading hits me on a deeper, more
emotional level. "The unloving are not so," it reads. "Turning from the
Heart of Love they will know suffering and pain. They will be isolated
from wisdom."
   After a period of silence, I speak up. "That reminds me of two events
of my youth," I tell my brethren. "The first was my parent's divorce,
which brought up some painful truths about my family."
   There's a long pause, then I start to choke up, and the tears begin to
well up—something that rarely happens to me.
   "The second . . . " Something stops me from saying it—the same thing
that keeps the tears from flowing. "The second," I say, "is really only an
echo of the first." That's true, but what I wanted to explain that morning
was how the second event—the suffering that followed my LSD-fueled
communion with my lover on a cliff at Big Sur—related to the death of
my brother, my parent's divorce, and my addiction.
   At Big Sur, my lover and I left walking hand and hand, brimming
with goodness and delight in the Spirit of Love. My subsequent bad trip
and psychotic break interrupted that dream. It reopened a wound that
had been festering since the death of my brother, ten months before my
birth, forming a shadow across the face of God. The original wound was
never treated. Forgiveness was never found.

My parents turned away from the Heart of Love. They did not fully experience their grief. They chose instead to bring new life into the world, which has been my blessing and my curse. I was born with the wound of my brother's death. My father and I stopped the bleeding, but only with the scab of cynicism. We erected a barrier around our hearts and souls, and then spent most of our lives trying to dissolve it with alcohol and other drugs.

It's time to forgive, time to heal.

.   .   .   .   .

My friend Kevin Griffin and I are winding down Highway 1 on our way to Esalen when I spot the small grove of Monterey pines between the road and the cliffs just before the Point Sur lighthouse.

"There it is," I say. "Pull over at that turnout right before that clump of trees."

It's been nearly forty years since my embryonic journey with my lover out on the edge of that cliff. I'd hoped to walk down and say a little prayer, but whoever owns this stretch of the Pacific Coast has erected a tall barbed wire fence and posted Danger and No Trespassing signs.

Kevin and I traipse up a small hill covered with ice plant to get a peak at the place where I saw God. Kevin gazes through the fog, but I see with greatest clarity when I close my eyes and let my mind drift back to that moment when there was no me, only white light, and I was at peace with that. It's taken me many years to realize I no longer have to take drugs to revisit that state of mind. I can get a taste by simply closing my eyes.

Something serendipitous always seems to happen to me at Big Sur, and this weekend will be no exception. Kevin is teaching a weekend workshop, "Buddhism and the Twelve Steps," at the Esalen Institute, but it turns out that the main event at the institute this weekend is a celebration to mark the eightieth birthday of Stan Grof, the Czech psychologist who did pioneering LSD research back in the late fifties and early sixties.

On Friday evening, as we gather in the living room of the Big House, people looking for the LSD celebration keep walking into our recovery meeting thinking that's where *they're* supposed to be. We send them on their merry way, and I sit down on my meditation cushion secure in the knowledge that I'm where *I'm* supposed to be. Twenty-five people have signed up for Kevin's workshop—mostly recovering alcoholics and drug addicts, but also a middle-aged man struggling with sex addiction and a young woman with an eating disorder. We come with varying amounts of sobriety, from two days to twenty-five years.

Kevin sits on a chair before a large fireplace. The rest of us find our places on firm meditation cushions, floppy corduroy pillows, or in chairs against the far wall. Kevin explains that the weekend will be a mix of sitting meditation and a presentation of his suggestions on how to combine the teachings of Buddhism with the program of recovery outlined by AA and other twelve-step fellowships. There will also be some small-group exercises and plenty of time for questions and discussion.

"Let's try to simply relax this weekend and see what emerges," he says. "Be present with your experience. Don't try to control it or do something with it. Just experience it—the raw human experience of life."

Serendipity arises with the first question, which comes from the sex addict. "I was down at the baths this afternoon, and someone from the Grof party told me that Bill Wilson took lots of LSD back in the sixties. I couldn't believe it! Do you know anything about that?"

Kevin, who'd just read an early draft of my book, shoots me a sideways glance and smiles. "He did, but we're not going to be passing out any acid at this workshop. If you want the mind-blowing experience, I suggest you go sit at the feet of Stan Grof."

My reason for coming to Big Sur was not to blow my mind—been there, done that—but to work on the eleventh step, which encourages us "through prayer and meditation to improve our conscious contact with God *as we understood Him,* praying only for knowledge of His will for us and the power to carry that out."

When I first read the Twelve Steps as a possible program for *my* recovery, I'd hit the brakes when I'd come upon language like "praying only for knowledge of His will." There's a woman here this weekend, the one with two days of sobriety, who reminds me of myself back then. She has the same reaction I had to the Bible-speak of the Big Book. She's been drinking two bottles of wine every night. She's been unable to stop, but unable to call herself an alcoholic. She's come here looking for another way. She starts crying when she tells me this over lunch. "I can't stand AA," she says. "It sounds like Christianity to me, and I've had enough of that. But I have to do *something.*"

Kevin has some advice. "When you come across a step asking you to 'know God's will,' think of it as letting go of your ego. This is about finding a way to deconstruct our old belief system, to deconstruct our old self, to have the intention and motivation to align ourselves with another power. Take God out of it and try to let go. It's about taking action to change our habitual patterns of thought and behavior. It doesn't have to be some God up there running the whole show."

Hearing Kevin's talk reminds me of the first time I met him. I couldn't stomach AA meetings and was looking for a Buddhist recovery group. At the time, they were not easy to find. I'd been going to a weekly meditation group near my house in Berkeley led by a teacher named James Barza. It was a large enough group that I was able to hide in the back and sneak out the door without having to talk to anyone. This was simply a generic meditation meeting, nothing to do with recovery, part of a network of California groups affiliated with Spirit Rock Meditation Center in Marin County.

My own study of Buddhism had convinced me that I could find a way out of my addiction through the Buddha's teachings about how our suffering and dissatisfaction stem from our attachments, cravings, and desire. At one of the Thursday night meetings, Barza jokingly mentioned his addiction to dark chocolate, which caused many in the *sangha* to chuckle. It inspired me to come back the next week and place an anonymous note in the basket Barza puts out for donations. "You struggle with chocolate. My problem is cocaine. Have you heard of anyone combining Buddhist meditation and recovery from serious substance abuse?" I signed the note with a false name, included a stamped envelope addressed to my P.O. box, and waited for an answer.

Months went by with no reply. I stopped going to the meditation group but didn't stop drinking and using. My downward spiral continued. I'd pretty much forgotten about James Barza when I finally got a note back in the mail telling me that one of his students, a guy named

Kevin, was writing a book about Buddhism and the Twelve Steps. If there were such a group, Kevin would probably know about it.

I called Kevin, who met me for lunch and took me to an AA meeting at a Quaker church in Berkeley. That was *not* what I had in mind. But Kevin also told me about the KooKoo Faktory, which turned out to be step 1 in my recovery.

So here I am eight years later, and five years clean and sober, sitting in Kevin's workshop, the first one he's offered at Esalen. There has been an explosion of Buddhist recovery groups since our first meeting. Kevin has published two books on the subject and now teaches workshops across the country. There's a chapter in Kevin's first book titled "Too Much Wisdom" that tells the story of a guy who calls him looking for an alternative to AA. When I read the chapter I thought the guy sounded a lot like me. Then I realized that the guy literally *was* me. That seems so long ago. I no longer have any real desire to drink or use, but I still have trouble finding a way to let go of my ego, quiet my mind, and establish a solid meditation practice. I still struggle daily with my own self-centeredness.

One of the most popular AA clichés is: "Keep coming back. It works." I'm trying to find the discipline to keep coming back to the meditation cushion. Five years ago I had almost come to the conclusion that I could never stop drinking and using. Then I did stop. Now I need to apply that same commitment to meditation. "It's about finding the confidence that there is the possibility for change," Kevin says. "If you don't believe you can get sober, you won't get sober. It's the same thing with meditation. You've got to trust that it's worth doing. You've got to quit saying you can't sit still, you can't calm your thoughts, you can't meditate."

At Esalen, we sit in meditation for half an hour at a time. I prefer the walking meditation, which reminds me of t'ai chi. I walk out of the Big House and onto a large deck perched on the edge of the cliff. I stand in one spot and slowly raise and lower my arms to the rising tide and the crashing waves. Huge beds of kelp surge up and down like they are breathing within me and without me. There's a feeling of oneness, a little reminder of what I felt on that Big Sur cliff four decades ago.

Unfortunately, we get to do walking meditation only once all weekend. My mind, as usual, won't shut up when I'm sitting on my *zafu*.

When I'm not thinking about what we might be having for lunch—or about the meditation room that I suddenly decide I need to build in my attic back home—I'm thinking about this book. I'd sent the final three chapters to my editor a few hours before Kevin swung by to pick me up for the trip down to Big Sur. I've decided that I need to rewrite the preface and introduction, so I start doing that in my head when I'm supposed to be meditating.

I catch myself and refocus on my breath. As usual, I'm not very good at being here now. I try my little mantra. I silently say "here" on the inhalation and "now" on the exhalation. In another ten seconds I'm thinking about some of the things I wrote about Ram Dass in my last book.

"Just sit," I tell myself. "Just sit."

We get a three-hour break on Saturday afternoon, so I head up into the canyon behind the retreat center. I cross a wooden bridge over a little river that flows through the canyon on its way to the Pacific and passes right through the Esalen property. This is where I used to sneak into the compound back in the 1970s to soak in the hot springs without paying for a workshop.

On my walk during our break, I ignore the Danger signs warning seminarians not to hike into the canyon alone. After a few minutes I leave the trail in search of a place I used to know by the river. I scramble up the steep ravine and find it—a sweet little spot nestled in the shadow of a giant redwood tree. I sit down on a soft bed of dry needles and look around.

Bright green ferns pop out of little crevices in a towering rock outcropping across the stream. The ferns dance as a cool breeze streams down the canyon. They come alive as the fog clears, smiling as they're bathed in the dappled sunlight. It's a comforting place to sit, not unlike my father's lap back in Chesterland, Ohio, more than half a century ago. I just sit. I look across the river. The water tumbles over rocks and fallen tree limbs, swirling about as it follows the path of least resistance on its journey to the sea.

Acknowledgments and Amends

One of the little tricks I learned in recovery may be worth mentioning here. You might even want to try it yourself. Begin your day by putting three or more pebbles in your left pocket. During your travels through the world over the next twelve hours, transfer a pebble from your left pocket to your right pocket whenever you feel grateful for something or someone. At the end of the day, notice how many pebbles have moved from left to right.

It's a simple little exercise. One of the things I've learned from it is how hard it is to be self-centered and thankful at the same time.

Right now, as I finish this book, I'm listing to the right with gratitude. I thank, first, the members of my family, not just for looking over early drafts of the manuscript, but also for their love and patience during the actual playing out of the scenes described in this memoir—and in many others I have chosen to leave out. Reading these stories and reliving some of the more painful chapters has not been easy. I especially thank my first wife, Antonia; my stepmother, Valeska; my sister, Denise; and, of course, Laura and the girls.

This book would not be in your hands without the wise counsel and persistent efforts of my literary agent, Amy Rennert, and my editor at the University of California Press, Reed Malcolm. It was not an easy book to pitch. Is it a group biography? Is it a memoir? Amy and Reed understood what I was trying to do before I completely figured it out. Many thanks to them, and to UC Press production editor Jacqueline Volin and copyeditor Bonita Hurd.

I also thank the monks at Ramakrishna Monastery in Trabuco Canyon, who kindly hosted me on three occasions during the researching and writing of this book. They are keeping the spirit of Aldous Huxley and Gerald Heard alive.

Annah Perch at the Stepping Stones Foundation Archives in Katonah/Bedford Hills, New York, the site of the historic home of Bill and Lois Wilson, generously supplied photos of Bill Wilson. I am also grateful for the assistance of John Roger Barrie, the literary executor of the Gerald Heard estate, who was an early supporter and a late fact-checker for this project. Readers wanting to learn more about Heard can do so at Geraldheard.org.

Many colleagues, friends, and family members were kind enough to look over early versions of the book, including Janis and James Crum, George Csicsery, Alison Falby, Steve Fields, Kevin Griffin, Myron Gulseth, Dick Hallgren, David and Cindy Hoffman, Jeffrey Kripal, Barbara Lewis, Patrick O'Neil, and Michael Taylor.

Finally, I express the deepest gratitude to all my friends in recovery. I couldn't have done it without you. Believe me, I tried.

If you think you might have a problem with alcohol or other drugs, you may want to go to a meeting or go online to explore Alcoholics Anonymous, Narcotics Anonymous, Cocaine Anonymous, or another support group. I found that it helps to keep an open mind. The twelve-step program encourages us to take "a searching and fearless moral inventory of ourselves" and then admit to God, ourselves, and at least one other human being "the exact nature of our wrongs." We are asked to make a list of all the persons we have harmed and to make amends "wherever possible, except when to do so would injure them or others."

Writing this book was, in some ways, like working the steps. This was not a tell-all memoir. Some stories could not be told without violating other people's privacy or creating more pain. Among the wreckage left in the wake of my drinking, drugging, and self-centeredness are a few ruined relationships from my work life, love life, and the rest of my life, and for that I am truly sorry.

Notes

INTRODUCTION

1 Epigraph: Heard 1924, p. 1.
2 *meeting was the tipping point:* Michael Murphy, interview by author, January 1987, and follow-up on June 27, 2011.
2 *tracked him down in Trabuco Canyon:* Huston Smith, interview by author, January 10, 2002, and follow-up on July 26, 2010.
6 *British mystical expatriates of Southern California:* Watts (1972) 2007, p. 167.
7 *a faith that works:* [Wilson] (1952) 2000, p. 34.
7 *greatest social architect of the twentieth century:* A. Huxley quoted in Thomsen 1975, p. 340.
8 *You use the same word for the highest religious experience:* Letter from Jung to B. Wilson, January 30, 1961, www.steppingstones.org/jung_letter.jpg.

ONE. WOUNDED

10 Epigraph: A. Huxley, in Baker and Sexton 2000, vol. 1, p. 5.

10 *at the U.S. National Cancer Institute:* Harner 2004.

11 *"Skin," he replied:* A. Huxley quoted in Francis Huxley, preface to Dunaway 1995, p. v.

11 *perhaps no conventional religion:* Bedford 1974, p. 9.

11 *no means of disproving it:* Letter from Thomas Henry Huxley to Charles Kingsley, September 23, 1860, http://alepho.clarku.edu/huxley/letters/60 .html.

12 *pretty strong conviction that the problem was insoluble:* T. Huxley 1901, pp. 237–39.

12 *mythology of their time and country:* L. Huxley quoted in Bedford 1974, p. 9.

14 *painful presence on my early life:* Heard quoted in Falby 2008, p. 6.

14 *English public-school boy is notorious:* Barrie's essay, "Who Is Gerald Heard?" 2002, is available at www.geraldheard.com. Copyright The Barrie Family Trust. The essay consolidates excerpts from "Some Reminiscences of Gerald Heard" by Jay Michael Barrie, published in *Parapsychology Review* 3, no. 3 (May–June 1975), along with the introduction to the 1975 edition of "Training for the Life of the Spirit."

14 *bullying haven of athleticism . . . keep the bullies at bay:* Falby 2008, p. 7.

15 *she was angry:* [Wilson] (1952) 2000, p. 9.

15 *never talked about it with anybody:* B. Wilson quoted in Cheever 2004, p. 23.

16 *on a matter of principle:* Kurtz 1979, p. 12.

16 *erased any vestiges:* Cheever 2004, p. 55.

22 *too much for him:* A. Huxley quoted in Murray 2002, p. 38.

22 *This meaningless catastrophe was the cause:* Birnbaum (1971) 2006, p. 131.

22 *scars left by the emotional ties of the family:* Dennis Gabor quoted in Murray 2002, p. 27.

22 *doctrines of Christianity:* Barrie, "Who Is Gerald Heard?" www.geraldheard .com.

22 *a frontal attack on the obstacles to these ends:* Ibid.

23 *suffocating under "the heavy pressure of inhibition":* Heard quoted in Falby 2008, p. 9.

23 *high road to his destiny:* [Wilson] (1952) 2000, pp. 50–51.

TWO. BLOOMSBURY

28 Epigraph: A. Huxley, in Baker and Sexton vol. 5, 2002, p. 223.

30 *Aldous Huxley sailed into my view:* Bedford 1974, p. 209.

30 *another session the following week:* Heard quoted in ibid., p. 209.

31 *Being with Rampion rather depresses me:* A. Huxley (1928) 1975, p. 322.

32 *where she can never take root:* Woolf quoted in Rosenbaum 1993, p. 45.

32 *and she often was:* Roiphe 2007, p. 181.
32 *her affectation is overwhelming:* A. Huxley quoted in G. Smith 1969, p. 86.
33 *of gentleness and depth:* Juliette Baillot quoted in Bedford 1974, p. 60.
33 *fidelity was not so strict:* Woolf quoted in Rosenbaum 1993, p. 368.
33 *scented, oiled and voluptuous:* Hutchinson quoted in Murray 2002, p. 73.
34 *The Times found his work "pleasantly offensive":* Murray 2002, p. 77.
34 *one is blasé and cynical:* A. Huxley quoted in ibid., p. 97.
35 *they could share each other's escapades:* Bedford 1974, p. 295.
35 *Maria was bisexual:* Ibid., p. 140.
35 *your air of impenetrable serenity that disquieted me:* A. Huxley quoted in Murray 2002, pp. 142–43.
35 *who attracted and charmed me:* Woolf and Hutchinson quoted in Murray 2002, pp. 142, 143.
36 *not to have husbands and wives:* Keynes quoted in Roiphe 2007, p. 8.
36 *communication for its own sake:* Roiphe 2007, p. 14.
44 *and his loquaciousness:* Falby 2008, p. 9.
44 *his style was far more remarkable:* Heard, "Memoir of Glyn Philpot," c. 1945, www.geraldheard.com/writings.htm. The following quotes in this passage about Heard and Philpot come from the same source.
45 *a "slyly exotic" style of dress:* Isherwood 1976, p. 102.
46 *young dilettante called Christopher Wood:* Parker 1989, p. 111.
46 *wavy hair "somehow appealing":* Heard quoted in Falby 2008, p. 12.
47 *would found Trabuco College:* John Roger Barrie, email to author, October 16, 2011.
47 *the heavy pressure of inhibition:* Heard quoted in Falby 2008, p. 9.
51 *dissolving the "family" in himself:* Laing 1970, p. 14.

THREE. REVELATION

53 Epigraph: [Wilson] (1952) 2000, p. 93.
54 *that strange barrier that had existed between me and all men and women:* Wilson 2000, p. 43.
54 *was loved and there was hope again:* [Wilson] 1984, p. 40.
55 *heavy component in her interest in me:* Wilson 2000, p. 35.
55 *symbol of prestige and power:* Ibid., p. 73.
55 *the habit of writing when drunk:* Ibid., p. 98.
56 *on my way to be cured:* Ibid., p. 140.
56 *the blazing thought, "You are a free man":* Ibid., p. 145.
61 *seek with all your might:* Ibid., p. 130.
62 *Perhaps you'd like to hear about it:* Ibid., p. 133.

66 *alcoholic insanity for religious insanity:* Ibid.

68 *the God of the preachers:* [Wilson] 1984, p. 121.

71 *Wasserman was the rascal:* Kinsolving, interview by the author, October 24, 2011.

71 *a blood alcohol level that was nearly three times the legal limit:* "The Report on Wasserman's Car Crash," *San Francisco Chronicle*, March 17, 1979.

72 *We're all over it—even if* you *are not:* Nolte, email to author, August 27, 2011.

75 *absolutism and one-sided dogmatism:* James (1902) 1982, p. 26.

76 *this Harvard professor, long in his grave:* Wilson 2000, p. 151.

76 *private blend that suited only his own soul:* Marty, introduction to James (1902) 1982, p. xi.

76 *The drunken consciousness is one bit of the mystic consciousness:* James (1902) 1982, p. 387.

76 *the only cure for "dipsomania is religio-mania":* James quoted in Kurtz 1979, p. 23.

77 *protective wall of human community:* Letter from Jung to B. Wilson, January 30, 1961, www.steppingstones.org/jung_letter.jpg.

FOUR. ABROAD

78 Epigraph: Heard 1941, pp. 3, 32.

78 *as much of this planet as possible:* A. Huxley quoted in Bedford 1974, p. 161.

79 *fewer Maharajas . . . and more schools:* Ibid., p. 165.

79 *to make us laugh as well:* Baker and Sexton 2002, vol. 6, p. 352.

80 *so sick I enjoyed it less:* A. Huxley 1994, p. 21.

83 *ordinary person increasingly superfluous:* A. Huxley, December 5, 1934.

84 *Cynicism is acceptance:* A. Huxley, September 3, 1932.

84 *the desire to transcend himself:* A. Huxley, November 28, 1934.

84 *greatest benefactors of suffering humanity:* A. Huxley, October 28, 1934.

89 *with an unconditional, ever-lasting love:* Lance Williams and Elizabeth Fernandez, "Pope Embraces the City," *San Francisco Examiner*, September 18, 1985.

90 *a considerable gloom about myself:* Letter from A. Huxley to E.M. Forster, January 17, 1935, in G. Smith 1969, p. 391.

91 *not only for Germany but for the whole world:* A. Huxley 1994, p. 96.

91 *a depressing news bulletin:* BBC radio broadcast, January 9, 1932, quoted in ibid.

92 *clear out to some safe spot in South America:* Letter from A. Huxley to J. Huxley, October 14, 1933, in G. Smith 1969, p. 375.

93 *if the speech happens to be my own:* Letter from A. Huxley to Jay Hubble, May 2, 1937, Rare Book, Manuscript, and Special Collections Library, Duke University Archives.

93 *pitifully small audience:* Jay Hubbell, "Aldous Huxley," personal memo, 1976, Rare Book, Manuscript, and Special Collections Library, Duke University Archives.

93 *I had had considerable doubt:* Letter from Heard to Charles Elwood, October 19, 1937, Rare Book, Manuscript, and Special Collections Library, Duke University Archives.

94 *Leisurely reading of carefully selected material:* "Huxley Criticizes Habits of Reading," *Durham Morning Herald,* May 5, 1937.

94 *a certain composite and synthetic Gothieness:* "An Englishman Looks at Duke," *Duke Alumni Register,* September 1937, p. 238, Rare Book, Manuscript, and Special Collections Library, Duke University Archives.

95 *never expect anything in particular to happen:* Ibid.

95 *a lugubrious and heavy-handed piece of propaganda:* M.C. Dawson quoted in Watt 1975, p. 16.

96 *vermin of diseased imaginations:* Douglas quoted in ibid, p. 82.

96 *the breakdown of forms:* Aiken quoted in ibid., p. 125.

96 *called* Point Counter Point *"illegible":* Gide quoted in ibid., p. 189.

96 *artificially constructed characters:* Hemingway quoted in ibid., p. 196.

96 *published since the war:* West quoted in ibid., p. 202.

96 *seems strained and even silly:* Bloom 2003, p. 1.

96 *I have learned the art of embodying the thing:* Transcript of Aldous Huxley speech, May 8, 1937, Lectures, Inside the College Speakers, Black Mountain College Records, North Carolina State Archive, Raleigh.

97 *where there is a hopeless depression and fear:* Ibid.

100 *the sun more and more vicious:* Letter from M. Huxley to Roy Fenton, October 13, 1937, in G. Smith 1969, p. 425.

101 *enormous efforts, pains and privations:* Letter from A. Huxley to Eugene Saxton, May 20, 1937, in Sexton 2007, pp. 338–39.

101 *the mad situation I have . . . put myself into:* M. Huxley quoted in Bedford 1974, p. 346.

102 *I do the washing up:* Ibid.

102 *when Gerald tries, and succeeds, in doing my housework:* Ibid.

102 *to see as few of them as possible:* Letter from A. Huxley to Eva Hermann, August 1, 1937, in Sexton 2007, p. 344.

103 *direct insight into the real nature of ultimate reality:* A. Huxley (1937) 1938, pp. 3–4.

103 *it interfered with our sexual freedom:* Ibid., p. 273.

104 *battle of rival propagandas grows ever fiercer:* Ibid., pp. 274–75.

104 *war is not a law of nature:* Ibid., p. 29.

FIVE. HOLLYWOOD

106 Epigraph: A. Huxley, in Baker and Sexton 2001, vol. 3, p. 318.

106 *date palms and red hot deserts:* Letter from A. Huxley to Flora Strousse, November 8, 1937, in Sexton 2007, p. 347.

107 *the really fabulous spectacle of San Francisco:* Letter from A. Huxley to Hutchinson, December 8, 1937, in ibid., p. 348.

107 *movie world in its own little suburb of Hollywood:* Ibid.

108 *in New York for about a fortnight:* Letter from A. Huxley to Loos, May 14, 1926, in G. Smith 1969, p. 269.

108 *above and beyond what ordinary mortals saw:* Loos 1974, p. 148.

108 *a very sporty Lesbian tailor-made:* Letter from A. Huxley to Hutchinson, December 8, 1937, in Sexton 2007, p. 348.

109 *disciples that attach themselves to a great man:* Loos 1974, pp. 148–49.

109 *an incredible salary in 1938:* Dunaway 1989, p. 83.

110 *I will protect you from the studio:* A. Huxley and Loos quoted in Bedford 1974, pp. 359–60.

110 *Garbo now wanted meatier, more mature roles:* Cukor and Garbo quoted in Swenson 1997, p. 380.

110 *It stinks:* Dunaway 1989, p. 103.

110 *Huxley felt he had failed Greta Garbo:* Isherwood quoted in Swenson 1997, p. 408.

111 *never sure how serious Garbo was about the idea:* A. Huxley quoted in ibid, p. 394.

111 *before her butterfly attention wandered away again:* Isherwood quoted in ibid, p. 401.

112 *I do not want followers:* J. Krishnamurti, "Truth Is a Pathless Land," n.d., www.jiddu-krishnamurti.net/en/1929-truth-is-a-pathless-land.

112 *he must suffer when he's treated as a prophet:* M. Huxley quoted in Bedford 1974, p. 381.

113 *sit together for long periods without saying a word:* Krishnamurti quoted in Lutyens 1983, p. 49.

113 *only one war, the war within ourselves:* "The Mirror of Relationship," First Talk in the Oak Grove, May 26, 1940, www.jiddu-krishnamurti.net/en/1936 -1944-the-mirror-of-relationship/krishnamurti-the-mirror-of-relationship -40.

114 *The patriot is allowed to indulge . . . in vanity and hatred:* Excerpt from "The Causes of War," on A. Huxley 2010, emphasis in the original. This is a CD of Huxley's BBC radio broadcasts.

115 *We'll be like escaping refugees:* Loos quoted in Isherwood 1997, p. 50.

116 *with someone who is wanted for murder:* Isherwood quoted in Parker 2004, p. 452.
116 *let's pretend we're two other people:* Isherwood 1997, p. 51.
116 *I think they were both scared:* Ibid., p. 50, italics in the original.
117 *before I arrest the slew of you:* Loos 1974, p. 151, italics in the original.
118 *Truth cannot be brought down:* Krishnamurti quoted in Blau 1995, p. 85.
124 *drugs were an illusory short cut:* Quinn quoted in ibid., p. 123.
125 *decisive gestures of a believer:* Isherwood 1981, p. 9.
125 *Gerald—disconcertingly, almost theatrically Christlike:* Isherwood 1997, pp. 22, 23.
126 *stopped seeing him unless it was absolutely necessary:* Isherwood 1981, p. 84.
126 *he muddled many of his friendships:* M. Huxley quoted in Bedford 1974, p. 423.
126 *Meditation takes for him the place of drugs:* Ibid., p. 391.
128 *sectarianism . . . and its horrible descendant:* Vivekananda, "Chicago Address," September 11, 1893, Vivekananda Vedanta Society, www.vedantasociety -chicago.org/chicago_address.htm.
130 *both of them were eclectics:* Isherwood 1981, p. 38.
131 *a constant corrective to my inherited puritanism:* Ibid., p. 39.
131 *It has no technique and therefore no authority:* Krishnamurti quoted in Lutyens 1983, p. 45.
131 *Aldous and Prabhavananda . . . were temperamentally far apart:* Isherwood 1981, p. 50.
132 *interpreter of Eastern thought for the modern world:* Watts (1972) 2007, cover.
132 *astonishment at the wondrous enormities of human folly:* Ibid., p. 168.
133 *subtle accommodation to social convention:* The extract and the following con- versation are from ibid., pp. 225–27, italics in the original.
134 *Krishnamurti never meditates on "objects":* Isherwood 1997, p. 114.
134 *part of its sabotage effort:* Ibid.
134 *such nonsense was regrettable:* Isherwood 1981, p. 7.
135 *nor approve of Gerald as a guru figure:* Bedford 1974, p. 425.
135 *he was a life-hater:* Isherwood 1981, p. 76.

SIX. TRABUCO

136 Epigraph: [Wilson] (1952) 2000, p. 76.
137 *a hopeless victim of "wet brain":* Elrick Davis, "Alcoholics Anonymous Makes Its Stand Here," pt. 1, *Cleveland Plain Dealer,* October 21, 1939.
138 *simply cogitate about "It" in the silence of their minds:* Elrick Davis, "Alcohol- ics Anonymous Makes Its Stand Here," pts. 1 and 2, *Cleveland Plain Dealer* October 21 and 23, 1939.

138 *rollicking rum pots, they were now sober:* Jack Alexander, "Jack Alexander of *Sat Eve Post* Fame Thought A.A.s Were Pulling His Leg," *A.A. Grapevine* 1, no. 12 (May 1945).

140 *"best example of spirituality" that he ever knew:* Letter from B. Wilson to Ed Dowling, April 21, 1950, in Falby 2008, p. 18.

140 *Heard spent around one hundred thousand dollars:* Falby 2008, p. 106.

141 *It will be a club for mystics:* Isherwood 1981, p. 96.

141 *Heard described his project as "un-denominational":* Heard quoted in Miller 2005, p. 88.

141 *there are no "prophets" among us:* Ibid.

141 *a new cult, Heardism, was being born:* Isherwood 1997, p. 235.

141 *a religious community that would forge "a new syncretism":* Falby 2008, p. 106.

141 *Humanity is failing:* Heard quoted in Miller 2005, p. 87.

142 *not as dark as Gerald thought it would:* William Forthman, interview by author, July 12, 2010. All quotes by Forthman in this chapter are from this interview.

142 *the Invisible Reality which we so glibly call God:* Heard (1942) 2008, p. 47.

143 *you must become Godlike:* Ibid., p. 34–35.

143 *he could never become a Christian:* Isherwood 1997, p. 28.

143 *mystically fertile soil of California:* Fremantle 1946, p. 386.

143 *Mr. Heard has always had a following:* Ibid., p. 385.

145 *I've always at least tried to practice:* Miriam King, "Life at Trabuco," n.d., Gerald Heard, http://geraldheard.com/recollections.htm#Life_At_Trabuco.

145 *Heard was "God-intoxicated":* Barrett, "The Perennial Pupil," *Parabola* (Fall 2000).

145 *He'd talk about the Christian mystics:* King n.d.

146 *they have cultivated distraction as a drug:* Heard (1942) 2008, p. 38.

146 *sexual appetite will not check itself:* Ibid., pp. 24–25.

146 *Heard maintained unbroken celibacy:* John Roger Barrie, October 16, 2011, email to author.

147 *an instant rapport was mutually recognized:* Jay Michael Barrie quoted in ibid.

147 *the two men were never "lovers":* John Roger Barrie, October 16, 2011, email to author.

147 *evolutionary energies sparkling in sex:* Kripal 2007, p. 93.

148 *Gerald is terribly upset about it:* Isherwood 1997, p. 376.

149 *our great English literature:* Maugham quoted in Falby 2008, p. 104.

149 *Yogi-journalese of the Gerald Heard type:* Koestler quoted in ibid, p. 103.

149 *it was not mystical dreaminess but cynicism:* Sawyer 2002, p. 128.

149 *Indifference is a form of sloth:* The extract and the following conversation are from A. Huxley (1936) 1968, pp. 10, 81, emphasis in the original.

151 *the pit was known as "Gerald's tomb":* J. Huxley 1965, p. 156.

151 *The Japanese have bombed Pearl Harbor:* Peggy Kiskadden quoted in Dunaway 1995, p. 56.

151 *he and Gerald are good friends again:* M. Huxley quoted in Bedford 1974, p. 424.

151 *runs wildly with the goats in the afternoon:* Ibid., p. 425.

152 *he pours out in love:* A. Huxley (1944) 1970, pp. 300–301.

152 *tired of hearing them yakking about God:* M. Huxley and Isherwood quoted in Bedford 1974, p. 441.

153 *become "loving, pure in heart, and poor in spirit":* A. Huxley (1944) 1970, p. iii.

153 *he should read Aristotle on moderation:* Joad 1946, p. 50.

153 *the selling-out of a once brilliant intellect:* Isherwood quoted in J. Huxley 1965, p. 158.

153 *People like their egos:* A. Huxley quoted in Isherwood 1945, p. 33.

157 *that book converted me . . . to the vaster world of the mystics:* Huston Smith, interview by author, July 26, 2010. Unless otherwise noted, all quotes by Smith in this chapter are from this interview.

158 *You wonder why someone would stay up all night:* H. Smith quoted in Lattin 2011.

158 *He would like you:* H. Smith 2009, p. 47.

159 *Life can only go downhill:* Ibid., pp. 47–48, italics in the original.

159 *if it had not been for that swami:* Ibid., p. 51.

165 *those words were carved in stone:* Yogeshananda, interview by author, August 15, 2009. All quotes by Yogeshananda in this chapter are from this interview.

167 *forgetting that God and Gerald were not the same thing:* M. Huxley quoted in Bedford 1974, p. 463.

168 *Why don't you choose your own conception of God:* reconstructed dialogue based on Wilson's writings and on King's account in "Life at Trabuco."

169 *advice from Gerald on what direction AA should:* Heard quoted in King, "Life at Trabuco."

169 *Keep it in discrete, small units:* Ibid.

170 *a new state of consciousness and being:* [Wilson] (1952) 2000, p. 107.

170 *This self-centered behavior blocked a partnership:* Ibid., p. 53.

170 *ultimate Reality that we glibly call "God":* Heard (1942) 2008, p. 47.

SEVEN. PSYCHEDELIC

183 Epigraph: Letter from B. Wilson to Heard and Michael Barrie on January 18, 1957. Published with the permission of the Barrie Family Trust. Provided by the UCLA Department of Special Collections.

184 *permitting the "other world" to rise into consciousness:* Letter from A. Huxley to Osmond, April 10, 1953, in G. Smith 1969, p. 668.

184 *we don't have a cook:* Ibid.

184 *I am eager to make the experiment:* Letter from A. Huxley to Osmond, April 19, 1953, in G. Smith 1969, p. 670.

185 *moment of naked existence:* A. Huxley (1954) 1970, p. 17.

185 *unspeakable and yet self-evident paradox:* Ibid.

185 *This is how one ought to see:* A. Huxley quoted in Stevens 1988, p. 46.

187 *this essence was not in me it was me:* Proust (1981) 2003, p. 60, emphasis in the original.

188 *The patterns of a lifetime's behaviors . . . all begin in this crucible:* Ackerman 2012, p. 1.

190 *doomed to suffer and enjoy in solitude:* A. Huxley (1954) 1970, p. 12.

190 *He had his psychedelic baptism . . . in November 1953:* John Roger Barrie, email to author, October 23, 2011.

191 *they had become more relaxed and human:* Watts (1972) 2007, p. 323.

192 *LSD was a device for saving humanity:* Janiger quoted in John Cody, "Postmodern Soul Guide," n.d., Island Views, http://island.org/ive/2/heard2.html.

192 *a secretive Canadian businessman named Al Hubbard:* Stevens 1988.

192 *According to some observers of the era:* Markoff 2005.

193 *some, like the witches of Macbeth, feel a prickling in their thumbs:* Heard 1963, p. 11.

193 *sober certainty of waking bliss:* This quote is actually taken from a 1956 TV interview with Heard by Dr. Sidney Cohen. To view it, go to the "Harvard Psychedelic Club" page at www.donlattin.com.

193 *Maybe that's an idea for Trabuco:* Letter from B. Wilson to Heard, July 9, 1948. All the Heard-Wilson letters quoted in this chapter are from the "Gerald Heard Papers, 1935–1971," Charles E. Young Research Library, Department of Special Collections, UCLA. Published with the permission of the Barrie Family Trust.

194 *or "spook sessions," as they termed them:* Wing 1992, p. 56.

194 *telepathic linkage:* Letter from Heard to B. Wilson, October 20, 1950.

194 *Mars is ruled by insects:* Heard (1950) 1953, p. 142.

195 *drunks who were given LSD recovered:* Hartigan 2000, p. 178.

195 *an adventurous kind of mind:* Osmond quoted in Lattin 2010a, p. 67.

196 *a lively correspondence for nearly two decades:* Wing 1992, p. 75.

196 *a lifelong personal friend and admirer:* L. Wilson 1979, p. 143.

196 *the freedom of which Krishnamurti speaks:* Letter from B. Wilson to A. Huxley, January 24, 1962. Reproduced with permission of the Stepping Stones Archives, Katonah, New York. No permission is granted for any other use or reproduction.

197 *border country of psychical research:* Letter from Heard to B. Wilson, October 20, 1950.

198 *Bill felt "an enormous enlargement":* Heard quoted in Cheever 2004, p. 241.

198 *this is going to be his therapy session:* Eisner quoted in Walsh and Grob 2005, p. 94, italics in the original.

198 *Lois Wilson participated in that first session:* L. Wilson quoted in Hartigan 2000, p. 178.

198 *the depression was pretty much absent:* B. Wilson to Cohen, September 25, 1956. Reproduced with permission of the Stepping Stones Archives, Katonah, New York. No permission is granted for any other use or reproduction.

198 *omitting my name when discussing LSD:* B. Wilson to Cohen, December 16, 1957. Reproduced with permission of the Stepping Stones Archives, Katonah, New York. No permission is granted for any other use or reproduction.

199 *his trip as "a dead ringer" for the epiphany:* Huston Smith, interview by author, December 12, 2007.

199 *The light, the ecstasy:* B. Wilson 2000, p. 145.

199 *given this potion every hour for fifty hours:* Pittman 1988, pp. 168–69.

200 *we ought to idealize and venerate it:* James (1902) 1982, p. 237, italics in the original.

201 *Visionary experience is not always blissful:* A. Huxley quoted in Baker and Sexton 2002, vol. 6, p. 27.

204 *he asked for a cigarette:* B. Wilson quoted in Cheever 2004, p. 241.

205 *a psychiatrist from Roosevelt Hospital in New York:* Hartigan 2000, p. 179.

206 *It was a great focuser of attention:* William Forthman, interview by author, July 12, 2010.

206 *LSD was then totally unfamiliar:* [Wilson] 1984, pp. 371–72.

206 *The material is about as harmless as aspirin:* Letter from B. Wilson to Sam Shoemaker, in ibid., p. 375.

207 *Do you have any of the stuff to spare?:* Letter from A. Huxley to Osmond, September 16, 1960 in G. Smith 1969, p. 895.

207 *I think more like a Protestant:* B. Wilson quoted in Cheever 2004, p. 202, italics in the original.

207 *the LSD business goes on apace:* B. Wilson quoted in Fitzgerald 1995, p. 95.

208 *Bill takes one pill to see God:* Ibid.

208 *evil spirit to assume the appearance of the angel of light:* Dowling quoted in Fitzgerald 1995, p. 98.

208 *When one has received the message, . . . one hangs up the phone:* Watts (1972) 2007, p. 327.

209 *conversion from total self-centeredness:* Kurtz 1979, p. 34, italics in the original.
211 *a gradually fading wonder:* Heard 1963, p. 16.

EIGHT. SIXTIES

212 Epigraph: A. Huxley, essay reprinted in Baker and Sexton 2002, vol. 4, p. 303.
213 *many religions can lead to eternal life:* Pew Forum on Religion and Public Life, "Many Americans Say Other Faiths Can Lead to Eternal Life," December 18, 2008, Pewforum.org.
213 *one of the following spiritual concepts or phenomena:* Pew Forum on Religion and Public Life, "Many Americans Mix Multiple Faiths—Eastern, New Age Beliefs Widespread," December 9, 2009, Pewforum.org.
214 *those who claimed no religious affiliation nearly doubled:* Cathy Lynn Grossman, "Most Religious Groups in USA Have Lost Ground, Survey Finds," March 17, 2009, *USA Today.*
214 *one-third of the American population now describe themselves as "spiritual but not religious":* George H. Gallup Jr., "Americans' Spiritual Searches Turn Inward," February 11, 2003, Gallup.com.
214 *God as "everywhere and in everything":* 2001 Beliefnet poll cited in Goldberg 2010, p. 37.
214 *shift from a "dwelling spirituality":* Wuthnow 1998, p. 3.
214 *one out of three of us had switched religions:* McKinney and Roof 1997, p. 172.
215 *more than twenty-three million Americans tried LSD: National Survey on Drug Use and Health: The NSDUH Report,* February 14, 2008, Substance Abuse and Mental Health Services Administration, oas.samhsa.gov/data/2k8/hallucinogens/hallucinogens.htm.
216 *compare his normal experiences with his drug-induced ones:* Letter from A. Huxley to Leary, June 13, 1961, in Forte 1999, p. 106.
216 *I would be grateful for a new supply:* Letter from A. Huxley to Leary, May 7, 1961, in ibid., p. 111.
216 *when the experience is what it always ought to be:* Letter from A. Huxley to Leary, February 2, 1962, in ibid., p. 109.
216 *Heard was signing his letters to Leary: "Love, Gerald":* Letter from Heard to Leary, July 17, 1962, in ibid., p. 109.
217 *there seems no doubt of their immense and growing value:* Letter from B. Wilson to Leary, July 17, 1961, Lattin 2010a, p. 67.
217 *the most dangerous man in America:* Ibid., p. 61.
217 *What one says on the air is bound to be misunderstood:* Letter from A. Huxley to Osmond, July 22, 1956, in G. Smith 1969, p. 803.

217 *why, does he have to be such an ass:* Letter from A. Huxley to Osmond, December 26, 1962, in ibid., p. 945.

218 *blossoming of new, government-approved research projects:* Lattin 2010b.

218 *men and women to achieve a radical self-transcendence:* A. Huxley quoted in Baker and Sexton 2002, vol. 6, p. 303.

219 *to love in an aware and knowledgeably directed way:* A. Huxley 1977, pp. 243, 249.

220 *Each trip got worse, more painful:* Murphy quoted in Forte 1999, p. 199.

222 *stood for art, rebellion, contemplative value, and transcendence:* Starr 2009, p. 314.

222 *concrete manifestation of the divine energy of the godhead:* Kripal 2007, p. 19.

224 *it invariably overcomes the rigid and hard:* Watts, introduction to Huang 1973, p. 2.

225 *enough to fully pour out our feelings:* Wang quoted in Lattin 1986.

227 *I mustn't die before Aldous:* M. Huxley quoted in Bedford 1974, p. 548.

227 *Maria is not getting better:* Letter from A. Huxley to Osmond, February 3, 1955, in G. Smith 1969, p. 730.

227 *Leave your body here like a bundle of old clothes:* Letter from A. Huxley to Osmond, February 21, 1955, in ibid., p. 736.

227 *wonderfully and gently brave through it all:* Murray 2002, p. 411.

227 *throw away all your baggage and go forward:* A. Huxley 1962, p. 302.

228 *words . . . have a kind of indecency:* Letter from A. Huxley to Osmond, October 24, 1955, in G. Smith 1969, p. 769.

228 *Don't ever be anyone but yourself:* A. Huxley quoted in Murray 2002, p. 416.

228 *plan a psychedelic session very carefully:* L. Huxley quoted in Dunaway 1995, p. 100.

229 *They are having tremendous visionary experiences:* A. Huxley 2008a, recorded on November 17, 1955.

229 *spirituality of small groups is a very high form of religion:* "The History of Tension," *A.A. Grapevine* (November 1957).

230 *I'm an essayist who writes novels: Look Here,* October 27, 1957, viewed at the Television and Motion Pictures Reading Room, Library of Congress.

230 *She is twenty years younger than I am:* Letter from A. Huxley to Matthew and Ellen Huxley, March 19, 1956, in G. Smith 1969, p. 794.

231 *He suffered from all kinds of ailments:* J. Huxley 1965, p. 157.

231 *Aldous looked like a withered old man:* A. Huxley quoted in Murray 2002, p. 452.

231 *you are going towards Maria's love:* L. Huxley quoted in ibid., p. 454.

231 *possibly the only person outside his family to receive it:* Wing 1992, p. 75.

231 *The tempered metal of Huxley's mind:* J. Huxley 1965, p. 101.

232 *union with the infinite sun of all being:* Heard 1961, available at www.myspace.com/geraldheard.

233 *she confessed to a "rage for fame":* Morris 1997, dust jacket.

233 *I wish that I could write with utmost frankness:* Letter from Luce to Heard, July 26, 1949. The Heard-Luce letters were obtained from the Clare Boothe Luce Collection, box 169, folder 2, Library of Congress, and used with the kind permission of the Barrie Family Trust.

234 *The LSD experience . . . is a profound communion:* Letter from Heard to Luce, December 15, 1959, box 38, folder 3, in ibid.

234 *we voyaged . . . to outer space:* Letter from Barrie to Luce, April 24, 1962, box 189, folder 5, in ibid.

234 *run about on the woodwork between the pigeonholes:* A. Huxley 2008b, recorded on April 3, 1955.

234 *birth a postmodern, psychologically aware mythos:* Cody 1993, pp. 64–70.

235 *his role was similar to that of a cuckoo bird:* J.M. Barrie quoted in Falby 2008, p. 196.

235 *Gerald Heard was a beautiful old gentleman:* Houston 1993, p. xviii.

235 *few great mythmakers and revealers of life's wonder:* Isherwood 1997, p. 304.

237 *Waves appear to be born and die:* Hanh 1995, p. 138.

237 *A business which takes no regular inventory usually goes broke:* [Wilson] (1939) 2001, p. 64.

238 *Sometimes there were other women:* Ibid., p. 106.

239 *we need deny them only the A.A. name:* B. Wilson 1971.

240 *doing to the women he was chasing:* Powers quoted in Hartigan 2000, p. 171.

240 *We must be willing to make amends:* [Wilson] (1939) 2001, pp. 68–69.

241 *was different than any he had before:* Hartigan 2000, pp. 190, 192.

241 *Bill never stopped loving Lois:* Ibid., p. 193.

242 *Wilson "asked for three shots of whiskey":* Cheever 2004, p. 248.

242 *We claim spiritual progress rather than spiritual perfection:* [Wilson] (1939) 2001, p. 60.

NINE. SOBER

243 Epigraph: [Wilson] (1952) 2000, p. 57.

246 *personal ambition has no place in A.A.:* Ibid., p. 183.

250 *It's the only way you become connected with yourself:* Lattin 1991, p. 17.

253 *self-centeredness . . . is the root of our troubles:* Wilson (1939) 2001, p. 62.

255 *short cut will prove to be a short circuit:* H. Smith 2000, p. 31.

256 *the Realm of Spirit is broad, roomy, all inclusive:* Wilson (1939) 2001, pp. 45, 46.

261 *He will be the first to blaspheme:* Isherwood 1945, p. 36.

263 *They are slowly killing us:* Keating 2003, pp. 73, 74.

264 *The idea of religious unity is wishful thinking:* Prothero 2010, p. 3.

Bibliography

Ackerman, Diane. 2012. "The Brain on Love." *New York Times Sunday Review,* March 25.

Anderson, Walter Truett. 1983. *The Upstart Spring: Esalen and the American Awakening.* Reading, MA: Addison-Wesley.

Atkins, John. 1967. *Aldous Huxley: A Literary Study.* London: Orion.

Baker, Robert, and James Sexton, eds. 2000–2002. *Aldous Huxley: Complete Essays.* Vols. 1–6. Chicago: Ivan R. Dee.

Bedford, Sybille. 1974. *Aldous Huxley: A Biography.* New York: Alfred A. Knopf.

Birnbaum, Milton. (1971) 2006. *Aldous Huxley: A Quest for Values.* Knoxville: University of Tennessee Press. Reprint, New Brunswick, NJ: Transaction.

Blau, Evelyne. 1995. *Krishnamurti: 100 Years.* New York: Stewart, Tabori and Chang.

Bloom, Harold, ed. 2003. *Aldous Huxley.* Broomall, PA: Chelsea House.

Cheever, Susan. 2004. *My Name Is Bill.* New York: Simon and Schuster.

Cody, John V. 1993. "Gerald Heard: Soul Guide to the Beyond Within." *Gnosis* (Winter): 64–70.

Dunaway, David King. 1989. *Huxley in Hollywood*. New York: Doubleday.
———. 1995. *Aldous Huxley Recollected: An Oral History*. New York: Carroll and Graf.
Eros, Paul. 2001. "'A Sort of Muff and Jeff': Gerald Heard, Aldous Huxley, and the New Pacifism," in *Aldous Huxley Annual*, vol. 1, ed. Jerome Meckier and Bernfried Nugel. Piscataway, NJ: Transaction.
Falby, Alison. 2008. *Gerald Heard: Between the Pigeonholes*. Newcastle, U.K.: Cambridge Scholars Publishing.
Fitzgerald, Robert. 1995. *The Soul of Sponsorship: The Friendship of Father Ed Dowling, S.J., and Bill Wilson in Letters*. Center City, MN: Hazelden Educational Services.
Forte, Robert, ed. 1999. *Timothy Leary: Outside Looking In*. Rochester, VT: Park Street Press.
Fremantle, Anne. 1946. "Heard Melodies." *Commonweal* 43, no. 15 (January 25): 384–87.
Goldberg, Philip. 2010. *American Veda: From Emerson and the Beatles to Yoga and Meditation: How Indian Spirituality Changed the West*. New York: Harmony Books.
Goldman, Marion. 2012. *The American Soul Rush: Esalen and the Rise of Spiritual Privilege*. New York: New York University Press.
Griffin, Kevin. 2004. *One Breath at a Time: Buddhism and the Twelve Steps*. Emmaus, PA: Rodale Books.
Hanh, Thich Nhat. 1995. *Living Buddha, Living Christ*. New York: Riverhead Books.
Harner, Dean. 2004. *The God Gene: How Faith Is Hardwired into Our Genes*. New York: Doubleday.
Hartigan, Francis. 2000. *Bill W*. New York: St. Martin's Press.
Heard, Gerald. 1924. *Narcissus: An Anatomy of Clothes*. New York: E. P. Dutton.
———. 1929. *The Ascent of Humanity*. New York: Harcourt, Brace and Company.
———. 1937. *The Source of Civilization*. New York: Harper and Brothers.
———. 1941. *Man the Master*. New York: Harper and Brothers.
———. (1941) 2009. *A Taste for Honey*. Nevada City, CA: Blue Dolphin.
———. (1942) 2008. *Training for the Life of the Spirit*. Eugene, OR: Wipf and Stock.
———. (1945) 2009. *The Gospel According to Gamaliel*. Eugene, OR: Wipf and Stock.
———. 1948. *Is God Evident?: An Essay Toward a Natural Theology*. New York: Harper and Brothers.
———. (1950) 1953. *Is Another World Watching? The Riddle of the Flying Saucers*. New York: Bantam.
———. 1951. *Immortality*. Garvin Lectures. Lancaster, PA: Garvin Trust.

———. 1961. *Explorations, Volume 2: Survival, Growth and Re-birth.* World Pacific Records. Album.

———. 1963. "Can This Drug Enlarge Man's Mind?" *Psychedelic Review* 1, no. 1 (June).

Houston, Jean. 1993. *Life Force: The Psycho-Historical Recovery of the Self.* Wheaton, IL: Theosophical Publishing House.

Huang, Al Chungliang. 1973. *Embrace Tiger, Return to Mountain—the Essence of T'ai Chi.* Moab, UT: Real People Press.

Huxley, Aldous. (1922) 1968. *Crome Yellow.* New York: Bantam.

———. 1923. *Antic Hay.* London: Chatto and Windus.

———. (1928) 1975. *Point Counter Point.* New York: Penguin.

———. 1929. *Do What You Will.* Garden City, NY: Country Life Press.

———. (1930) n.d. *After the Fireworks.* New York: Avon. Originally titled *Brief Candles.* New York: Harper and Brothers.

———. (1932) 1968. *Brave New World.* New York: Bantam.

———. (1934) 1984. *Beyond the Mexique Bay.* London: Granada Publishing.

———. (1936) 1968. *Eyeless in Gaza.* New York: Bantam.

———. (1937) 1938. *Ends and Means: An Inquiry into the Nature of Ideals and into the Methods Employed for Their Realization.* London: Chatto and Windus.

———. 1939. *After Many a Summer Dies the Swan.* New York: Avon.

———. (1942) 1975. *The Art of Seeing.* Seattle: Montana Books.

———. (1944) 1970. *The Perennial Philosophy.* New York: Harper Colophon.

———. 1944. *Time Must Have a Stop.* New York: Harper and Brothers.

———. (1948) 1968. *Ape and Essence.* New York: Bantam.

———. 1948. *Mortal Coils.* New York: Harper and Brothers.

———. 1952. *The Devils of Loudun.* New York: Harper and Brothers.

———. (1954) 1970. *The Doors of Perception.* New York: Harper and Row.

———. 1955. *The Genius and the Goddess.* New York: Harper and Brothers.

———. 1956. *Tomorrow and Tomorrow and Tomorrow.* New York: Signet.

———. 1958a. *Brave New World Revisited.* New York: Harper and Brothers.

———. 1958b. *Collected Essays.* New York: Harper and Row.

———. 1962. *Island.* New York: Harper and Bros.

———. 1977. *The Human Situation: Lectures at Santa Barbara, 1959.* New York: Harper and Row.

———. 1994. *Aldous Huxley between the Wars: Essays and Letters.* Edited by David Bradshaw. Chicago: Ivan R. Dee.

———. 2008a. *Knowledge and Understanding: A Lecture by Aldous Huxley, plus Selections from Question/Answer Session.* Recorded on November 27, 1955, at the Vedanta Society, Hollywood, CA. Hollywood, CA: Vedanta Press. CD.

———. 2008b. *Who Are We? A Lecture by Aldous Huxley plus Q and A.* Recorded on April 3, 1955, at the Vedanta Society, Hollywood, CA. Hollywood, CA: Vedanta Press. CD.

———. 2010. *The Spoken Word—Aldous Huxley*. London: British Library Publishing. CD.

Huxley, Julian. 1965. *Aldous Huxley, 1894–1963*. New York: Harper and Row.

Huxley, Thomas H. 1901. *Collected Essays*. Vol. 1. New York: D. Appleton.

Isherwood, Christopher. 1935. *Berlin Stories*. New York: New Directions.

———, ed. 1945. *Vedanta for the Western World*. Hollywood, CA: Vedanta Press.

———. 1976. *Christopher and His Kind*. New York: Farrar, Straus and Giroux.

———. 1981. *My Guru and His Disciple*. New York: Penguin.

———. 1997. *Diaries, Volume One, 1939–1960*. New York: HarperCollins.

Izzo, David Garrett. 2001. "'Dear Gerald': Letters to and from Aldous Huxley, Gerald Heard, and Friends," in *Aldous Huxley Annual*, vol. 1, ed. Jerome Meckier and Bernfried Nugel. Piscataway, NJ: Transaction.

James, William. (1902) 1982. *The Varieties of Religious Experience: A Study in Human Nature*. New York: Penguin Books.

Joad, C. E. M. 1946. "Huxley Gone Sour." Review of *The Perennial Philosophy*, by Aldous Huxley. *New Statesman and Nation* 32 (October 5): 50.

Keating, Thomas. 2003. *Intimacy with God: An Introduction to Centering Prayer*. New York: Crossroad.

Kripal, Jeffrey. 2007. *Esalen and the Religion of No Religion*. Chicago: University of Chicago Press.

Kripal, Jeffrey, and Glenn Shuck, eds. 2005. *On the Edge of the Future: Esalen and the Evolution of American Culture*. Bloomington: Indiana University Press.

Kurtz, Ernest. 1979. *Not-God: A History of Alcoholics Anonymous*. Center City, MN: Hazelden Educational Services.

Laing, R. D. 1970. *The Politics of the Family*. New York: Basic Books.

Lattin, Don. 1986. "Old Chinese Arts Find New Vigor on Mystic Mountain." *San Francisco Examiner*, March 7, A1.

———. 1990. "Going to Church the 12-Step Way." *San Francisco Chronicle*, December 17, A1.

———. 1991. "The Need to Cry Out." *Common Boundary* (May–June): 16–22.

———. 1998. *Shopping for Faith: American Religion in the New Millennium*. San Francisco: Jossey-Bass.

———. 2003. *Following Our Bliss: How the Spiritual Ideals of the Sixties Shape Our Lives Today*. San Francisco: HarperSanFrancisco.

———. 2010a. *The Harvard Psychedelic Club: How Timothy Leary, Ram Dass, Huston Smith, and Andrew Weil Killed the Fifties and Ushered in a New Age for America*. San Francisco: HarperOne.

———. 2010b. "Leary's Legacy," *California Magazine*, Fall.

———. 2011. "Chasing the Divine: The Seekers of Trabuco Canyon." *California Magazine*, Spring.

Loos, Anita. 1974. *Kiss Hollywood Good-by*. New York: Viking.

Lutyens, Mary. 1983. *Krishnamurti: The Years of Fulfillment*. New York: Farrar, Straus and Giroux.

Markoff, John. 2005. *What the Dormouse Said: How the Sixties Counterculture Shaped the Personal Computer Industry*. New York: Penguin.

McKinney, William, and Wade Clark Roof. 1997. *American Mainline Religion*. New Brunswick, NJ: Rutgers University Press.

Mencken, H. L. 1940. *Newspaper Days*. New York: Alfred A. Knopf.

Miller, Timothy. 2005. "Notes on the Prehistory of the Human Potential Movement: The Vedanta Society and Gerald Heard's Trabuco College." In *On the Edge of the Future: Esalen and the Evolution of American Culture*, ed. Jeffrey Kripal and Glenn Shuck. Bloomington: Indiana University Press.

Morris, Sylvia Juke. 1997. *Rage for Fame: The Ascent of Clare Boothe Luce*. New York: Random House.

Murray, Nicholas. 2002. *Aldous Huxley: A Biography*. New York: St. Martin's Press.

Parker, Peter. 1989. *A Life of J. R. Ackerley*. London: Constable.

———. 2004. *Isherwood: A Life*. London: Picador.

Pittman, Bill. 1988. *AA: The Way It Began*. Seattle, WA: Glen Abbey Books.

Prothero, Stephen. 2010. *God Is Not One*. San Francisco: HarperOne.

Proust, Marcel. (1981) 2003. *Swann's Way: In Search of Lost Time*. Vol. 1. New York: Modern Library.

Roiphe, Katie. 2007. *Uncommon Arrangements: Seven Portraits of Married Life in London Literary Circles, 1910–1939*. New York: Dial Press.

Roof, Wade Clark. 1993. *A Generation of Seekers*. San Francisco: HarperSanFrancisco.

Rosenbaum, S. P. 1993. *A Bloomsbury Group Reader*. Oxford: Blackwell.

Sawyer, Dana. 2002. *Aldous Huxley: A Biography*. New York: Crossroad.

Sexton, James. 2007. *Aldous Huxley: Selected Letters*. Chicago: Ivan R. Dee.

Smith, Grover. 1969. *The Letters of Aldous Huxley*. New York: Harper and Row.

Smith, Huston. (1958) 1991. *The World's Religions*. San Francisco: HarperSanFrancisco.

———. 2000. *Cleansing the Doors of Perception*. New York: Tarcher/Putnam.

———. 2009. *Tales of Wonder: Adventures Chasing the Divine*. New York: HarperOne.

Starr, Kevin. 2009. *Golden Dreams: California in an Age of Abundance, 1950 – 1953*. Cambridge: Oxford University Press.

Stevens, Jay. 1988. *Storming Heaven: LSD and the American Dream.* New York: Harper and Row.

Strachey, Lytton. (1918) 2000. *Eminent Victorians.* Champaign, IL: Project Gutenberg.

Swenson, Karen. 1997. *Greta Garbo: A Life Apart.* New York: Scribner.

Thomsen, Robert. 1975. *Bill W.* New York: Harper and Row.

Vann, Gerald. 1934. *On Being Human: St. Thomas and Mr. Aldous Huxley.* New York: Sheed and Ward.

Vieira, Mark. 2005. *Greta Garbo: A Cinematic Legacy.* New York: Harry N. Abrams.

Walsh, Roger, and Charles Grob. 2005. *Higher Wisdom: Eminent Elders Explore the Continuing Impact of Psychedelics.* Albany: State University of New York Press.

Washington, Peter. 1993. *Madame Blavatsky's Baboon.* New York: Schocken Books.

Watt, Donald, ed. 1975. *Aldous Huxley: The Critical Heritage.* New York: Routledge.

Watts, Alan. 1957. *The Way of Zen.* New York: Pantheon.

———. (1972) 2007. *In My Own Way.* Novato, CA: New World Library.

Watts, Alan, with Al Chungliang Huang. 1975. *Tao: The Watercourse Way.* New York: Pantheon.

[Wilson, Bill]. (1939) 2001. *Alcoholics Anonymous* [The Big Book]. New York: Alcoholics Anonymous World Services.

———. (1952) 2000. *Twelve Steps and Twelve Traditions.* New York: Alcoholics Anonymous World Services.

———. 1957. *Alcoholics Anonymous Comes of Age.* New York: Alcoholics Anonymous World Services.

Wilson, Bill [Bill W.]. 1967. *As Bill Sees It.* New York: Alcoholics Anonymous World Services.

———. 1971. "Bill W.'s Letter about Hippies in A.A." *A.A. Grapevine* 61, no. 1 (March).

[Wilson, Bill]. 1984. *"Pass It On": The Story of Bill Wilson and How the A. A. Message Reached the World.* New York: Alcoholics Anonymous World Services.

Wilson, Bill [Bill W.]. 2000. *Bill W.: My First Forty Years.* Center City, MN: Hazelden Educational Services.

Wilson, Lois. 1979. *Lois Remembers.* Don Mills, Canada: T. H. Best Printing.

Wing, Nell. 1992. *Grateful to Have Been There.* Park Ridge, IL: Parkside.

Wuthnow, Robert. 1998. *After Heaven: Spirituality in America since the 1950s.* Berkeley: University of California Press.

Index

Text:	10/14 Palatino
Display:	Bauer Bodoni, Univers Condensed Light
Compositor:	BookMatters, Berkeley
Indexer:	Andrew Joron
Printer and binder:	Maple-Vail Book Manufacturing Group

12/12